THE
HIDDEN
YOU

Sol,
Wishing you health
& Happiness
Love Alex

For information about Alexandra Rose's workshops, lectures, consulting and public relations services, employee relations programs, upcoming books or

to order The Hidden You Pocket Size Symbol Cards and additional journal pages, write:

Imagery Publishing
P.O. Box 60011
1515 Rebecca Street
Oakville, Ontario, Canada
L6L 5G0
Please send a stamped, self-addressed envelope.

E-mail: imagery@globalserve.net

or call (416) 410-9992.

BECOME YOUR POTENTIAL
Symbols, Interpretations, and Journal

ALEXANDRA ROSE

IMAGERY
PUBLISHING
Oakville, Ontario, Canada

Canadian Cataloguing in Publication Data

Rose, Alexandra, 1966-
    The hidden you : become your potential :
symbols, interpretations and journal

ISBN 0-9682906-1-2

    1. Self-actualization (Psychology) 2. Self-help
techniques. 3. Diaries--Therapeutic use. I. Title.

BF637.S4R76 2000   158.1   C99-901680-6

Readers should assume responsibility for their health and choices. Consult your
physician, therapist, and/or a natural health expert for assisting your individual
needs. The author and publisher assume no responsibility for unintentional errors
or inaccuracy of information.

Quantity discounts are available on bulk purchases.

FOR INFORMATION CONTACT:
Imagery Publishing
P.O. Box 60011, 1515 Rebecca Street, Oakville, Ontario, Canada L6L 5G0
(416) 410-9992
E-mail: imagery@globalserve.net

Consulting and Review by: Pam Champagne, M.S.W., C.S.W.,
and Linda Simmonds, M.S.W.

Editing by: Mark Champagne

ENDORSEMENTS

DEDICATIONS

I dedicate this book to you the reader.
This piece of art that you hold in your hands is my life
-- a journey that you have guided for many years.
I had the courage to find my Potential -- my Hidden me --
because I knew that you would be there in the end.
You gave me reason and desire to not only write, but to live this book.

I dedicate the Awakening symbol to a great man
whose work touched my soul so deeply -- it Awakened it --
Robin Williams, the actor, comedian, and humanitarian.
His work gave me reason to believe in and hold onto the essence
of my true-self as I followed in his footsteps.

In loving memory of my mother, Eleanor Ruth,
who encouraged, believed in, and supported me
while I studied to become a writer.
As my best friend and an astounding artist,
she was the finest mother I could have ever asked for.
Thank you mom.

A special thank you to our ancestors for
being our forerunners and leaving us their wisdom.

Quotation is the highest compliment you can pay to an author.
-- Dr. Sam'l Johnson

ACKNOWLEDGMENTS

*Pam Champagne and Ric Hollowell are the wind beneath my wings.
This book was guided by their belief in me, Pam's clinical interest,
and her loving desire to help others. Their support during my
journey is the essence of The Hidden You.*

*Linda Simmonds gives me strength just being in her presence. Her
personal and professional interest in The Hidden You evoked a
power that emanates from cover to cover.*

*David Kazdan, a great doctor and humanitarian,
gave my mother her dignity back when illness took it away,
and guided the healing of my body, mind, and spirit.*

*Thank you to the many clients who contributed their time to
researching the symbols. Their devotion to helping their fellow
humankind gave life to The Hidden You.*

*To Mark Champagne, who devoted his time to editing this manuscript.
His friendship and authenticity gave me the strength to complete my work.*

*To my family -- from the darkness came light!
John, my heart bound father, Celine, my beautiful stepmother, Susan,
Dayna, Roslyn and Andrea, my valiant sisters, Little Lisa, Lindie, Colleen,
Megan and Christopher, my angelic nieces and nephew, and Martin and
Billy, my charming stepbrothers, will live in my heart forever!*

*Afshin Afshari exudes the strength of an honorable, devoted man and a
great father! He has brought new life into my life!*

*To Anna F. and Lee Morino, whose friendship will never be forgotten,
Bob & Jackie Hissett, the Burke family, and Kathy Williams,
for each being a pillar in my life!*

John Bradshaw's teachings helped me heal my inner child.

John Hogan introduced me to my spirit! I will never forget him!

TABLE OF CONTENTS

Message to the Reader

INTRODUCTION

Our fight for wellness begins the day that we are born. To me, this means we fight to keep our spirit -- our true-selves -- alive which in turn keeps the mind and body well. As we grow, our true-selves may become Hidden for various reasons, including: rules, regulations, religious beliefs, childhood trauma, or "dysfunctional" family life. As adults, most of us need a boost to reclaim our Hidden selves and Become our Potential!

As a child, my true-self was limitless. I was captured by my fellow kind and loved life with a passion. I was aware of my spirit and its connection to life. I loved nature and the essence of our world. I desired to understand the spirit of people and explored it every chance I could. Unfortunately, my life was a dance that only I knew the steps to and I was greatly misunderstood. Before the age of twelve, my true-self had Hidden.

Ten years later, I found myself spiritless and wandering aimlessly through life. This awareness began my journey to reclaim my Hidden self and Become My Potential.

My mother was a great influence. She reminded me constantly that writing and art were my Potential from the time I was a child and this is where I would find my Hidden Me. I returned to school and received honors in a three year public relations writing program. I also took night courses in graphic art and studied psychology in my spare time.

She was right. I found my Hidden self and my passions as they burned in my soul, but that is where they remained! I had more work to do to free my Hidden self and Become my Potential.

Upon completion of my schooling, I entrenched myself in books for the next four years. I studied spirituality and world religions that led me to great healers and healing methods of our time. My mind, although, continued to store old memories and habits burdening my Hidden self from being free. I began to examine spirituality and psychology as two elements working together. This bore the creation of the symbols. My Hidden self began to awaken.

My mother became terminally ill and my focus turned to studying medicine, which included: natural, holistic, and conventional. I began to see that physical, mental, and spiritual health were prerequisites for becoming well, freeing my Hidden me, and Becoming my Potential.

I applied my findings to the symbol's interpretations and put them into clinical study. The study showed an accuracy of 97% and still holds true when used in therapy today.

To Become Your Potential, you must not only find, but free your Hidden You -- your true-self -- the child within.

The pillars for Becoming Your Potential are wellness of your mind, body, and spirit. The same state we experience as children -- limitless -- adventurous -- exploratory -- alive! This is being the best that you can be! This is being Your Potential.

I don't claim to be a doctor or psychologist. I don't claim to be the know all or end all. I do claim to have saved my own life by freeing my Hidden self and Becoming My Potential.

I wish you all the best in your journey to wellness and remember -- you are in control of your destiny!

Live well, but more importantly, live!

INTRODUCTION

Heal your spirit by finding The Hidden You. Heal your mind by freeing The Hidden You. Heal your body by Becoming Your Potential. This is an awakening to the memory of who you really are.

Seven years of research, one in clinical study with Pam Champagne, M.S.W., C.S.W., Psychotherapist, show an accuracy of 97%. Pam continues to use the symbols as a resource in her practice.

The 9 unique **SYMBOLS** represent characteristics of The Hidden You that are vital for reaching your Potential. They represent Awakening, Balance, Energy, Faith, Freedom, Hope, Spirit, Strength, and Vision. All symbols are equal. One is not better than the other. There are no right or wrong answers. <u>The symbols you choose change as your mood changes.</u>

The **INTERPRETATIONS** describe the symbol's meanings and give simple advice to free your Hidden You and Become Your Potential!

The **JOURNAL** is used to document your findings and overall health. It gives you the opportunity to assess and make changes to your personal health patterns quickly and accurately. Physical, mental, and spiritual health are the pillars for freeing your Hidden You and Becoming Your Potential! The information you gather in the journal can be helpful for assisting your medical practitioner, counselor, or natural health expert.

You will begin to care for and listen to your body, mind, and spirit as they communicate to you through the journal.

This book will assist you to alleviate emotional distress that is the root to many physical and mental health disorders. You will learn to listen to your inner voices as they cry out for your attention. Healing begins with the spirit, moves to the mind, and empowers the body.

It takes courage to grow up and turn out to be who you really are.
                                    -- e.e. cummings

SYMBOL & INTERPRETATION INSTRUCTIONS

(1) RELAX. Breathe deeply into your stomach.

(2) CHOOSE YOUR SYMBOL(S). Look at the symbols on the next page.

If you are in a **good mood** and **want to Become Your Potential**, choose the symbol(s) you find yourself most attracted to. If you are attracted equally to <u>all</u> the symbols, you are living your Potential at this moment. Make the most of it!

If you are in a **good mood**, but **something is bothering you** and you **want to Become Your Potential**, think about what is bothering you and choose the symbol(s) you find yourself least attracted to.

If you are in a **bad mood** and **want to Become Your Potential**, choose the symbol(s) you find yourself least attracted to. If <u>all</u> the symbols are equally unattractive, you are under great stress. Relax and follow the advice of the Awakening symbol (page 6). Try again later.

<u>This is not a guessing game!</u> **The symbol(s) you choose should be <u>obviously</u> more or less attractive than the other symbols. If this is not the case, your choice may not be accurate. Try again later.**

(3) READ THE INTERPRETATION(S). You have now chosen your symbol(s). Read the page suggested beneath each symbol for the symbol's interpretation. Refer to the page indicated as "attractive" when you find yourself attracted to a symbol. Refer to the page indicated as "unattractive" when you find a symbol unattractive.

• When reading the interpretation of the symbol you are attracted to, it may not describe what you <u>presently think of yourself</u>. Look deep within yourself and you will find The Hidden You!

• If you are not attracted to a symbol, read the "unattractive" section suggested and then the "attractive" section. This will further boost you Becoming Your Potential by freeing your Hidden You!

1

THE
SYMBOLS

Attractive: Page 4
Unattractive: Page 6

Attractive: Page 8
Unattractive: Page 10

Attractive: Page 12
Unattractive: Page 14

Attractive: Page 16
Unattractive: Page 18

Attractive: Page 20
Unattractive: Page 22

You are connected to your higher self and reason using the wisdom that you have gained throughout your lifetime. Your decision making is unbiased and admired by others. You are the witness or observer on the outside looking in.

❋ You live in the moment. You do not live in the past or in the future. In this state, you are thankful and appreciate life's little blessings. You do not waste your time thinking about what you may have missed, the mistakes you have made, or the mistakes you might make. In the moment, your thoughts are pure, majestic, and blissful.

❋ If there is heaven on earth, it is the state you are experiencing right now. You are detached, yet completely attached to the rhythm of life.

You enjoy life, but do not get caught up in it. You prefer to watch and listen. You see the potential in almost everyone and everything. Life is a dance that surrounds you in all your glory. You have the freedom to dance a while, but sometimes choose to just stand back and watch.

❋ You are free of emotional and intellectual turmoil. You know what is best for you and you make wise decisions.

❋ As an understanding and accepting person of human limitation, people are comfortable in your presence.

❋ You have incredible visionary skills. May it be visualizing the future of a corporation or seeing beyond what the typical person sees. It is natural. You have a gift.

❋ Have you experienced a change in your life or yourself? Do you have a new awareness? Possibly, you are experiencing an awakening.

Awakening is to rise from a state of unconsciousness. In other words, you notice the beauty in everything around you.

❋ Some people have experienced an "awakening" in near death experiences. This happens when a person dies, typically has a beautiful, peaceful, enlightened experience, and then is brought back to life. This "awakening" brings with it a new awareness. After this type of experience, some people have been known to drastically change their lives and become better people for it.

❋ This is an excellent time to meditate.

Buddhists have used meditation for centuries to experience inner peace. Buddha means "awakened one". Some use meditation to find spiritual direction.

Common meditation exercises include: a quiet environment, sitting in an alert, formal position, and relaxing by focusing on an object that keeps your attention, for instance, your breathing. If your mind drifts, regain your concentration by reminding yourself to focus.

Yoga assists to embrace a meditative state. Yoga is a beautiful art that is healthy for your mind, body, and spirit. Sunrise yoga comes highly recommended.

❋ Each morning, we all experience a daily awakening. For the first few seconds after waking, our minds are quiet. This in itself is a meditative state. Stay in it as long as you can. You will experience inner peace and may receive some spiritual guidance. In this state, anything is possible!

Your body is precious.
It is our vehicle for awakening.
Treat it with care.
-- Buddha

You are all the Buddha.
-- last words of Buddha

5

Lift the heaviness off your shoulders by forgiving those who have hurt you. Free yourself by accepting human limitation. If you are judging yourself or anyone else, stop! Block out all the chatter in your head and take the time for peace of mind.

✺ Love guides the road to forgiveness. We all want to be forgiven and therefore must learn to forgive. North American Indians understand the essence of forgiveness as they speak of not judging a person until you have walked in that person's shoes. To forgive and forget is an act of great kindness, understanding, and love. Forgiveness rids us of emotional turmoil that interferes with our own personal happiness. It allows our spirit to grow and expand within the realm of love.

✺ Since the beginning of time, there have been wise, old souls. Stop and look into a mirror. Stand tall and proud. Hold your chin up and shoulders back. Look into the depths of your being. There you will find your brilliant, wise, old soul.

✺ You may feel confused or overwhelmed. Sometimes we get too emotionally or intellectually involved in a situation and are unable to see what is right in front of our eyes. It is time to step outside your situation and take a look at the bigger picture. Bring your attention to the beauty within yourself and in the life around you. This will take your attention away from the situation and re-energize you. Then take a new look at your situation. If your mind starts to chatter, tell it to stop until you are able to see the situation with a quiet mind. Know that your situation is not good or bad, it just is! You will find clarity.

✺ Your true-self and intuition are undivided. Listen to your instincts and gut feelings. These inner voices are your personal needs calling out to you.

It can be difficult to put your own needs ahead of others, but your health must always come first. One's health includes the wellness of the body, mind, and spirit. This means the body needs good, healthy food and exercise, the mind needs peace and positive thinking, and the spirit needs love and freedom.

✳ Maybe you would like a new perspective. Are you living the life you have always dreamt of living? Can you alter what you are doing now to improve the quality of your life? Anything is possible. Do not judge your desires. Love them. Let them be. They are there for a reason. That reason is to live.

✳ This is a good time to experience new things and expand your horizons. Have you ever thought of traveling? Do you ever dream of getting away? Do it! Go hiking in the country, dancing in the city, swimming in a lake, or skiing down a mountain. The change and awakening will do you well. The experience will live with you always.

Culture is another form of new experience. Eat new foods and awaken to new tastes and smells. Open up your senses. Go to a concert or relax in a sexy jazz bar. Spread edible flowers on your next salad or try exotic fruits and vegetables. Just go wild!

✳ You are your own best friend. Create a sacred space for yourself. This is a great time to indulge in candles, aroma therapy, or a foam bath. Relax and turn off your mind. Only allow thoughts of your passions to enter it and meditate on those thoughts. Begin imagining what it would feel like to live out your passions. Enjoy! Your Hidden You will awaken. You will Become Your Potential!

May you live all the days of your life.
-- Jonathan Swift

Reflect on your present blessings, of which every man has many, not on your past misfortunes, of which all men have some.
-- **Charles Dickens**

You understand life's enchantment and are able to handle stress without stress. While idling in neutral, you weigh the pros and cons of situations enabling you to make good decisions. Your masculine and feminine are in harmony.

❈ You are settled in life and stand tall in your personal convictions. Your calm and peaceful demeanor creates a pleasant atmosphere. Others see your reasoning and are more balanced in your presence.

❈ This is a great time for decision making.

❈ You see the positive and negative of situations, but stay centered without judgment. This balance allows all of your thoughts to flow comfortably in and out of your mind.

❈ One of the greatest strengths of balance is the pride of standing behind what you do, whether right or wrong. Nothing is good or bad, positive or negative. It just is. Balance brings equilibrium to the thought process. Your emotions are calm and energy is high.

❈ Balance means holding your composure which brings harmony to all things. It offers stability to thoughts, feelings, and emotions.

❈ Some eastern therapies believe balance means that our energy flows along pathways in our body that connect all our organs and bodily systems. Stress and other influences can disturb the flow causing imbalance.

A traditional Chinese doctor may treat the imbalance that produces symptoms of illness instead of treating the symptoms. Traditional Chinese medicine uses herbs, acupuncture, and other healing methods to increase the flow of energy moving along our body's pathways.

The harmony that comes with balance is also known as the "yin & yang" of Chinese philosophy. Harmony, leading to health, relies on balancing the yin and yang. In order for our bodies to stay well, we must constantly make changes and adjustments to maintain balance. We become ill when we are unable to adjust to changes around us, including: change in weather, increased or decreased stress, or the attack of an infection.

Chinese practitioners recognize approximately 6000 medicinal substances composed of botanical, mineral, and animal products. These substances are used to help rebuild and sustain balance.

Movement is an element of Chinese preventative medicine. Tai-chi, a flowing movement of the body, and the use of breathing techniques encourage a steady flow of energy through the body.

❋ Moderation is the key to being balanced, maintaining health, and preventing illness.

❋ For humanity's sake, balance is a vital characteristic needed to maintain peace among human kind. No matter what race, belief structure, or religion, we are born alike. We are all the same animal -- humans -- equal.

❋ You are balanced and a great humanitarian. You are an asset to the world!

To many abstinence is easier than perfect moderation.
-- St. Augustine

Let every man be respected as an individual and no man idolized. It is an irony of fate that I myself have been the recipient of excessive admiration and reverence from my fellow-beings, through no fault, and no merit, of my own.
-- Albert Einstein

We hold these truths to be self-evident, that all men are created equal.
-- Thomas Jefferson

Life may seem black and white,
but there is a possibility that things are not quite as they seem.
There is always grey area. You inevitably have choices.

✳ Equilibrium is an equal balance between forces. If you want to achieve equilibrium, live your life in moderation. If you are doing anything in excess, cut back and you will regain balance. You may be sleeping too much or too little, eating too much or too little, or working too much or too little. Take a look at your life and observe your habits. Make changes where necessary and your balance will be restored.

✳ Balance is understanding life's enchantment and being challenged by happiness and sadness. Loving is sometimes a challenge. When we lose love, for instance, we may become sad, close-up and stop loving, but there is another choice. The choice to see that what happened is sad, but it is time to learn, grow, and move on. Look at what went right and what went wrong. Take this experience with you on your journey and accept the wisdom that you have gained.

✳ When making decisions, listen to your gut feelings or intuition. Sit back, relax, and breathe deeply into your stomach for a while. Once your stomach relaxes, ask yourself how it feels to make your decision. If your stomach stays relaxed or feels good, you are probably making a good decision. If your stomach tightens or gets upset in any way, it most likely is not a good decision for your personal wellness.

✳ Also, when making decisions, consider if they are congruent with the needs of your personal journey. Ask yourself who you are and what you want out of life. Then, base your decisions on those two elements. If the answer to your decision is against who you are or what you want out of life then it will create an obstacle interfering with you Becoming Your Potential. You can now base your decision on what is truly best for you.

If you have a hard time figuring out who you are, check again. The Hidden You lives in your heart. It lives in your laughter and tears. It lives in the child -- your inner child. Do you remember the first time you saw a butterfly or your blood from a skinned knee? Remember and you will remember who you are.

Your personal morals, values, and boundaries are also major components of who you are. Believe in them and live every moment of your life by them.

✸ Be proud of yourself and of being human. We are creatures who create and explore unknown territory. We are animals with instinct, curiosity, and supreme intelligence. Also, be proud when you try because when you try, you never fail. When you try, you live! Respect who you are and let yourself make mistakes. Allow yourself to be human and enjoy it!

✸ Never put yourself down. These thoughts will become etched in your mind and you will begin to believe them. Be your own best friend. Speak lovingly to yourself and stand behind everything you do. Even in your weakest moments, you are still a wonderful, beautiful human being.

✸ You are sometimes selfish and good for you! One needs to be selfish to care for themselves. Selfishness, as all things, only becomes unhealthy when taken to an extreme. One can be selfish and selfless at the same time. As long as you come first and are healthy, you can give freely and selflessly. Take good care of yourself and you will Become Your Potential.

Deal with the faults of others as gently as with your own.
-- Chinese Proverb

The best and most beautiful things in the world cannot be seen or even touched. They must be felt with the heart.
-- Helen Keller

11

ENERGY Attractive

While your creative juices flow,
your body feels invigorated and fortified.
Your inner-child is alive and feeling playful and happy.
Beauty is vivid and life is fun.

✳ A pulse within your soul is beating with healthy, clear energy. Your power, stamina, and vitality are in full force. Excitement and laughter are your driving forces.

✳ Has anyone ever said that you are wild or crazy? Take it as a compliment. This expression of self through the body's own energy is creative and beautiful. This is the essence or breath of life. Where others are content staying in one place, you are always on an adventure indulging in stimulating activities. You are alive and living proof that one can be truly "full of life".

✳ Your wild soul is free and heats the fire for magnificent sex. This is a good time to slip into something more comfortable. Your sexual energy is in prime form. While respecting yourself and your body, allow your sexual energy the freedom to express itself. If without a partner at this time, still explore your senses. Pleasure yourself. Love yourself. Become risqué and write a seductive story or draw a sensuous picture. Delight and rollick in the luxury of your sexuality.

✳ We all have a luminous energy field. This energy is heat that our bodies radiate. The more energy we have the more vibrant the energy is leaving our bodies. This is our aura. Specialized photography shows the energy in colour depending upon the level of heat. This experimentation with energy has shown that our energy changes with our moods.

Throughout history, our aura has been documented. Ancient pictures of Jesus Christ and saints indicate a white light surrounding their bodies. White signifies clean, clear energy. This type of energy has been noted to indicate healing qualities. People with this energy are known to have healing hands.

✳ In this state, you too have healing hands. If you concentrate or meditate and visualize the energy in your body being forced to your hands, the palms of your hands will become warm. Practice. This is the healing energy used by hands-on-healers.

Reiki is a hands-on-healing tool used to transfer energy. The art of Reiki came from the ancient Sanskrit manuscripts. Pronounced as "ray-key", this word comes from the Japanese words rei, meaning universal and ki, meaning vital force. When this energy is channeled properly, healing has occurred.

✳ Children are a perfect example of energy in motion. Babies are born moving, kicking, and crying. Toddlers have exuberant amounts of energy. They are constantly active. When held back from running and playing, the child may have a tantrum, get a headache, stomach-ache, or even feel depressed and lethargic. This is the child's way of dealing with their pent-up energy.

✳ Eat as many live foods as possible to increase your intake of energy. These include uncooked fruits and vegetables. Juicing is an excellent way to intake these foods.

✳ This majestic state is empowering and fun. Express yourself and bask in your creative forces. Draw or paint a picture, whittle a piece of wood, arrange fresh flowers, redecorate your home, cook a beautiful dinner, or take pictures of nature. Let your creative juices flow. Indulge!

Follow your bliss.
-- Joseph Campbell

Conformity is the jailer of freedom and the enemy of growth.
-- John F. Kennedy

Laugh with friends, go dancing, take up a new sport,
meditate, listen to music and let yourself be free.
Radiate all the great energy from inside your body.
Stand tall with courage and take a leap of faith.
It is fun out there. Go for it!
Let go! Be proud!

✳ This symbol may remind you of squirming snakes. It may seem creepy, scary, or wicked. This is the feeling that one acquires when holding excessive energy inside the body.

Are your hands shaking? Do you have a headache? Are you tired? Do your joints ache? It is important to release the excess energy from your body. Go for a walk, stretch like a cat, cry like a baby, scream in your car, dance in your living room, or laugh in hysterics to free the overabundance of energy. Dance and challenge your body. Read a book and challenge your mind. Meditate and challenge your spirit. Bring life into your life and express yourself!

Have you been holding onto problems? For instance, are you angry with someone? Maybe all you have to do is tell them. Whatever you may be holding onto, let it go gently.

✳ Our whole world revolves around energy. Energy creates movement. It is measured and is a natural power. Use your energy to its fullest capacity and you will be well.

✳ Do you find your relationships boring? If so, it is time to bring new energy into them. Begin by doing more activities together. Joke around and have fun. Play sports or games together. Read to each other. The energy will begin flowing and your relationships will become more alive and exciting.

✳ If you want to spark the fires of intimacy with your partner, indulge in the pleasures shared only with a loved one. Buy scented oils and massage each other. This includes every part of the body, not just the back. Massage each other's hands one day and each other's head another. Share in the simplicity of life. Shower and bathe together. Tell your loved one how beautiful their body is and how much you enjoy touching them. Stroke their hair and caress their face. Touch those spots rarely touched, including: the eyelids, the back of the neck, behind the ears, in-between the fingers or toes, the inside of the thigh, and behind the knees. Wash their hair and/or brush it for them. Undress them before bed. Play with your partner and enjoy them to the fullest. This is why we have a partner. It gives us the opportunity to share with them a love and intimacy not shared with others.

✴ You enjoy being your Hidden You, the kid, the scientist, the music lover, the nature girl or boy, etc. We are multifaceted creatures and have many desires and passions. Look deep within yourself and you will find The Hidden You. If not behind a wall, you will find The Hidden You within your heart.

✴ Always know that you are beautiful in whatever form you take. A piece of art is a creation from the soul and so are you. Let your Hidden You be free and your beauty will radiate for all to see.

✴ There is always more to life than meets the eye. We typically perceive our limitations as those which others have taught or told us. Go beyond these beliefs and let yourself be free. You have few limitations and can do anything you put your mind to! Give your being the freedom to express itself through the mind, body, and spirit. You will feel re-energized, revitalized, youthful, and happy. You will Become Your Potential!

Life was meant to be lived and curiosity must be kept alive.
One must never, for whatever reason, turn his back on life.
-- Eleanor Roosevelt

Energy and persistence conquer all things.
-- Benjamin Franklin

You are a survivor of a cruel, but innocent world.
You honor the sacredness of your true-self.
Your purpose, vision, and focus are clear.

✳ With your torch of will and determination held high, you fight with heart and soul to create your own destiny.

✳ You are a star and have much to be proud of. You warrant respect. You stand for pride and dignity. Your humility is an inspiration.

✳ While connected to the rhythm of life, you have faith in your knowing. You know more than most, see more than most, and hear more than most. Your wisdom and intelligence exceed your elders.

✳ Encompassed by instinct and intuition, you are a believer in endless possibilities.

✳ Most of humanity have faith in something, may it be a God, many Gods, the God within ourselves, love, trust, or honesty.

Faith, more often than not, creates what we desire. When we believe to the point of conviction, desires and dreams become reality. It is created from one single thought. A thought based on faith.

Faith is believing in something or trusting without any proof. It is a state-of-mind, not governed by religions or institutions. Our own personal beliefs govern faith.

✳ Your faith has always taken care of you. Your perseverance and trust have guided many travels. Your faith has led the way to you reaching your goals.

✳ Faith eliminates obstacles that we create by worrying. Faith does not give worry the opportunity to become a solid thought and therefore worry has no power.

✴ Faith is a tool used to keep the body healthy. Thoughts of wellness flow from the mind and are delivered to the core of our cellular structure. The mind is a powerful vehicle and the body responds quickly to our inherent thought process. Have faith that you are well and you will be well.

✴ Faith healing calls upon a higher power to remedy and heal the patient's illness. It is based on the patient's belief and trust in the healer. The earliest faith healers were priests, Shamans, and medicine men. Science believes that faith healing is psychological and triggers a healing response in the body. Whether based on psychology or divine intervention, faith healing can heal. So, let it heal!

✴ Humans did not evolve by reading books. We evolved through experiencing life and by learning through success and failure. Whether pushed to learn because of curiosity and intrigue or just the plain desire for something more, faith has moved us forth through the ages. Faith has created medicine, scientific discovery, planetary exploration, and so much more. Those with faith have led the way for evolution.

If faith has the power to guide evolution, imagine what it is doing for you. Keep having faith in yourself and you will evolve to whatever state you desire. Your Potential is limitless!

It's better to light a candle than to curse the darkness.
-- Eleanor Roosevelt

The important thing is not to stop questioning.
-- Albert Einstein

I find out what the world needs.
Then I go and try to invent it.
-- Thomas Edison

Obtain faith by trusting yourself.
Make yourself a promise and keep it.
Pick a road and travel it.

✳ Faith is something that takes time. Sit back, take it easy, and just imagine the greatest things that could ever happen to you. Have faith in yourself and they will happen to you! You will Become Your Potential!

✳ You are a focused person with a deep sense of intelligence. It is necessary to keep your mind active. Take night courses, read books, or watch the learning channels on television. Take up a mentally stimulating activity such as tai-chi, karate, or chess. Play games that challenge your mind, including: crossword puzzles, brain teasers, trivia, and board games.

✳ Do you fear something? List the positives of living with this fear and the negatives of living with this fear. You will be in a more insightful position to decide whether to be afraid or not to be afraid. If you are unable to break free from your fear, speak to a holistic practitioner, or counselor.

Fear hinders you from freeing your Hidden You and Becoming Your Potential. Fear causes undue stress on the whole of your being. To dissolve fear, you must walk through your fear.

Fear is part of our natural make-up and warns us of danger. The body and mind know if there is something to fear. When we are frightened by what we think about, we are creating a fear that is not natural to the body. Trust your body and know that it will tell you when there is something to fear. Ease your mind as you are in good hands.

✳ Faith is a wonderful tool, but be aware of situations where faith can make you hold on too tight. Let go just a little and re-evaluate the situation from time-to-time. Make sure your faith is not clouding your reality. For example, if you have faith in the institution of marriage and your spouse physically harms you, do you remain married because you have faith in the institution of marriage or do you leave because you have faith in yourself?

✳ Live up to your promises to yourself and you will learn to trust again. It all begins with you trusting you.

✳ Sometimes proof and evidence are not readily available and you just have to trust. This trust is faith. When you have faith that something is going to happen, it usually will, but at its own pace. Be patient.

✳ When your heart is open and you are a loving person, your instinct and intuition will move through you easily. Let these inner voices guide your faith.

✳ Faith has a deep impact on our spiritual essence. Belief in something great and powerful, for example, love, harmony, or a higher power, gives the spirit the freedom to soar above all things.

✳ There is a big shining star inside you. The same one that has been there since you were a child. Maybe it is time for your star to emerge. You have so much to share with the world. It is waiting for you. It is calling for you. Your Hidden You wants to be free and shine for all the world to see!

Where there is a will there is a way.
-- Scott

Kind hearts are the garden; kind thoughts are the roots; kind words are the flowers; kind deeds are the fruits.
-- English Proverb

When it is dark enough, you can see the stars.
-- Charles A. Beard

FREEDOM

While under no one's control and controlling of no one,
you have the strength to hold onto personal rights.
You see life in a broad sense; life is not literal.
You are gracefully frank and unreserved.

❋ Spontaneity and independence are your driving forces giving you the freedom to assert a strong sense of self.

❋ Freedom represents a state in which the mind, body, and spirit are open to express freely. Your senses are truly alive. Freedom will take you anywhere you want to go. You can do anything, be anyone, and go anywhere.

❋ You are in harmony with life. This state is one of the most glorious to experience. People watch you in awe. You are a wonderful example of humanity in its purest form.

❋ You may be unique or different. Being unique is wonderful. You are one-of-a-kind, an experience rather than one of the crowd. You are a creation all of your own. It is wonderful to see a person who is comfortable in their own skin. You are proud of who you are and stand tall in your personal conviction to love yourself -- your Hidden You!

❋ Freedom relieves the body of stress and anxiety. Unhealthy pressure on the body, mind, and spirit is avoided and sometimes eliminated. You are healthy in this state.

❋ You may feel full. You are beaming with love and immersed in your own life energy. This beauty shines from the core of your being. Your Hidden You is free!

❋ Your creativity is in full force. Feed it often. Creativity takes many forms, including: cooking, gardening, decorating, playing an instrument, singing, dancing, painting, drawing, writing, etc.

Indulge in your creative forces as you will achieve outstanding results. You will experience a union between yourself and your creation. It is a stimulating experience.

❋ Freedom brings the power of flight. Have you been flying in your dreams? This is an incredible experience. Try going to sleep with thoughts of flying on your mind. It may evoke such dreams.

❋ Children love being in your presence as your innocence is still alive. The child within is safe and loved by your adult self. Your Hidden You -- the child -- is held sacred in your heart.

❋ You are independent, yet love the company of others. You love being loved and you love loving.

❋ You are in your own presence and quite delighted with yourself. This state you are experiencing is close to the state we are born in. A state by which there are no laws governing your being. You are living your Potential to its fullest capacity. You are in the moment, outside the moment, and overseeing the moment all at the same time. It is possible that you are the moment!

❋ You will live a long, healthy life in this state. You are one person who will have few regrets, if any. You make the most of your life. In fact, you are life! You won't just Become Your Potential. You are Potential!

You give but little when you give of your possessions.
It is when you give of yourself that you truly give.
-- Kahlil Gibran

Your heart's desires be with you!
-- Shakespeare

Beauty is not caused. It is.
-- Emily Dickinson

FREEDOM

Unattractive

Grab a mirror and look straight in your eyes.
That is you in there. Free yourself!
Let the innocence of love and life live
before you lose your desire to fly.

❋ You are not alone nor have you ever been. There is someone who loves you more than anything and will be with you forever. This someone is your Hidden You. You are never alone as long as you have yourself.

You are not empty when you love yourself. Loving yourself fills you with a passion to be loyal to your needs. When consumed with love, you share it as freely as you create it.

Say good morning to the paper boy, bus driver, or other passing stranger. Put your loneliness aside and open up to others. Share your love with others and others will share their love with you. Your energy will increase and your heart will fill.

❋ Do something that you think is rather wild. Dance in the rain. Go to a movie or dinner by yourself. Sing in your car. Let your thoughts and judgments go. Live on the edge for a moment. Once you have done it a few times, you will get better and better at it. It will become easy, almost second nature, a personal challenge or adventure. In no time, you will feel free as a bird.

Whether it is dancing, singing, exercising, crafts, art, team sports, adventures, spontaneity, or just enjoying the moment, live every day as if it were your first!

❋ Are you involved in a relationship or situation in which you are not being yourself? The true-self knows when it is locked away. The mind has to work hard to keep it down. When your mind is free, your true-self -- The Hidden You -- is free.

22

❋ You are growing. Have faith! You will get there. Your tears and/or feelings deserve approval. Focus on loving yourself and respecting your needs. Direction will be yours. Your Hidden You will always guide you. Trust!

❋ Freedom in relationships is the essence of success. Humans do not like being controlled. We are born free and thus inherit the need for freedom. Freedom is to do what makes us happy with the intent to promote the well being of our fellow humans. This is being a humanitarian. We are born free, but must always stand for humanity. This should be a universal law!

Bathing in the waters of freedom means one must take responsibility for one's choices. Be free and enjoy it, but do not forget to fulfill your obligations. Therefore, you will not end up flying alone. It is more fun flying with your friends and loved ones.

❋ Play with your spirit. Enjoy your sensuality and inner fire. Be all consuming now and then. Take an hour to yourself. Tantalize your senses with an aromatic, hot, deep bath. Light some candles and turn on some relaxing music to create your own personal mood. You are there, alone, under the soothing, gentle waves of the water. Your body feels free, light, and buoyant. Your mind is being caressed by the gentleness around you. ENJOY! Let your Hidden You be free!

My only sketch, profile, of Heaven is a large blue sky,
and larger than the biggest I have seen in June
- and in it are my friends - every one of them.
-- Emily Dickinson

A man's friendships are
one of the best measures of his worth.
-- Charles Darwin

There is light at the end of the tunnel.
You are the master of bravery.
Your humble and adoring heart
declares your spiritual conviction.

✴ These may be trying times, but hope is guiding you. Listen to your inner voice, instinct, intuition, and gut feelings as they are your pathfinders. They have led you all of your life and will continue to direct your journeys.

✴ As a child, you may have had a personal experience with a higher power. Whether or not you have memory, you know your instincts well and are on alert for inner wisdom.

✴ Hope is the light beneath the darkness. One single thought -- "I hope". This one thought pulls the light up from the darkness. Hope is a powerful human expression. This one creative thought can provide discovery and endless possibilities.

"I give-up" is a sign of lost hope. Again, it is one single thought. Our thoughts have a great influence on how we live our lives. If we consistently think that we give-up, we are conditioning our mind. Our body will respond simultaneously with feelings of depression, loneliness, anger, etc. "I hope" brings upon the light. There is a possibility! There is a chance!

✴ The power of hope proves itself in the terminally ill. If there is a chance for cure, the person may far exceed life expectancy. Once told there is no chance for cure, people have been known to die overnight -- lost hope!

✴ Hope is our guardian and rescues us from falling into the darkness of despair. Whether from ill health or the loss of a loved one, hope gives us the opportunity to move on and keep living. It gives us the chance to see that there is always light even in our darkest moments. Hope governs life and is a great influence on the growth of human kind. Without hope, all is lost. In our human existence, this is almost never the case. Humans are resilient and can get through almost any tragedy with the hope for a brighter tomorrow. This has carried us through the ages and will continue for as long as we exist.

✴ You know all is safe and that you are fine. You have always had an innate ability of knowing.

✴ There is light at the end of the tunnel. Hope lights the way for endless possibilities and is the spark of life. It gives us the strength to survive. Your hopefulness fortifies others. You never give up. Your strength is dynamic and encouraging.

✴ Hope does, although, bestow a shadow of a doubt. Faith bestows no doubt. Hope is the essence of life and faith creates life. Hope usually indicates the possibility that our desires may not come our way. If your desire is 100% under your control, you may consider moving out of this state and into a state of faith (see page 16). Hope is the origin of faith.

✴ Live up to your promises to yourself and others. When you say you are going to do something, do it! Your Hidden You will feel safe and freedom will be yours. Build faith in yourself and you will have faith in Becoming Your Potential!

Hope is the parent of faith.
-- Cyrus A. Bartol

In all things it is better to hope than to despair.
-- Johann Wolfgang von Goethe

Self-trust is the first secret of success.
-- Emerson

Your dance is humble and graceful.
To build strength, feed yourself with positive energy.

✳ Do not allow the little obstacles to be deterrents. As water rushes down a river, it does not stop for anything that is in its way. It immediately creates a new path and continues to flow as if there were no obstacle at all. Spend some time observing a river. Imagine that you are the river. Obstacles are only challenges that make us create a new path. The more obstacles, the clearer our path becomes and stronger our course runs. Put less thought towards the obstacle and more thought towards creating a path around it. Where there is a will, there is a way.

✳ You may feel like a caged bird. Your wings want to open and your spirit wants to fly. There is a door by which you can leave your cage. Unlock it and free yourself. If you are waiting for someone else to open the door, it may not happen. You are in control of your destiny. You are the captain of your ship. If you want something, take action. Take your focus off your problems and free the caged bird.

✳ Worries keep you caged. Do you worry? What do you worry about? List the positives of living with this worry and the negatives of living with this worry. This will give you insight to worry or not to worry. If you are unable to break free from worry, speak to a doctor, holistic practitioner, or counselor.

Negative thinking is the root of worry which is a powerful emotion. Worry is expecting something bad to happen. This type of thinking will destroy the body. It brings on nervousness, upset stomach, panic attacks, anxiety disorders, heart ailments, sleeping disorders, etc.

We create most of our worries by getting involved in other peoples worries and troubles. This undue stress will take a toll on your body. Alone, this stress can be a killer.

✳ Every day that we are alive is a blessing. Share the beauty of your life with others and ask that they share the beauty of their life with you.

✳ You love being fed with positive energy. Get out with people who like you for you. Meet new friends. Join a gym. Take part in a social group. Take courses. Hang out at the library. Change your job. If an idea makes you happy, do it!

✳ Bring out the warrior within. Utilize your personal boundaries and stand tall. When you walk, pull your shoulders back -- hold your head high -- raise your chin. This will give your body and mind a feeling of power and strength. Look at your posture and assume an open, strong stance. Your body will pick-up on your desire for strength. If slouched over or hiding behind crossed arms and legs, your inner power has no way out. Your body releases inner strength when you stand tall and open.

✳ Patience brings a quiet mind and a peaceful soul. It gives us the opportunity to stay on our journey. When there is a lack of patience, there is a disturbance of the mind, body, and spirit. Our journey becomes unclear and guided by the mind instead of the heart. Be patient! You will free your Hidden You and Become Your Potential!

✳ Others admire your dynamic impulse to hope for great things. Action feeds hope. If you hope for love, be loving. If you hope for success, be successful. If you hope for health, be healthy. If you hope for happiness, be happy. Make the decision to go after your desires. Do not stop until you get what you want!

Act like a lamb and the wolves will eat you.
-- Anon femme

You gain strength, courage and confidence by every experience in which you really stop to look fear in the face.
-- Eleanor Roosevelt

You are free to fly in mind, body, and spirit.
The innocence of the child within you is alive.
You are light and buoyant with positive, clean, clear energy.
You are nurturing and love being nurtured.

✴ You are accepting of human limitation and are not judgmental. You are loving, gentle, strong, and clear. You are all beautiful things combined into one. Your light heart and desire to live in the moment are enchanting. You are in a glorious state.

✴ Your spirit conveys strong intuition and pure knowing. It links you to destiny. This is a good time to make life decisions.

Intuition is a beautiful experience. It is your spirit talking to you and caring for you. It is the mind that causes confusion, especially when we doubt ourselves. To connect to your intuition, turn off the chatter in your mind and let your spirit be free through loving yourself and the world around you.

✴ To have spirit is to have life. The spirit gives you the power to do anything you want to do. It feeds the body and mind with ultimate bliss. As long as we live to love, there is no right or wrong sense of spirituality.

The essence of spirit is love. When loving, spirit is alive. Love is unconditional. It does not waiver. Giving love and receiving love is as easy as drinking milk and eating cookies. It is enjoyable and comes naturally. You love yourself and others at no cost. You do not take advantage of love and do not put any restraints on love. Your love is not demanding. It is merely sharing your spirit and feeling good about doing so.

✴ Delve deeply into the wells of your mind to help link into the bliss of spirituality. All nations, creeds, and religions, in one way or another, have found spirit. Spirit is the essence of strength, world peace, and healing.

✴ Shamanism is known to be the world's oldest system of mind-body healing. Shamans (a word meaning wise ones) are highly trained healers. If you believe and seek the wisdom of Shamanism, you too may have the power to heal.

✴ Your steps are light as if you are walking on clouds. At this moment, you know your spirit as you always have. You know your dreams and desires. You know what makes you happy and you know what you want out of life. Write it all down and remind yourself everyday. Believe and your spirit will lead the way.

✴ You are kind to all life, plant and animal. Born onto the same earth, humankind shares this world with all living things. To survive, we fundamentally need all creatures great and small. We need the air we breath, the water we drink, and the insects that cause our plants to bear fruit. If we hurt these dynamics, we are in essence destroying ourselves. You are a highly evolved humanitarian and give hope to all life for a peaceful existence.

Good to forgive, best to forget.
-- Browning

I have made a decision, on the presumption that my offer of love has been accepted and reciprocated, I am now by my own free choice committed to the happiness, security, and well-being of the person I love. I will do everything I can to help you build whatever dreams you have. It is this commitment which I make when I offer you my love. I have always said that I would die for you and never said that for anyone before. "No one can give a greater proof of love than by laying down his life for his friends."
John 15:13

You may be longing for inner peace. Look at yourself and your surroundings. Find the beauty in everything you see. Listen to your instinct and always follow it.

✳ Become aware of your relationships. Are they positive, loving, supportive, and nurturing? Surround yourself with healthy, caring, supportive, happy people who love you for you. Focus your energy on building positive relationships -- relationships that give as well as take.

It is important to feel comfortable when asking your friends for help and know that you are being loved when they give it to you. We all need a shoulder to lean on now and then. When you need a little love and support, ask a "friend" and you will receive it.

Giving exudes love from the spirit. The spirit is barren without loving others and sharing with others.

✳ When we think of spirit, we may think of ghost, apparition, vision, or animation. Spirit may embody courage, enthusiasm, purpose, heart, vision, life, mood, substance, nature, essence, psyche, or soul. Spirit may be all. When you have spirit, you have a connection to all things great!

✳ Many of us have been raised with stories of bad spirits that may injure us or of a judgmental God who may, if we are BAD, throw us into the fires of hell. This is not spirituality! Spirituality is not frightening, unbelievable, or overpowering. Rather, it is a feeling of pureness within the heart and soul!

✳ Give spirituality a chance! You have nothing to lose. It has taken years to reach a point where modern society accepts individual spirituality. It has gained respect from both men and women. Fifty years from now, it will be a different world as spirituality will have had more time to become an accepted aspect of ourselves.

✳ You may feel alone or abandoned when disconnected from the spirit. This is the loss of connection to the true-self. When connected, you are never alone.

✳ Do you feel guilt or shame? If so, accept yourself and your human limitations. It does not matter who you have been. Who you are today is all that matters. You have a beautiful heart and deserve love. Share all you can with others who love you. The shame and guilt, once shared and accepted by those who love you, will evaporate.

✳ Know that you are beautiful in your own form. No matter what, you are just as wonderful as everyone else. Comparing yourself to others can only hurt you. Be happy with what you have. List all the wonderful things in your life and be thankful. Sometimes it is easy to forget how extraordinary our lives are. If you judge yourself by what others have, you will stifle your growth and lessen the self pride that you truly deserve. Be proud of yourself and your accomplishments.

✳ Within each of us is spirit. We may be aware of it everyday or just for moments during our life. Whichever it is, feed your spirit. Your spirit needs change, love, respect, new horizons, and play. The more you feed your spirit, the more your spirit will feed you.

✳ Care for your spirit. Love it and give it the opportunity to be free. Look at others who are alive and have spirit. Love their laughter and joy. Indulge in humor and your sexual energy. There is nothing to be ashamed of. Open up and be free. You will become more youthful, full of life, and happier in the presence of yourself. You will free your Hidden You and Become Your Potential!

If we really want to love, we must learn how to forgive.
-- Mother Theresa

I am not now that which I have been.
-- Byron

You are solid as a rock and sure of your self greatness.
You are emotionally calm as confidence and security
reside within. You are aware of and driven by goals
making you a strong decision maker.
This is a great time for deep meditation.

✳ Do not be concerned with your attraction to this symbol. Powerful people do great acts and deserve to be proud of their strength. Your powers are love, wisdom, intelligence, and calm emotions.

✳ Solid, well-built boundaries and a strong sense of self are the signs of great strength. You know who you are, where you come from, and where you are going. While your feet are planted firmly on the ground, you take direction and are focused.

✳ Before making a decision, you think long and hard about your goals. When it is time to take action, you drive as a bull and stop at nothing to reach your destination.

✳ You are a crusader and charge into success with victory. You will achieve much in your lifetime. You have great entrepreneurial skills and are good at anything you put your heart and soul into.

✳ Others are aware of your strength as it is a powerful energy. People feel bigger and stronger when in your presence. Some may feel a little intimidated at first, but are soon enlightened by the greatness of your soul. You are a great humanitarian and care for as many people as you can. If you could heal the world, you would!

✳ Do not allow anyone to take advantage of you or attempt to steal your energy. If you are around people and your energy is being depleted, avoid them. Your Hidden You is talking to you.

✳ Your commitment to excellence shines through your love of family.

Your own family is or will be the best it can be. Do not ever settle for second best!

✳ You maintain a quiet and controlled mind. You typically think before answering a question. You are sturdy in your thoughts not just on your feet.

✳ Take good care of your heart. Strength can take a toll on the heart muscle. Keep stress out of your life, eat healthy, exercise, and love as often as you can. Listen to your body. Do not ignore little aches and pains as they are the subtle inner voices telling you to slow down.

✳ When giving, you, in return, receive the greatest gift of all -- your own self-worth. You give to others from your heart and others give to you from theirs.

✳ As strong as you are, remember that you still need others to care for you. Sometimes it is easy to forget as you take such good care of yourself. Indulge in the touch of another and the care given through loving acts. You are a rock, but so much more alive when bathed in the waters of life.

✳ Have you ever noticed that you get everything you want? When you put your mind to something, does everything fall into place? This is because you stop at nothing to achieve your goals. You are the master of your destiny and take charge of what you want out of life. If life does not offer you something that you want, you create it! You are creating and Becoming Your Potential!

Trust me, but look to thyself.
-- Irish proverb

Alone I did it.
-- Shakespeare

*Take time out to smell the flowers, touch the rain,
hear the wind, watch the sun rise or set, and
taste the dew from an early morning blossom.
As a new sun rises every day so will the strength within you.*

✴ This is a time to reflect and capture a moment from your past. Look for the beauty in yourself and believe in the wisdom that you have gained.

✴ Does your body feel ragged or tired? Is your mind clouded? Do you feel emotionally exhausted? It is time to rebuild your strength. Nurture your body with activity. Nurture your mind with silence. Nurture your emotions with happiness. Gain strength by feeding yourself with these strong influential forces.

✴ Stand behind and acknowledge what you do -- right or wrong. This is pure strength, confidence, and self respect.

✴ You may feel the need to lighten-up. Is there a darkness in your heart or soul? It may be time to turn on some light. Take time out to appreciate what is going well in your life. Spend more time with loved ones and avoid isolation. You are stronger than you think and will do just fine.

✴ Respect is a large part of strength. Respect your body, mind, and soul, and others will respect you.

✴ Weakness is not failure. Weakness gives strength the possibility to grow. If you accept and respect your weaknesses, you can convert them into strengths.

✴ True strength comes from within. It is not the body's muscle structure or the stern tone in your voice. It is the art of loving and believing in yourself. It is the power to hold onto personal rights and stand behind your desires, wants, and needs.

✳ If you are feeling weak, your boundaries and beliefs may be taking a toll on you. It may be time to look at your belief structure and examine your beliefs to confirm that they are really yours -- not just beliefs that others have taught you. Go easy on yourself. Allow yourself the freedom to live in harmony with all life.

✳ Walls of iron bring protection. Sometimes we need to protect ourselves from outside forces, but can usually handle it with good, strong boundaries. Write down how you want others to treat you. These are your boundaries. Then, live every day of your life by them.

✳ When we are self absorbed and give little, we deprive ourselves of love. Sharing of oneself -- one's Hidden self -- is the essence of love.

✳ Anger brings darkness to the soul and hurts the body. Anger and lack of control over oneself can grow to be hatred. Be patient and understand that humans make mistakes. Do not judge yourself or others. Anger brings stress to the body, mind, and spirit. When you apply love instead of anger, you eliminate undue stress.

Anger turned inward is depression and can grow to be an explosive emotion. Deal with anger moment-by-moment. This way it will not build-up. If you feel an explosive anger building, work it off physically. Leave the situation you are in and release your anger though exercise, including: running, walking, cycling, push-ups, sit-ups, chin-ups, and swimming. If need be, beat-up a pillow!

✳ You have much to be proud of and deserve the opportunity to live in the greatness of yourself!

Peace cannot be kept by force.
It can only be achieved by understanding.
-- Albert Einstein

Remember that we often repent of what we have said, but never,
never of that which we have not.
-- Thomas Jefferson

*You are able to think clearly about multifaceted details.
This is a good time for strong decision making,
implementing new ideas, organizing, and planning.*

✹ Your self trust and reliability leave others feeling safe and secure. You carry magnificent inspiration.

✹ Strong visualization abilities give your desires the opportunity for fulfillment. If you want something, you go out and get it. Your confidence reigns over your fears.

✹ Vision is not only seeing with your eyes, but also with your heart. It is feeling what is seen. Some people call this psychic, but it is also seen as pure visionary skills. You see, understand, and "know" the big picture.

✹ To have vision is to have strength. You have infinite trust in instinct and intuition. You hold all the keys in your mind and use them when needed. You have the wisdom to know what to do and when to do it. Your connection to pure knowledge links you to a higher form of intelligence.

✹ You are sure of yourself and your decisions in life. Everything you do is well thought-out. You base your decisions on hard facts, understanding, inner-knowing, and reasoning. This is a good time to make sound decisions.

✹ You work best on one project at a time. Your focus is unbreakable and you are thorough covering every aspect of a project to make it the best it can possibly be.

✹ Having focus and concentration is a wonderful skill, but can easily become all consuming. Although your mind is a multi-faceted piece of art, there is another piece of art just as amazing and that is your sense of freedom. Freedom to laugh, play and enjoy the physical activities available to your beautiful body. There is more to you than just your mind, as magnificent as it is. If you can bring vision and freedom together, you will have balance to carry you through your years satisfied and fulfilled.

✳ When focus is in full force, you may not be listening to your body. Your body cries out all the time. It feels thirsty when it needs water and hungry when it needs food. It gives you a headache when your head is too full and feels lethargic when it is tired and bored. It feels weak when you are not having fun and it feels pressure when you are not free. Listen to your body as intensely as you focus on other things. Take care of your body and it will take care of your mind.

✳ Many visionaries have healing capabilities. You may want to invest a little time in researching courses on reiki and hands-on healing. You are a perfect candidate.

✳ When you get too close to something, you can lose sight of it. Do not take anything for granted. Focus on everything that is important to you. Remember your friends, family, and loved ones.

✳ You have expanded the use of your mind. You allow all history and information to down-load while focusing clearly on your mission. You consume and record information. You are a highly intelligent human being with a supreme sense of vision. Nourish and maintain the freedom of your Hidden You and your Potential is limitless!

The best thing about the future
is that it only comes one day at a time.
-- Abraham Lincoln

The farther back you look, the farther forward you are likely to see.
-- Winston Churchill

The world may feel as if it is closing in on you.
Slow down and prioritize conflicts.
Work on them one at a time and one step at a time.
Slow and steady as you go.

✳ Are you feeling confused? Make some time for yourself. Relax and shut off your mind. When you feel comfortable, take a new look at your situation.

✳ When your mind is quiet, intuition and self love will flow. A chattering mind leaves little room for the quietness of love and peace of mind. Thought stopping is an art. When thoughts cloud your ability to feel the beauty in life, turn off your mind. Take more time to feel with your heart and less time to think with your head. Tell your mind to STOP! After a few short days, you will have conditioned your mind. You will gain more control over your life.

✳ Prioritize conflicts. Make a list of everything you need to do and the issues that are bothering you. Evaluate them one-by-one. Use your time efficiently on issues you can control. If a problem is out of your control, let it go. Do not procrastinate. The sooner you deal with issues that you have control over the sooner you will be well.

✳ Do not obsess or focus too hard on problems. If unable to come up with a solution to care for a problem, talk to loved ones and, if needed, ask for help. Sometimes all we need is to hear ourselves talk. Once a problem is shared, the mind is free and you are able to see more clearly.

✳ Tunnel vision is a hard focus also seen as determination. If the focus is too hard, one may tend to avoid outside life. Give yourself the opportunity to see outside of your focus so that you can let new ideas and information into your focus.

✳ Look beyond what is right in front of you. Expand your awareness and see the whole scheme of things -- the big picture. You may have more choices than you think. Open up and the world will open up to you.

✸ Are you having difficulty staying focused on your goals? Re-affirm your goals and reasons for setting them. List all the benefits of reaching your goals. If your goals make you feel happy and content, then feed your desire to reach these goals by reading your list often. Begin your journey to Become Your Potential.

✸ Look for the beauty in everything. Look into people's eyes and see the splendor within. Ignore the facade or outer expression. Who do you see inside? Who is behind those eyes? Vision gives you the opportunity to see with your heart and then use your mind to confirm what you are seeing.

✸ Listen to your inner feelings and intuition. When you ignore the truth -- your true-self -- confusion and self imposed rejection result. The truth is sometimes hard to accept, but truth brings peace of mind and leads you to freeing your Hidden You.

✸ Get in touch with nature and the simplicity it brings. Seeing the beauty in nature, loving it, and embracing it comes from the essence of our being. It gives us the oxygen we breath, the material we build our homes with, the food that keeps us alive, and the beauty that surrounds us everyday.

✸ To free yourself, your Hidden You, face what you need to face. You will Become Your Potential!

Whatever you are, be a good one.
-- Abraham Lincoln

Don't look back in anger, look forward in fury.
-- LLL

JOURNAL INSTRUCTIONS

<u>MORNING</u>

DATE_____

Sleep Time ____:____ Wake Time ____:____ Hours of Sleep _____

DREAMS _____

(1) Enter the **DATE**, time you went to sleep (**Sleep Time**), time you woke-up (**Wake Time**), and number of hours you slept (**Hours of Sleep**).

(2) If you remember a dream, fill in the **DREAMS** section.

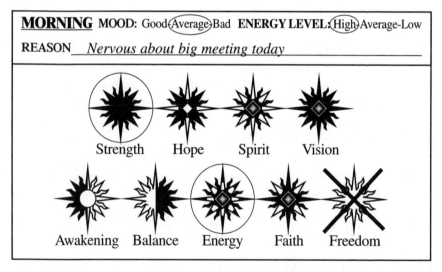

MORNING MOOD: Good Average Bad **ENERGY LEVEL:** High Average-Low

REASON _Nervous about big meeting today_

Strength Hope Spirit Vision

Awakening Balance Energy Faith Freedom

(3) Fill in the section titled **MORNING**. Circle whether you are in a good, average, or bad **MOOD**. Circle whether your **ENERGY LEVEL** is high, average, or low. Write a **REASON** if there is one, for example: slept well, did not sleep well, bad dreams, good dreams, rainy day, sunny day, back hurts, or feel physically great, etc.

(4) Follow **SYMBOL & INTERPRETATION** instructions on page one. Then, **circle** the symbol(s) on your journal page that you are most attracted to and/or **place an X** through the symbols(s) that you are least attracted to. *(When choosing the symbols, use the larger symbols on page two rather than the smaller symbols found in the journal pages.)*

DIET

Meat	☐	☐	☐	☐	☐	☐	☐	☐	☐	☐	☐
Bread	☑	☑	☐	☐	☐	☐	☐	☐	☐	☐	☐
Dairy	☑	☑	☐	☐	☐	☐	☐	☐	☐	☐	
Vegetables	☑	☑	☑	☑	☐	☐	☐	☐	☐	☐	
Fruit	☑	☐	☐	☐	☐	☐	☐	☐	☐	☐	
Water	☐	☐	☐	☐	☐	☐	☐	☐	☐	☐	☐
Vitamins	☑	☐	☐	☐	☐	☐	☐	☐	☐	☐	

PHYSICAL DISCOMFORT

PLAY

Exercise	☐	Laugh	☐	Read	☐
Meditation	☑	Dance	☑	_____	☐
Sex	☐	Sing	☑	*Golf*	☑

CYCLE DAY

_____

(5) Fill in the **DIET** section by placing check marks in the boxes following the food, water, and vitamins that you ingested. Fill in the **PLAY** section by placing check marks in the boxes following the play activity you took part in. There are spaces available to fill in other personal play activities. Mark the areas of your body where you are feeling **PHYSICAL DISCOMFORT**.

(6) If you experience a menstrual cycle, fill in **CYCLE DAY.** The first day of your period is the first day of your cycle.

AFFIRMATION _____

(7) Fill in your daily **AFFIRMATION**. This is a single thought that will empower you for the day, for example: I'm strong, I'm free, I'm proud of myself, etc.

NIGHT

(1) Fill in the section titled **NIGHT**. Follow the instructions for MORNING numbers 3 through 5.

CONTINUED..................

```
┌─────────────────────────────────────────────────────────┐
│ DAILY  DISCOVERIES _____        │
│ HEALTH  PATTERNS _____        │
│ ACHIEVEMENT _____         │
│ ACT OF KINDNESS _____         │
└─────────────────────────────────────────────────────────┘
```

(2) Use the **DAILY DISCOVERIES** section as a diary or journal. Record anything you want.

(3) Use the **HEALTH PATTERNS** section to note patterns that you will notice after a few days of journaling. These patterns are broken by taking the advice in the interpretations. The following are examples:

(a) "When under stress, I choose the unattractive Energy symbol a lot. I don't eat. I get head-aches and my knees hurt. I feel better when I follow the advice from the interpretation."

(b) "I have noticed that my arthritis isn't bad when I'm attracted to the Freedom symbol. I practice following the advice of the Freedom unattractive and attractive symbol to keep my arthritis under control."

(c) "I'm chronically ill and my symptoms are worse when I'm not attracted to the Faith symbol. My symptoms lessen when I am attracted to the Freedom, Spirit, and Awakening symbols. I try to stay in the positive states expressed in those symbol's interpretations."

(d) "I fight with my husband every time I'm not attracted to the Balance symbol. I'm keeping a close eye on it now and working on staying balanced."

(4) Record your personal **ACHIEVEMENT** of the day, for example, you broke through your shyness by saying hello to a stranger or you asked for a raise.

(5) Record a random **ACT OF KINDNESS** you received or gave, for instance, you helped someone cross the road or you called a loved one just to say I love you.

> *When you have to make a choice and don't make it,*
> *that is in itself a choice.*
> **-- William James**

THE
JOURNAL

DATE_____

Sleep Time ____:____ Wake Time ____:____ Hours of Sleep _____

DREAMS _____
_____
_____
_____
_____
_____
_____
_____
_____
_____

<u>**MORNING**</u>   **MOOD:** Good-Average-Bad   **ENERGY LEVEL:** High-Average-Low

REASON _____

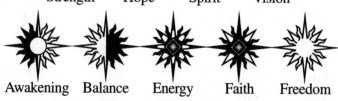

| Strength | Hope | Spirit | Vision |

| Awakening | Balance | Energy | Faith | Freedom |

AFFIRMATION _____

<u>**NIGHT**</u>   **MOOD:** Good-Average-Bad   **ENERGY LEVEL:** High-Average-Low

REASON _____

| Strength | Hope | Spirit | Vision |

| Awakening | Balance | Energy | Faith | Freedom |

DAILY DISCOVERIES _____

_____
_____
_____
_____
_____
_____
_____
_____
_____
_____
_____
_____
_____
_____
_____
_____
_____
_____
_____
_____
_____
_____

HEALTH PATTERNS _____

_____
_____
_____
_____
_____
_____
_____

ACHIEVEMENT _____

ACT OF KINDNESS _____

DIET

Meat	☐	☐	☐	☐	☐	☐	☐	☐	☐	☐	☐
Bread	☐	☐	☐	☐	☐	☐	☐	☐	☐	☐	☐
Dairy	☐	☐	☐	☐	☐	☐	☐	☐	☐	☐	☐
Vegetables	☐	☐	☐	☐	☐	☐	☐	☐	☐	☐	☐
Fruit	☐	☐	☐	☐	☐	☐	☐	☐	☐	☐	☐
Water	☐	☐	☐	☐	☐	☐	☐	☐	☐	☐	☐
Vitamins	☐	☐	☐	☐	☐	☐	☐	☐	☐	☐	☐

PHYSICAL DISCOMFORT

PLAY

Exercise	☐	Laugh	☐	Read	☐	
Meditation	☐	Dance	☐	_____	☐	
Sex	☐	Sing	☐	_____	☐	

CYCLE DAY

_____

DATE_____

Sleep Time ____:____ Wake Time ____:____ Hours of Sleep _____

DREAMS _____
_____
_____
_____
_____
_____
_____
_____
_____

MORNING   **MOOD:** Good-Average-Bad   **ENERGY LEVEL:** High-Average-Low

REASON _____

Strength	Hope	Spirit	Vision	
Awakening	Balance	Energy	Faith	Freedom

AFFIRMATION _____

NIGHT   **MOOD:** Good-Average-Bad   **ENERGY LEVEL:** High-Average-Low

REASON _____

Strength	Hope	Spirit	Vision	
Awakening	Balance	Energy	Faith	Freedom

DAILY DISCOVERIES _____

_____
_____
_____
_____
_____
_____
_____
_____
_____
_____
_____
_____
_____
_____
_____
_____
_____
_____
_____
_____
_____

HEALTH PATTERNS _____

_____
_____
_____
_____
_____
_____

ACHIEVEMENT _____

ACT OF KINDNESS _____

DIET

Meat	□	□	□	□	□	□	□	□	□	□	□
Bread	□	□	□	□	□	□	□	□	□	□	□
Dairy	□	□	□	□	□	□	□	□	□	□	□
Vegetables	□	□	□	□	□	□	□	□	□	□	□
Fruit	□	□	□	□	□	□	□	□	□	□	□
Water	□	□	□	□	□	□	□	□	□	□	□
Vitamins	□	□	□	□	□	□	□	□	□	□	□

PHYSICAL DISCOMFORT

PLAY

Exercise	□	Laugh	□	Read	□
Meditation	□	Dance	□	_____	□
Sex	□	Sing	□	_____	□

CYCLE DAY

_____

DATE_____

Sleep Time ____:____ Wake Time ____:____ Hours of Sleep _____

DREAMS _____
_____
_____
_____
_____
_____
_____
_____
_____

MORNING   MOOD: Good-Average-Bad   ENERGY LEVEL: High-Average-Low

REASON _____

Strength	Hope	Spirit	Vision

Awakening	Balance	Energy	Faith	Freedom

AFFIRMATION _____

NIGHT   MOOD: Good-Average-Bad   ENERGY LEVEL: High-Average-Low

REASON _____

Strength	Hope	Spirit	Vision

Awakening	Balance	Energy	Faith	Freedom

DAILY DISCOVERIES _____
_____
_____
_____
_____
_____
_____
_____
_____
_____
_____
_____
_____
_____
_____
_____
_____
_____
_____
_____
_____
_____
_____

HEALTH PATTERNS _____
_____
_____
_____
_____
_____
_____
_____

ACHIEVEMENT _____
ACT OF KINDNESS _____

DIET

Meat	☐	☐	☐	☐	☐	☐	☐	☐	☐	☐	☐
Bread	☐	☐	☐	☐	☐	☐	☐	☐	☐	☐	☐
Dairy	☐	☐	☐	☐	☐	☐	☐	☐	☐	☐	☐
Vegetables	☐	☐	☐	☐	☐	☐	☐	☐	☐	☐	☐
Fruit	☐	☐	☐	☐	☐	☐	☐	☐	☐	☐	☐
Water	☐	☐	☐	☐	☐	☐	☐	☐	☐	☐	☐
Vitamins	☐	☐	☐	☐	☐	☐	☐	☐	☐	☐	☐

PHYSICAL DISCOMFORT

PLAY

Exercise	☐	Laugh	☐	Read	☐
Meditation	☐	Dance	☐	_____	☐
Sex	☐	Sing	☐	_____	☐

CYCLE DAY

_____

DATE_____

Sleep Time ____:____ Wake Time ____:____ Hours of Sleep _____

DREAMS _____
_____
_____
_____
_____
_____
_____
_____
_____

MORNING MOOD: Good-Average-Bad ENERGY LEVEL: High-Average-Low

REASON _____

Strength	Hope	Spirit	Vision

Awakening	Balance	Energy	Faith	Freedom

AFFIRMATION _____

NIGHT MOOD: Good-Average-Bad ENERGY LEVEL: High-Average-Low

REASON _____

Strength	Hope	Spirit	Vision

Awakening	Balance	Energy	Faith	Freedom

DAILY DISCOVERIES _____

_____
_____
_____
_____
_____
_____
_____
_____
_____
_____
_____
_____
_____
_____
_____
_____
_____
_____
_____
_____

HEALTH PATTERNS _____

_____
_____
_____
_____
_____
_____
_____

ACHIEVEMENT _____

ACT OF KINDNESS _____

DIET

Meat	☐	☐	☐	☐	☐	☐	☐	☐	☐	☐	☐	☐
Bread	☐	☐	☐	☐	☐	☐	☐	☐	☐	☐	☐	☐
Dairy	☐	☐	☐	☐	☐	☐	☐	☐	☐	☐	☐	☐
Vegetables	☐	☐	☐	☐	☐	☐	☐	☐	☐	☐	☐	☐
Fruit	☐	☐	☐	☐	☐	☐	☐	☐	☐	☐	☐	☐
Water	☐	☐	☐	☐	☐	☐	☐	☐	☐	☐	☐	☐
Vitamins	☐	☐	☐	☐	☐	☐	☐	☐	☐	☐	☐	☐

PHYSICAL DISCOMFORT

PLAY

Exercise	☐	Laugh	☐	Read	☐
Meditation	☐	Dance	☐	_____	☐
Sex	☐	Sing	☐	_____	☐

CYCLE DAY

_____

DATE_____

Sleep Time ____:____ **Wake Time** ____:____ **Hours of Sleep** _____

DREAMS _____
_____
_____
_____
_____
_____
_____
_____
_____
_____

MORNING   MOOD: Good-Average-Bad   ENERGY LEVEL: High-Average-Low

REASON _____

Strength	Hope	Spirit	Vision	
Awakening	Balance	Energy	Faith	Freedom

AFFIRMATION _____

NIGHT   MOOD: Good-Average-Bad   ENERGY LEVEL: High-Average-Low

REASON _____

Strength	Hope	Spirit	Vision	
Awakening	Balance	Energy	Faith	Freedom

DAILY DISCOVERIES _____

_____
_____
_____
_____
_____
_____
_____
_____
_____
_____
_____
_____
_____
_____
_____
_____
_____
_____
_____
_____
_____
_____

HEALTH PATTERNS _____

_____
_____
_____
_____
_____
_____

ACHIEVEMENT _____
ACT OF KINDNESS _____

DIET
Meat   ☐☐☐☐☐☐☐☐☐☐☐☐
Bread   ☐☐☐☐☐☐☐☐☐☐☐☐
Dairy   ☐☐☐☐☐☐☐☐☐☐☐☐
Vegetables ☐☐☐☐☐☐☐☐☐☐☐☐
Fruit   ☐☐☐☐☐☐☐☐☐☐☐☐
Water   ☐☐☐☐☐☐☐☐☐☐☐☐
Vitamins   ☐☐☐☐☐☐☐☐☐☐☐☐

PHYSICAL DISCOMFORT

PLAY
Exercise ☐   Laugh ☐   Read ☐
Meditation ☐   Dance ☐   _____ ☐
Sex ☐   Sing ☐   _____ ☐

CYCLE DAY
_____

DATE_____

Sleep Time ____:____   Wake Time ____:____   Hours of Sleep _____

DREAMS _____
_____
_____
_____
_____
_____
_____
_____
_____

<u>**MORNING**</u>   **MOOD:** Good-Average-Bad   **ENERGY LEVEL:** High-Average-Low

REASON _____

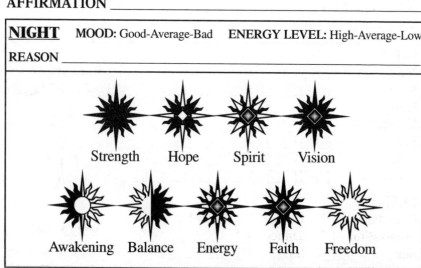

Strength	Hope	Spirit	Vision

Awakening	Balance	Energy	Faith	Freedom

AFFIRMATION _____

<u>**NIGHT**</u>   **MOOD:** Good-Average-Bad   **ENERGY LEVEL:** High-Average-Low

REASON _____

Strength	Hope	Spirit	Vision

Awakening	Balance	Energy	Faith	Freedom

DAILY DISCOVERIES _____

_____
_____
_____
_____
_____
_____
_____
_____
_____
_____
_____
_____
_____
_____
_____
_____
_____
_____
_____
_____
_____
_____

HEALTH PATTERNS _____

_____
_____
_____
_____
_____
_____

ACHIEVEMENT _____
ACT OF KINDNESS _____

DIET		**PHYSICAL**
Meat	□□□□□□□□□□□	**DISCOMFORT**
Bread	□□□□□□□□□□□	
Dairy	□□□□□□□□□□	
Vegetables	□□□□□□□□□□	
Fruit	□□□□□□□□□□	
Water	□□□□□□□□□□	
Vitamins	□□□□□□□□□□	

PLAY

Exercise □	Laugh □	Read □
Meditation □	Dance □	_____ □
Sex □	Sing □	_____ □

CYCLE DAY

_____

DATE_____

Sleep Time ____:____ Wake Time ____:____ Hours of Sleep _____

DREAMS _____
_____
_____
_____
_____
_____
_____
_____
_____

MORNING   **MOOD:** Good-Average-Bad   **ENERGY LEVEL:** High-Average-Low

REASON _____

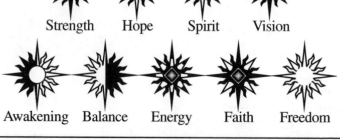

Strength	Hope	Spirit	Vision

| Awakening | Balance | Energy | Faith | Freedom |

AFFIRMATION _____

NIGHT   **MOOD:** Good-Average-Bad   **ENERGY LEVEL:** High-Average-Low

REASON _____

| Strength | Hope | Spirit | Vision |

| Awakening | Balance | Energy | Faith | Freedom |

DAILY DISCOVERIES _____

_____
_____
_____
_____
_____
_____
_____
_____
_____
_____
_____
_____
_____
_____
_____
_____
_____
_____
_____
_____
_____

HEALTH PATTERNS _____

_____
_____
_____
_____
_____
_____

ACHIEVEMENT _____

ACT OF KINDNESS _____

DIET

Meat	☐	☐	☐	☐	☐	☐	☐	☐	☐	☐	☐	☐
Bread	☐	☐	☐	☐	☐	☐	☐	☐	☐	☐	☐	☐
Dairy	☐	☐	☐	☐	☐	☐	☐	☐	☐	☐	☐	☐
Vegetables	☐	☐	☐	☐	☐	☐	☐	☐	☐	☐	☐	☐
Fruit	☐	☐	☐	☐	☐	☐	☐	☐	☐	☐	☐	☐
Water	☐	☐	☐	☐	☐	☐	☐	☐	☐	☐	☐	☐
Vitamins	☐	☐	☐	☐	☐	☐	☐	☐	☐	☐	☐	☐

PHYSICAL DISCOMFORT

PLAY

Exercise	☐	Laugh	☐	Read	☐
Meditation	☐	Dance	☐	_____	☐
Sex	☐	Sing	☐	_____	☐

CYCLE DAY

_____

DATE_____

Sleep Time ____:____ Wake Time ____:____ Hours of Sleep _____

DREAMS _____

_____

_____

_____

_____

_____

_____

_____

<u>**MORNING**</u>   MOOD: Good-Average-Bad   ENERGY LEVEL: High-Average-Low

REASON _____

Strength	Hope	Spirit	Vision	
Awakening	Balance	Energy	Faith	Freedom

AFFIRMATION _____

<u>**NIGHT**</u>   MOOD: Good-Average-Bad   ENERGY LEVEL: High-Average-Low

REASON _____

Strength	Hope	Spirit	Vision	
Awakening	Balance	Energy	Faith	Freedom

DAILY DISCOVERIES _____

_____
_____
_____
_____
_____
_____
_____
_____
_____
_____
_____
_____
_____
_____
_____
_____
_____
_____
_____
_____
_____
_____

HEALTH PATTERNS _____

_____
_____
_____
_____
_____
_____
_____

ACHIEVEMENT _____
ACT OF KINDNESS _____

DIET		
Meat	□□□□□□□□□□□	**PHYSICAL**
Bread	□□□□□□□□□□□	**DISCOMFORT**
Dairy	□□□□□□□□□□□	
Vegetables	□□□□□□□□□□□	
Fruit	□□□□□□□□□□□	
Water	□□□□□□□□□□□	
Vitamins	□□□□□□□□□□□	

PLAY

Exercise	□	Laugh	□	Read	□
Meditation	□	Dance	□	_____	□
Sex	□	Sing	□	_____	□

CYCLE DAY

_____

DATE_____

Sleep Time ____:____ **Wake Time** ____:____ **Hours of Sleep** _____

DREAMS _____
_____
_____
_____
_____
_____
_____
_____
_____

MORNING   MOOD: Good-Average-Bad   ENERGY LEVEL: High-Average-Low

REASON _____

Strength   Hope   Spirit   Vision

Awakening   Balance   Energy   Faith   Freedom

AFFIRMATION _____

NIGHT   MOOD: Good-Average-Bad   ENERGY LEVEL: High-Average-Low

REASON _____

Strength   Hope   Spirit   Vision

Awakening   Balance   Energy   Faith   Freedom

DAILY DISCOVERIES _____

_____
_____
_____
_____
_____
_____
_____
_____
_____
_____
_____
_____
_____
_____
_____
_____
_____
_____
_____
_____
_____

HEALTH PATTERNS _____

_____
_____
_____
_____
_____
_____

ACHIEVEMENT _____
ACT OF KINDNESS _____

DIET		**PHYSICAL**
Meat	☐☐☐☐☐☐☐☐☐☐☐	**DISCOMFORT**
Bread	☐☐☐☐☐☐☐☐☐☐☐	
Dairy	☐☐☐☐☐☐☐☐☐☐☐	
Vegetables	☐☐☐☐☐☐☐☐☐☐☐	
Fruit	☐☐☐☐☐☐☐☐☐☐☐	
Water	☐☐☐☐☐☐☐☐☐☐☐	
Vitamins	☐☐☐☐☐☐☐☐☐☐☐	

PLAY

Exercise	☐	Laugh	☐	Read	☐
Meditation	☐	Dance	☐	_____	☐
Sex	☐	Sing	☐	_____	☐

CYCLE DAY

_____

DATE_____

Sleep Time ____:____ Wake Time ____:____ Hours of Sleep _____

DREAMS _____
_____
_____
_____
_____
_____
_____
_____
_____

MORNING   MOOD: Good-Average-Bad   ENERGY LEVEL: High-Average-Low

REASON _____

Strength   Hope   Spirit   Vision

Awakening   Balance   Energy   Faith   Freedom

AFFIRMATION _____

NIGHT   MOOD: Good-Average-Bad   ENERGY LEVEL: High-Average-Low

REASON _____

Strength   Hope   Spirit   Vision

Awakening   Balance   Energy   Faith   Freedom

DAILY DISCOVERIES _____

_____
_____
_____
_____
_____
_____
_____
_____
_____
_____
_____
_____
_____
_____
_____
_____
_____
_____
_____
_____
_____
_____

HEALTH PATTERNS _____

_____
_____
_____
_____
_____
_____

ACHIEVEMENT _____
ACT OF KINDNESS _____

DIET		**PHYSICAL**
Meat	☐☐☐☐☐☐☐☐☐☐☐☐	**DISCOMFORT**
Bread	☐☐☐☐☐☐☐☐☐☐☐☐	
Dairy	☐☐☐☐☐☐☐☐☐☐☐☐	
Vegetables	☐☐☐☐☐☐☐☐☐☐☐☐	
Fruit	☐☐☐☐☐☐☐☐☐☐☐☐	
Water	☐☐☐☐☐☐☐☐☐☐☐☐	
Vitamins	☐☐☐☐☐☐☐☐☐☐☐☐	

PLAY

Exercise	☐	Laugh	☐	Read	☐
Meditation	☐	Dance	☐	_____	☐
Sex	☐	Sing	☐	_____	☐

CYCLE DAY

_____

DATE_____

Sleep Time ____:____   Wake Time ____:____   Hours of Sleep _____

DREAMS _____

_____
_____
_____
_____
_____
_____
_____
_____

<u>MORNING</u>   **MOOD:** Good-Average-Bad   **ENERGY LEVEL:** High-Average-Low

REASON _____

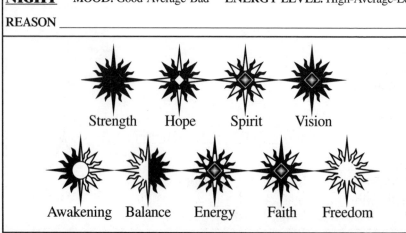

Strength	Hope	Spirit	Vision

Awakening	Balance	Energy	Faith	Freedom

AFFIRMATION _____

<u>NIGHT</u>   **MOOD:** Good-Average-Bad   **ENERGY LEVEL:** High-Average-Low

REASON _____

Strength	Hope	Spirit	Vision

Awakening	Balance	Energy	Faith	Freedom

DAILY DISCOVERIES _____

_____
_____
_____
_____
_____
_____
_____
_____
_____
_____
_____
_____
_____
_____
_____
_____
_____
_____
_____
_____

HEALTH PATTERNS _____

_____
_____
_____
_____
_____
_____

ACHIEVEMENT _____
ACT OF KINDNESS _____

DIET		**PHYSICAL**
Meat	☐☐☐☐☐☐☐☐☐☐☐☐	**DISCOMFORT**
Bread	☐☐☐☐☐☐☐☐☐☐☐☐	
Dairy	☐☐☐☐☐☐☐☐☐☐☐☐	
Vegetables	☐☐☐☐☐☐☐☐☐☐☐☐	
Fruit	☐☐☐☐☐☐☐☐☐☐☐☐	
Water	☐☐☐☐☐☐☐☐☐☐☐☐	
Vitamins	☐☐☐☐☐☐☐☐☐☐☐☐	

PLAY

Exercise	☐	Laugh	☐	Read	☐
Meditation	☐	Dance	☐	_____	☐
Sex	☐	Sing	☐	_____	☐

CYCLE DAY

_____

DATE_____

Sleep Time ____:____   Wake Time ____:____   **Hours of Sleep** _____

DREAMS _____
_____
_____
_____
_____
_____
_____
_____
_____

<u>**MORNING**</u>   **MOOD:** Good-Average-Bad   **ENERGY LEVEL:** High-Average-Low

REASON _____

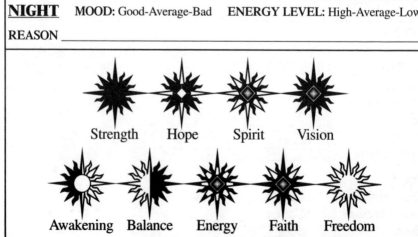

Strength	Hope	Spirit	Vision	
Awakening	Balance	Energy	Faith	Freedom

AFFIRMATION _____

<u>**NIGHT**</u>   **MOOD:** Good-Average-Bad   **ENERGY LEVEL:** High-Average-Low

REASON _____

Strength	Hope	Spirit	Vision	
Awakening	Balance	Energy	Faith	Freedom

DAILY DISCOVERIES _____

_____
_____
_____
_____
_____
_____
_____
_____
_____
_____
_____
_____
_____
_____
_____
_____
_____
_____
_____
_____

HEALTH PATTERNS _____

_____
_____
_____
_____
_____
_____

ACHIEVEMENT _____

ACT OF KINDNESS _____

DIET													
Meat	☐	☐	☐	☐	☐	☐	☐	☐	☐	☐	☐	☐	☐
Bread	☐	☐	☐	☐	☐	☐	☐	☐	☐	☐	☐	☐	☐
Dairy	☐	☐	☐	☐	☐	☐	☐	☐	☐	☐	☐	☐	☐
Vegetables	☐	☐	☐	☐	☐	☐	☐	☐	☐	☐	☐	☐	☐
Fruit	☐	☐	☐	☐	☐	☐	☐	☐	☐	☐	☐	☐	☐
Water	☐	☐	☐	☐	☐	☐	☐	☐	☐	☐	☐	☐	☐
Vitamins	☐	☐	☐	☐	☐	☐	☐	☐	☐	☐	☐	☐	☐

PHYSICAL DISCOMFORT

PLAY

Exercise	☐	Laugh	☐	Read	☐
Meditation	☐	Dance	☐	_____	☐
Sex	☐	Sing	☐	_____	☐

CYCLE DAY

_____

DATE_____

Sleep Time ____:____ Wake Time ____:____ Hours of Sleep _____

DREAMS _____
_____
_____
_____
_____
_____
_____
_____

<u>MORNING</u>   **MOOD:** Good-Average-Bad   **ENERGY LEVEL:** High-Average-Low

REASON _____

Strength	Hope	Spirit	Vision

Awakening	Balance	Energy	Faith	Freedom

AFFIRMATION _____

<u>NIGHT</u>   **MOOD:** Good-Average-Bad   **ENERGY LEVEL:** High-Average-Low

REASON _____

Strength	Hope	Spirit	Vision

Awakening	Balance	Energy	Faith	Freedom

DAILY DISCOVERIES _____

_____
_____
_____
_____
_____
_____
_____
_____
_____
_____
_____
_____
_____
_____
_____
_____
_____
_____
_____
_____

HEALTH PATTERNS _____

_____
_____
_____
_____
_____
_____
_____

ACHIEVEMENT _____

ACT OF KINDNESS _____

DIET

Meat	☐	☐	☐	☐	☐	☐	☐	☐	☐	☐	☐	☐
Bread	☐	☐	☐	☐	☐	☐	☐	☐	☐	☐	☐	☐
Dairy	☐	☐	☐	☐	☐	☐	☐	☐	☐	☐	☐	☐
Vegetables	☐	☐	☐	☐	☐	☐	☐	☐	☐	☐	☐	☐
Fruit	☐	☐	☐	☐	☐	☐	☐	☐	☐	☐	☐	☐
Water	☐	☐	☐	☐	☐	☐	☐	☐	☐	☐	☐	☐
Vitamins	☐	☐	☐	☐	☐	☐	☐	☐	☐	☐	☐	☐

PHYSICAL DISCOMFORT

PLAY

Exercise	☐	Laugh	☐	Read	☐
Meditation	☐	Dance	☐	_____	☐
Sex	☐	Sing	☐	_____	☐

CYCLE DAY

_____

DATE_____

Sleep Time ____:____ Wake Time ____:____ Hours of Sleep _____

DREAMS _____
_____
_____
_____
_____
_____
_____
_____

MORNING   MOOD: Good-Average-Bad   ENERGY LEVEL: High-Average-Low

REASON _____

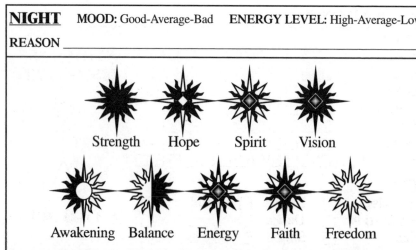

Strength	Hope	Spirit	Vision	
Awakening	Balance	Energy	Faith	Freedom

AFFIRMATION _____

NIGHT   MOOD: Good-Average-Bad   ENERGY LEVEL: High-Average-Low

REASON _____

Strength	Hope	Spirit	Vision	
Awakening	Balance	Energy	Faith	Freedom

DAILY DISCOVERIES _____

_____
_____
_____
_____
_____
_____
_____
_____
_____
_____
_____
_____
_____
_____
_____
_____
_____
_____
_____
_____
_____

HEALTH PATTERNS _____

_____
_____
_____
_____
_____
_____

ACHIEVEMENT _____

ACT OF KINDNESS _____

DIET

Meat	☐	☐	☐	☐	☐	☐	☐	☐	☐	☐	☐	☐
Bread	☐	☐	☐	☐	☐	☐	☐	☐	☐	☐	☐	☐
Dairy	☐	☐	☐	☐	☐	☐	☐	☐	☐	☐	☐	
Vegetables	☐	☐	☐	☐	☐	☐	☐	☐	☐	☐	☐	
Fruit	☐	☐	☐	☐	☐	☐	☐	☐	☐	☐	☐	
Water	☐	☐	☐	☐	☐	☐	☐	☐	☐	☐	☐	
Vitamins	☐	☐	☐	☐	☐	☐	☐	☐	☐	☐	☐	

PHYSICAL DISCOMFORT

PLAY

Exercise	☐	Laugh	☐	Read	☐
Meditation	☐	Dance	☐	_____	☐
Sex	☐	Sing	☐	_____	☐

CYCLE DAY

_____

DATE_____

Sleep Time ____:____   Wake Time ____:____   Hours of Sleep _____

DREAMS _____
_____
_____
_____
_____
_____
_____
_____
_____

MORNING   MOOD: Good-Average-Bad   ENERGY LEVEL: High-Average-Low

REASON _____

Strength	Hope	Spirit	Vision

Awakening	Balance	Energy	Faith	Freedom

AFFIRMATION _____

NIGHT   MOOD: Good-Average-Bad   ENERGY LEVEL: High-Average-Low

REASON _____

Strength	Hope	Spirit	Vision

Awakening	Balance	Energy	Faith	Freedom

DAILY DISCOVERIES _____

_____
_____
_____
_____
_____
_____
_____
_____
_____
_____
_____
_____
_____
_____
_____
_____
_____
_____
_____
_____
_____

HEALTH PATTERNS _____

_____
_____
_____
_____
_____
_____

ACHIEVEMENT _____
ACT OF KINDNESS _____

DIET

Meat	☐	☐	☐	☐	☐	☐	☐	☐	☐	☐	☐	☐
Bread	☐	☐	☐	☐	☐	☐	☐	☐	☐	☐	☐	☐
Dairy	☐	☐	☐	☐	☐	☐	☐	☐	☐	☐	☐	☐
Vegetables	☐	☐	☐	☐	☐	☐	☐	☐	☐	☐	☐	☐
Fruit	☐	☐	☐	☐	☐	☐	☐	☐	☐	☐	☐	☐
Water	☐	☐	☐	☐	☐	☐	☐	☐	☐	☐	☐	☐
Vitamins	☐	☐	☐	☐	☐	☐	☐	☐	☐	☐	☐	☐

PHYSICAL DISCOMFORT

PLAY

Exercise	☐	Laugh	☐	Read	☐	
Meditation	☐	Dance	☐	_____	☐	
Sex	☐	Sing	☐	_____	☐	

CYCLE DAY

_____

DATE_____

Sleep Time ____:____   Wake Time ____:____   Hours of Sleep _____

DREAMS _____

_____

_____

_____

_____

_____

_____

_____

_____

MORNING   **MOOD:** Good-Average-Bad   **ENERGY LEVEL:** High-Average-Low

REASON _____

Strength   Hope   Spirit   Vision

Awakening   Balance   Energy   Faith   Freedom

AFFIRMATION _____

NIGHT   **MOOD:** Good-Average-Bad   **ENERGY LEVEL:** High-Average-Low

REASON _____

Strength   Hope   Spirit   Vision

Awakening   Balance   Energy   Faith   Freedom

DAILY DISCOVERIES _____

_____
_____
_____
_____
_____
_____
_____
_____
_____
_____
_____
_____
_____
_____
_____
_____
_____
_____
_____
_____
_____
_____
_____

HEALTH PATTERNS _____

_____
_____
_____
_____
_____
_____

ACHIEVEMENT _____

ACT OF KINDNESS _____

DIET

		PHYSICAL
Meat	☐☐☐☐☐☐☐☐☐☐☐☐	**PHYSICAL DISCOMFORT**
Bread	☐☐☐☐☐☐☐☐☐☐☐☐	
Dairy	☐☐☐☐☐☐☐☐☐☐☐	
Vegetables	☐☐☐☐☐☐☐☐☐☐☐	
Fruit	☐☐☐☐☐☐☐☐☐☐☐	
Water	☐☐☐☐☐☐☐☐☐☐☐	
Vitamins	☐☐☐☐☐☐☐☐☐☐☐	

PLAY

Exercise	☐	Laugh	☐	Read	☐
Meditation	☐	Dance	☐	_____	☐
Sex	☐	Sing	☐	_____	☐

CYCLE DAY

_____

DATE_____

Sleep Time ____:____ Wake Time ____:____ Hours of Sleep _____

DREAMS _____
_____
_____
_____
_____
_____
_____
_____

MORNING   MOOD: Good-Average-Bad   ENERGY LEVEL: High-Average-Low

REASON _____

Strength	Hope	Spirit	Vision

Awakening	Balance	Energy	Faith	Freedom

AFFIRMATION _____

NIGHT   MOOD: Good-Average-Bad   ENERGY LEVEL: High-Average-Low

REASON _____

Strength	Hope	Spirit	Vision

Awakening	Balance	Energy	Faith	Freedom

DAILY DISCOVERIES _____

_____
_____
_____
_____
_____
_____
_____
_____
_____
_____
_____
_____
_____
_____
_____
_____
_____
_____
_____
_____
_____

HEALTH PATTERNS _____

_____
_____
_____
_____
_____
_____

ACHIEVEMENT _____

ACT OF KINDNESS _____

DIET													
Meat	☐ ☐ ☐ ☐ ☐ ☐ ☐ ☐ ☐ ☐ ☐ ☐												
Bread	☐ ☐ ☐ ☐ ☐ ☐ ☐ ☐ ☐ ☐ ☐ ☐												
Dairy	☐ ☐ ☐ ☐ ☐ ☐ ☐ ☐ ☐ ☐ ☐												
Vegetables	☐ ☐ ☐ ☐ ☐ ☐ ☐ ☐ ☐ ☐ ☐												
Fruit	☐ ☐ ☐ ☐ ☐ ☐ ☐ ☐ ☐ ☐ ☐												
Water	☐ ☐ ☐ ☐ ☐ ☐ ☐ ☐ ☐ ☐ ☐												
Vitamins	☐ ☐ ☐ ☐ ☐ ☐ ☐ ☐ ☐ ☐ ☐												

PHYSICAL DISCOMFORT

PLAY

Exercise	☐	Laugh	☐	Read	☐
Meditation	☐	Dance	☐	_____	☐
Sex	☐	Sing	☐	_____	☐

CYCLE DAY

_____

DATE_____

Sleep Time _____:_____ Wake Time _____:_____ Hours of Sleep _____

DREAMS _____
_____
_____
_____
_____
_____
_____
_____
_____

MORNING   MOOD: Good-Average-Bad   ENERGY LEVEL: High-Average-Low

REASON _____

Strength	Hope	Spirit	Vision

Awakening	Balance	Energy	Faith	Freedom

AFFIRMATION _____

NIGHT   MOOD: Good-Average-Bad   ENERGY LEVEL: High-Average-Low

REASON _____

Strength	Hope	Spirit	Vision

Awakening	Balance	Energy	Faith	Freedom

DAILY DISCOVERIES _____

_____
_____
_____
_____
_____
_____
_____
_____
_____
_____
_____
_____
_____
_____
_____
_____
_____
_____
_____
_____
_____
_____

HEALTH PATTERNS _____

_____
_____
_____
_____
_____
_____
_____

ACHIEVEMENT _____
ACT OF KINDNESS _____

DIET		**PHYSICAL**
Meat	☐☐☐☐☐☐☐☐☐☐☐	**DISCOMFORT**
Bread	☐☐☐☐☐☐☐☐☐☐☐	
Dairy	☐☐☐☐☐☐☐☐☐☐☐	
Vegetables	☐☐☐☐☐☐☐☐☐☐☐	
Fruit	☐☐☐☐☐☐☐☐☐☐☐	
Water	☐☐☐☐☐☐☐☐☐☐☐	
Vitamins	☐☐☐☐☐☐☐☐☐☐☐	

PLAY

Exercise	☐	Laugh	☐	Read	☐
Meditation	☐	Dance	☐	_____	☐
Sex	☐	Sing	☐	_____	☐

CYCLE DAY

_____

DATE_____

Sleep Time ____:____   Wake Time ____:____   Hours of Sleep _____

DREAMS _____
_____
_____
_____
_____
_____
_____
_____
_____

MORNING   MOOD: Good-Average-Bad   ENERGY LEVEL: High-Average-Low

REASON _____

Strength	Hope	Spirit	Vision

Awakening	Balance	Energy	Faith	Freedom

AFFIRMATION _____

NIGHT   MOOD: Good-Average-Bad   ENERGY LEVEL: High-Average-Low

REASON _____

Strength	Hope	Spirit	Vision

Awakening	Balance	Energy	Faith	Freedom

DAILY DISCOVERIES _____

_____
_____
_____
_____
_____
_____
_____
_____
_____
_____
_____
_____
_____
_____
_____
_____
_____
_____
_____
_____
_____
_____

HEALTH PATTERNS _____

_____
_____
_____
_____
_____
_____
_____

ACHIEVEMENT _____

ACT OF KINDNESS _____

DIET

		PHYSICAL DISCOMFORT
Meat	☐☐☐☐☐☐☐☐☐☐☐☐	
Bread	☐☐☐☐☐☐☐☐☐☐☐☐	
Dairy	☐☐☐☐☐☐☐☐☐☐☐☐	
Vegetables	☐☐☐☐☐☐☐☐☐☐☐☐	
Fruit	☐☐☐☐☐☐☐☐☐☐☐☐	
Water	☐☐☐☐☐☐☐☐☐☐☐☐	
Vitamins	☐☐☐☐☐☐☐☐☐☐☐☐	

PLAY

Exercise ☐	Laugh ☐	Read ☐	
Meditation ☐	Dance ☐	_____ ☐	**CYCLE DAY**
Sex ☐	Sing ☐	_____ ☐	_____

DATE_____

Sleep Time ____:____ Wake Time ____:____ Hours of Sleep _____

DREAMS _____
_____
_____
_____
_____
_____
_____
_____

MORNING   MOOD: Good-Average-Bad   ENERGY LEVEL: High-Average-Low

REASON _____

Strength	Hope	Spirit	Vision

Awakening	Balance	Energy	Faith	Freedom

AFFIRMATION _____

NIGHT   MOOD: Good-Average-Bad   ENERGY LEVEL: High-Average-Low

REASON _____

Strength	Hope	Spirit	Vision

Awakening	Balance	Energy	Faith	Freedom

DAILY DISCOVERIES _____

_____
_____
_____
_____
_____
_____
_____
_____
_____
_____
_____
_____
_____
_____
_____
_____
_____
_____
_____
_____
_____

HEALTH PATTERNS _____

_____
_____
_____
_____
_____
_____

ACHIEVEMENT _____

ACT OF KINDNESS _____

DIET

Meat	☐	☐	☐	☐	☐	☐	☐	☐	☐	☐	☐
Bread	☐	☐	☐	☐	☐	☐	☐	☐	☐	☐	☐
Dairy	☐	☐	☐	☐	☐	☐	☐	☐	☐	☐	☐
Vegetables	☐	☐	☐	☐	☐	☐	☐	☐	☐	☐	☐
Fruit	☐	☐	☐	☐	☐	☐	☐	☐	☐	☐	☐
Water	☐	☐	☐	☐	☐	☐	☐	☐	☐	☐	☐
Vitamins	☐	☐	☐	☐	☐	☐	☐	☐	☐	☐	☐

PHYSICAL DISCOMFORT

PLAY

Exercise	☐	Laugh	☐	Read	☐
Meditation	☐	Dance	☐	_____	☐
Sex	☐	Sing	☐	_____	☐

CYCLE DAY

_____

DATE_____

Sleep Time ____:____ Wake Time ____:____ Hours of Sleep _____

DREAMS _____
_____
_____
_____
_____
_____
_____
_____
_____

MORNING   MOOD: Good-Average-Bad   ENERGY LEVEL: High-Average-Low

REASON _____

Strength   Hope   Spirit   Vision

Awakening   Balance   Energy   Faith   Freedom

AFFIRMATION _____

NIGHT   MOOD: Good-Average-Bad   ENERGY LEVEL: High-Average-Low

REASON _____

Strength   Hope   Spirit   Vision

Awakening   Balance   Energy   Faith   Freedom

DAILY DISCOVERIES _____

_____
_____
_____
_____
_____
_____
_____
_____
_____
_____
_____
_____
_____
_____
_____
_____
_____
_____
_____
_____
_____

HEALTH PATTERNS _____

_____
_____
_____
_____
_____
_____
_____

ACHIEVEMENT _____

ACT OF KINDNESS _____

DIET		**PHYSICAL**
Meat	□□□□□□□□□□□	**DISCOMFORT**
Bread	□□□□□□□□□□□	
Dairy	□□□□□□□□□□	
Vegetables	□□□□□□□□□□	
Fruit	□□□□□□□□□□	
Water	□□□□□□□□□□	
Vitamins	□□□□□□□□□□	

PLAY

Exercise	□	Laugh	□	Read	□	
Meditation	□	Dance	□	_____	□	**CYCLE DAY**
Sex	□	Sing	□	_____	□	_____

DATE_____

Sleep Time ____:____   Wake Time ____:____   Hours of Sleep _____

DREAMS _____
_____
_____
_____
_____
_____
_____
_____
_____

MORNING   MOOD: Good-Average-Bad   ENERGY LEVEL: High-Average-Low

REASON _____

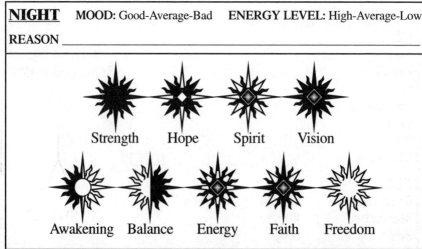

Strength	Hope	Spirit	Vision

Awakening	Balance	Energy	Faith	Freedom

AFFIRMATION _____

NIGHT   MOOD: Good-Average-Bad   ENERGY LEVEL: High-Average-Low

REASON _____

Strength	Hope	Spirit	Vision

Awakening	Balance	Energy	Faith	Freedom

DAILY DISCOVERIES _____

_____
_____
_____
_____
_____
_____
_____
_____
_____
_____
_____
_____
_____
_____
_____
_____
_____
_____
_____
_____
_____
_____
_____

HEALTH PATTERNS _____

_____
_____
_____
_____
_____
_____
_____

ACHIEVEMENT _____

ACT OF KINDNESS _____

DIET

Meat	☐☐☐☐☐☐☐☐☐☐☐☐	
Bread	☐☐☐☐☐☐☐☐☐☐☐☐	
Dairy	☐☐☐☐☐☐☐☐☐☐☐	
Vegetables	☐☐☐☐☐☐☐☐☐☐☐	
Fruit	☐☐☐☐☐☐☐☐☐☐☐	
Water	☐☐☐☐☐☐☐☐☐☐☐	
Vitamins	☐☐☐☐☐☐☐☐☐☐☐	

PHYSICAL DISCOMFORT

PLAY

Exercise	☐	Laugh	☐	Read	☐
Meditation	☐	Dance	☐	_____	☐
Sex	☐	Sing	☐	_____	☐

CYCLE DAY

_____

DATE_____

Sleep Time ____:____   Wake Time ____:____   Hours of Sleep _____

DREAMS _____

_____

_____

_____

_____

_____

_____

_____

_____

MORNING   MOOD: Good-Average-Bad   ENERGY LEVEL: High-Average-Low

REASON _____

Strength	Hope	Spirit	Vision

Awakening	Balance	Energy	Faith	Freedom

AFFIRMATION _____

NIGHT   MOOD: Good-Average-Bad   ENERGY LEVEL: High-Average-Low

REASON _____

Strength	Hope	Spirit	Vision

Awakening	Balance	Energy	Faith	Freedom

DAILY DISCOVERIES _____

_____
_____
_____
_____
_____
_____
_____
_____
_____
_____
_____
_____
_____
_____
_____
_____
_____
_____
_____
_____
_____

HEALTH PATTERNS _____

_____
_____
_____
_____
_____
_____

ACHIEVEMENT _____

ACT OF KINDNESS _____

DIET		**PHYSICAL**
Meat	□□□□□□□□□□□	**DISCOMFORT**
Bread	□□□□□□□□□□□	
Dairy	□□□□□□□□□□	
Vegetables	□□□□□□□□□□	
Fruit	□□□□□□□□□□□	
Water	□□□□□□□□□□	
Vitamins	□□□□□□□□□□	

PLAY

Exercise	□	Laugh	□	Read	□
Meditation	□	Dance	□	_____	□
Sex	□	Sing	□	_____	□

CYCLE DAY

_____

DATE_____

Sleep Time ____:____   Wake Time ____:____   Hours of Sleep _____

DREAMS _____
_____
_____
_____
_____
_____
_____
_____
_____

MORNING   MOOD: Good-Average-Bad   ENERGY LEVEL: High-Average-Low

REASON _____

Strength	Hope	Spirit	Vision

Awakening	Balance	Energy	Faith	Freedom

AFFIRMATION _____

NIGHT   MOOD: Good-Average-Bad   ENERGY LEVEL: High-Average-Low

REASON _____

Strength	Hope	Spirit	Vision

Awakening	Balance	Energy	Faith	Freedom

DAILY DISCOVERIES _____

_____
_____
_____
_____
_____
_____
_____
_____
_____
_____
_____
_____
_____
_____
_____
_____
_____
_____
_____

HEALTH PATTERNS _____

_____
_____
_____
_____
_____
_____

ACHIEVEMENT _____

ACT OF KINDNESS _____

DIET

Meat	☐☐☐☐☐☐☐☐☐☐☐☐		
Bread	☐☐☐☐☐☐☐☐☐☐☐☐		
Dairy	☐☐☐☐☐☐☐☐☐☐☐		
Vegetables	☐☐☐☐☐☐☐☐☐☐☐		
Fruit	☐☐☐☐☐☐☐☐☐☐☐☐		
Water	☐☐☐☐☐☐☐☐☐☐☐☐		
Vitamins	☐☐☐☐☐☐☐☐☐☐☐		

PHYSICAL DISCOMFORT

PLAY

Exercise	☐	Laugh	☐	Read	☐
Meditation	☐	Dance	☐	_____	☐
Sex	☐	Sing	☐	_____	☐

CYCLE DAY

_____

DATE_____

Sleep Time ____:____ Wake Time ____:____ Hours of Sleep _____

DREAMS _____
_____
_____
_____
_____
_____
_____
_____
_____

MORNING   MOOD: Good-Average-Bad ENERGY LEVEL: High-Average-Low

REASON _____

Strength   Hope   Spirit   Vision

Awakening Balance   Energy   Faith   Freedom

AFFIRMATION _____

NIGHT   MOOD: Good-Average-Bad   ENERGY LEVEL: High-Average-Low

REASON _____

Strength   Hope   Spirit   Vision

Awakening Balance   Energy   Faith   Freedom

DAILY DISCOVERIES _____

_____
_____
_____
_____
_____
_____
_____
_____
_____
_____
_____
_____
_____
_____
_____
_____
_____
_____
_____
_____
_____

HEALTH PATTERNS _____

_____
_____
_____
_____
_____
_____

ACHIEVEMENT _____

ACT OF KINDNESS _____

DIET		**PHYSICAL DISCOMFORT**
Meat	☐☐☐☐☐☐☐☐☐☐☐☐	
Bread	☐☐☐☐☐☐☐☐☐☐☐☐	
Dairy	☐☐☐☐☐☐☐☐☐☐☐☐	
Vegetables	☐☐☐☐☐☐☐☐☐☐☐☐	
Fruit	☐☐☐☐☐☐☐☐☐☐☐☐	
Water	☐☐☐☐☐☐☐☐☐☐☐☐	
Vitamins	☐☐☐☐☐☐☐☐☐☐☐☐	

PLAY

Exercise	☐	Laugh	☐	Read	☐
Meditation	☐	Dance	☐	_____	☐
Sex	☐	Sing	☐	_____	☐

CYCLE DAY

_____

DATE_____

Sleep Time _____:_____ Wake Time _____:_____ Hours of Sleep _____

DREAMS _____
_____
_____
_____
_____
_____
_____
_____

MORNING   MOOD: Good-Average-Bad   **ENERGY LEVEL:** High-Average-Low

REASON _____

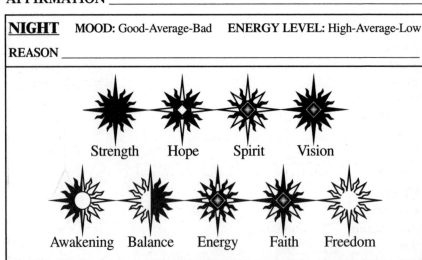

Strength   Hope   Spirit   Vision

Awakening Balance Energy Faith Freedom

AFFIRMATION _____

NIGHT   MOOD: Good-Average-Bad   **ENERGY LEVEL:** High-Average-Low

REASON _____

Strength   Hope   Spirit   Vision

Awakening Balance Energy Faith Freedom

DAILY DISCOVERIES _____

_____
_____
_____
_____
_____
_____
_____
_____
_____
_____
_____
_____
_____
_____
_____
_____
_____
_____
_____
_____
_____

HEALTH PATTERNS _____

_____
_____
_____
_____
_____
_____

ACHIEVEMENT _____

ACT OF KINDNESS _____

DIET													
Meat	☐	☐	☐	☐	☐	☐	☐	☐	☐	☐	☐	☐	☐
Bread	☐	☐	☐	☐	☐	☐	☐	☐	☐	☐	☐	☐	☐
Dairy	☐	☐	☐	☐	☐	☐	☐	☐	☐	☐	☐	☐	
Vegetables	☐	☐	☐	☐	☐	☐	☐	☐	☐	☐	☐	☐	
Fruit	☐	☐	☐	☐	☐	☐	☐	☐	☐	☐	☐	☐	
Water	☐	☐	☐	☐	☐	☐	☐	☐	☐	☐	☐	☐	
Vitamins	☐	☐	☐	☐	☐	☐	☐	☐	☐	☐	☐	☐	

PHYSICAL DISCOMFORT

PLAY

Exercise	☐	Laugh	☐	Read	☐
Meditation	☐	Dance	☐	_____	☐
Sex	☐	Sing	☐	_____	☐

CYCLE DAY
_____

DATE_____

Sleep Time ____:____   Wake Time ____:____   Hours of Sleep _____

DREAMS _____
_____
_____
_____
_____
_____
_____
_____

MORNING   MOOD: Good-Average-Bad   ENERGY LEVEL: High-Average-Low

REASON _____

Strength   Hope   Spirit   Vision

Awakening   Balance   Energy   Faith   Freedom

AFFIRMATION _____

NIGHT   MOOD: Good-Average-Bad   ENERGY LEVEL: High-Average-Low

REASON _____

Strength   Hope   Spirit   Vision

Awakening   Balance   Energy   Faith   Freedom

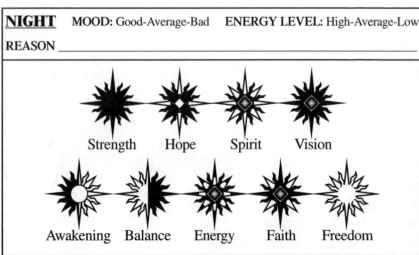

DAILY DISCOVERIES _____

_____
_____
_____
_____
_____
_____
_____
_____
_____
_____
_____
_____
_____
_____
_____
_____
_____
_____
_____
_____
_____

HEALTH PATTERNS _____

_____
_____
_____
_____
_____
_____
_____

ACHIEVEMENT _____

ACT OF KINDNESS _____

DIET

Meat	☐	☐	☐	☐	☐	☐	☐	☐	☐	☐	☐	☐	☐
Bread	☐	☐	☐	☐	☐	☐	☐	☐	☐	☐	☐	☐	☐
Dairy	☐	☐	☐	☐	☐	☐	☐	☐	☐	☐	☐	☐	☐
Vegetables	☐	☐	☐	☐	☐	☐	☐	☐	☐	☐	☐	☐	☐
Fruit	☐	☐	☐	☐	☐	☐	☐	☐	☐	☐	☐	☐	☐
Water	☐	☐	☐	☐	☐	☐	☐	☐	☐	☐	☐	☐	☐
Vitamins	☐	☐	☐	☐	☐	☐	☐	☐	☐	☐	☐	☐	☐

PHYSICAL DISCOMFORT

PLAY

Exercise	☐	Laugh	☐	Read	☐
Meditation	☐	Dance	☐	_____	☐
Sex	☐	Sing	☐	_____	☐

CYCLE DAY

_____

DATE_____

Sleep Time ____:____   Wake Time ____:____   Hours of Sleep _____

DREAMS _____
_____
_____
_____
_____
_____
_____
_____
_____

MORNING   MOOD: Good-Average-Bad   ENERGY LEVEL: High-Average-Low

REASON _____

        Strength   Hope   Spirit   Vision

    Awakening   Balance   Energy   Faith   Freedom

AFFIRMATION _____

NIGHT   MOOD: Good-Average-Bad   ENERGY LEVEL: High-Average-Low

REASON _____

        Strength   Hope   Spirit   Vision

    Awakening   Balance   Energy   Faith   Freedom

DAILY DISCOVERIES _____

_____
_____
_____
_____
_____
_____
_____
_____
_____
_____
_____
_____
_____
_____
_____
_____
_____
_____
_____
_____
_____
_____
_____

HEALTH PATTERNS _____

_____
_____
_____
_____
_____
_____

ACHIEVEMENT _____

ACT OF KINDNESS _____

DIET												
Meat	☐	☐	☐	☐	☐	☐	☐	☐	☐	☐	☐	☐
Bread	☐	☐	☐	☐	☐	☐	☐	☐	☐	☐	☐	☐
Dairy	☐	☐	☐	☐	☐	☐	☐	☐	☐	☐	☐	
Vegetables	☐	☐	☐	☐	☐	☐	☐	☐	☐	☐	☐	
Fruit	☐	☐	☐	☐	☐	☐	☐	☐	☐	☐	☐	
Water	☐	☐	☐	☐	☐	☐	☐	☐	☐	☐	☐	
Vitamins	☐	☐	☐	☐	☐	☐	☐	☐	☐	☐	☐	

PHYSICAL DISCOMFORT

PLAY

Exercise	☐	Laugh	☐	Read	☐
Meditation	☐	Dance	☐	_____	☐
Sex	☐	Sing	☐	_____	☐

CYCLE DAY

_____

DATE_____

Sleep Time ____ : ____ Wake Time ____ : ____ Hours of Sleep _____

DREAMS _____
_____
_____
_____
_____
_____
_____
_____
_____

MORNING   MOOD: Good-Average-Bad   ENERGY LEVEL: High-Average-Low

REASON _____

Strength   Hope   Spirit   Vision

Awakening   Balance   Energy   Faith   Freedom

AFFIRMATION _____

NIGHT   MOOD: Good-Average-Bad   ENERGY LEVEL: High-Average-Low

REASON _____

Strength   Hope   Spirit   Vision

Awakening   Balance   Energy   Faith   Freedom

DAILY DISCOVERIES _____

_____
_____
_____
_____
_____
_____
_____
_____
_____
_____
_____
_____
_____
_____
_____
_____
_____
_____
_____

HEALTH PATTERNS _____

_____
_____
_____
_____
_____
_____
_____

ACHIEVEMENT _____

ACT OF KINDNESS _____

DIET

Meat	☐ ☐ ☐ ☐ ☐ ☐ ☐ ☐ ☐ ☐ ☐
Bread	☐ ☐ ☐ ☐ ☐ ☐ ☐ ☐ ☐ ☐ ☐
Dairy	☐ ☐ ☐ ☐ ☐ ☐ ☐ ☐ ☐ ☐ ☐
Vegetables	☐ ☐ ☐ ☐ ☐ ☐ ☐ ☐ ☐ ☐ ☐
Fruit	☐ ☐ ☐ ☐ ☐ ☐ ☐ ☐ ☐ ☐ ☐
Water	☐ ☐ ☐ ☐ ☐ ☐ ☐ ☐ ☐ ☐ ☐
Vitamins	☐ ☐ ☐ ☐ ☐ ☐ ☐ ☐ ☐ ☐ ☐

PHYSICAL DISCOMFORT

PLAY

Exercise	☐	Laugh	☐	Read	☐
Meditation	☐	Dance	☐	_____	☐
Sex	☐	Sing	☐	_____	☐

CYCLE DAY

_____

DATE_____

Sleep Time _____:_____   Wake Time _____:_____   Hours of Sleep _____

DREAMS _____
_____
_____
_____
_____
_____
_____
_____
_____

MORNING   MOOD: Good-Average-Bad   ENERGY LEVEL: High-Average-Low

REASON _____

Strength   Hope   Spirit   Vision

Awakening   Balance   Energy   Faith   Freedom

AFFIRMATION _____

NIGHT   MOOD: Good-Average-Bad   ENERGY LEVEL: High-Average-Low

REASON _____

Strength   Hope   Spirit   Vision

Awakening   Balance   Energy   Faith   Freedom

DAILY DISCOVERIES _____

_____
_____
_____
_____
_____
_____
_____
_____
_____
_____
_____
_____
_____
_____
_____
_____
_____
_____
_____
_____

HEALTH PATTERNS _____

_____
_____
_____
_____
_____
_____

ACHIEVEMENT _____

ACT OF KINDNESS _____

DIET		**PHYSICAL**
Meat	☐☐☐☐☐☐☐☐☐☐☐	**DISCOMFORT**
Bread	☐☐☐☐☐☐☐☐☐☐☐	
Dairy	☐☐☐☐☐☐☐☐☐☐☐	
Vegetables	☐☐☐☐☐☐☐☐☐☐☐	
Fruit	☐☐☐☐☐☐☐☐☐☐☐	
Water	☐☐☐☐☐☐☐☐☐☐☐	
Vitamins	☐☐☐☐☐☐☐☐☐☐☐	

PLAY

Exercise	☐	Laugh	☐	Read	☐
Meditation	☐	Dance	☐	_____	☐
Sex	☐	Sing	☐	_____	☐

CYCLE DAY

_____

DATE_____

Sleep Time ____:____   Wake Time ____:____   Hours of Sleep _____

DREAMS _____
_____
_____
_____
_____
_____
_____
_____
_____
_____

MORNING   MOOD: Good-Average-Bad   **ENERGY LEVEL:** High-Average-Low

REASON _____

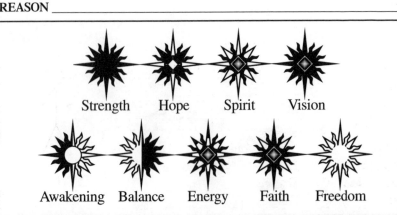

Strength   Hope   Spirit   Vision

Awakening   Balance   Energy   Faith   Freedom

AFFIRMATION _____

NIGHT   MOOD: Good-Average-Bad   **ENERGY LEVEL:** High-Average-Low

REASON _____

Strength   Hope   Spirit   Vision

Awakening   Balance   Energy   Faith   Freedom

DAILY DISCOVERIES _____

_____
_____
_____
_____
_____
_____
_____
_____
_____
_____
_____
_____
_____
_____
_____
_____
_____
_____
_____
_____
_____

HEALTH PATTERNS _____

_____
_____
_____
_____
_____
_____
_____

ACHIEVEMENT _____

ACT OF KINDNESS _____

DIET

Meat	□	□	□	□	□	□	□	□	□	□	□	□
Bread	□	□	□	□	□	□	□	□	□	□	□	□
Dairy	□	□	□	□	□	□	□	□	□	□	□	□
Vegetables	□	□	□	□	□	□	□	□	□	□	□	□
Fruit	□	□	□	□	□	□	□	□	□	□	□	□
Water	□	□	□	□	□	□	□	□	□	□	□	□
Vitamins	□	□	□	□	□	□	□	□	□	□	□	□

PHYSICAL DISCOMFORT

PLAY

Exercise	□	Laugh	□	Read	□
Meditation	□	Dance	□	_____	□
Sex	□	Sing	□	_____	□

CYCLE DAY

_____

DATE_____

Sleep Time ____:____ Wake Time ____:____ Hours of Sleep _____

DREAMS _____
_____
_____
_____
_____
_____
_____
_____

MORNING   MOOD: Good-Average-Bad   ENERGY LEVEL: High-Average-Low

REASON _____

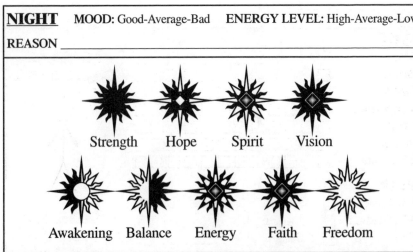

Strength   Hope   Spirit   Vision

Awakening   Balance   Energy   Faith   Freedom

AFFIRMATION _____

NIGHT   MOOD: Good-Average-Bad   ENERGY LEVEL: High-Average-Low

REASON _____

Strength   Hope   Spirit   Vision

Awakening   Balance   Energy   Faith   Freedom

DAILY DISCOVERIES _____

_____
_____
_____
_____
_____
_____
_____
_____
_____
_____
_____
_____
_____
_____
_____
_____
_____
_____
_____
_____

HEALTH PATTERNS _____

_____
_____
_____
_____
_____
_____
_____

ACHIEVEMENT _____

ACT OF KINDNESS _____

DIET

Meat	☐	☐	☐	☐	☐	☐	☐	☐	☐	☐	☐
Bread	☐	☐	☐	☐	☐	☐	☐	☐	☐	☐	☐
Dairy	☐	☐	☐	☐	☐	☐	☐	☐	☐	☐	
Vegetables	☐	☐	☐	☐	☐	☐	☐	☐	☐	☐	
Fruit	☐	☐	☐	☐	☐	☐	☐	☐	☐	☐	☐
Water	☐	☐	☐	☐	☐	☐	☐	☐	☐	☐	☐
Vitamins	☐	☐	☐	☐	☐	☐	☐	☐	☐	☐	

PHYSICAL DISCOMFORT

PLAY

Exercise	☐	Laugh	☐	Read	☐	
Meditation	☐	Dance	☐	_____	☐	
Sex	☐	Sing	☐	_____	☐	

CYCLE DAY

_____

DATE_____

Sleep Time ____:____ Wake Time ____:____ Hours of Sleep _____

DREAMS _____
_____
_____
_____
_____
_____
_____
_____
_____

MORNING   MOOD: Good-Average-Bad   ENERGY LEVEL: High-Average-Low

REASON _____

Strength	Hope	Spirit	Vision

Awakening	Balance	Energy	Faith	Freedom

AFFIRMATION _____

NIGHT   MOOD: Good-Average-Bad   ENERGY LEVEL: High-Average-Low

REASON _____

Strength	Hope	Spirit	Vision

Awakening	Balance	Energy	Faith	Freedom

DAILY DISCOVERIES _____

_____
_____
_____
_____
_____
_____
_____
_____
_____
_____
_____
_____
_____
_____
_____
_____
_____
_____
_____
_____

HEALTH PATTERNS _____

_____
_____
_____
_____
_____
_____

ACHIEVEMENT _____
ACT OF KINDNESS _____

DIET		**PHYSICAL DISCOMFORT**
Meat	☐☐☐☐☐☐☐☐☐☐☐☐	
Bread	☐☐☐☐☐☐☐☐☐☐☐☐	
Dairy	☐☐☐☐☐☐☐☐☐☐☐	
Vegetables	☐☐☐☐☐☐☐☐☐☐☐	
Fruit	☐☐☐☐☐☐☐☐☐☐☐☐	
Water	☐☐☐☐☐☐☐☐☐☐☐	
Vitamins	☐☐☐☐☐☐☐☐☐☐☐	

PLAY

Exercise	☐	Laugh	☐	Read	☐
Meditation	☐	Dance	☐	_____	☐
Sex	☐	Sing	☐	_____	☐

CYCLE DAY
_____

DATE_____

Sleep Time ____:____ Wake Time ____:____ Hours of Sleep _____

DREAMS _____
_____
_____
_____
_____
_____
_____
_____
_____

MORNING   MOOD: Good-Average-Bad   ENERGY LEVEL: High-Average-Low

REASON _____

Strength   Hope   Spirit   Vision

Awakening   Balance   Energy   Faith   Freedom

AFFIRMATION _____

NIGHT   MOOD: Good-Average-Bad   ENERGY LEVEL: High-Average-Low

REASON _____

Strength   Hope   Spirit   Vision

Awakening   Balance   Energy   Faith   Freedom

DAILY DISCOVERIES _____

_____
_____
_____
_____
_____
_____
_____
_____
_____
_____
_____
_____
_____
_____
_____
_____
_____
_____
_____
_____
_____
_____

HEALTH PATTERNS _____

_____
_____
_____
_____
_____
_____
_____

ACHIEVEMENT _____

ACT OF KINDNESS _____

DIET		**PHYSICAL DISCOMFORT**
Meat	☐☐☐☐☐☐☐☐☐☐☐☐	
Bread	☐☐☐☐☐☐☐☐☐☐☐☐	
Dairy	☐☐☐☐☐☐☐☐☐☐☐☐	
Vegetables	☐☐☐☐☐☐☐☐☐☐☐☐	
Fruit	☐☐☐☐☐☐☐☐☐☐☐☐	
Water	☐☐☐☐☐☐☐☐☐☐☐☐	
Vitamins	☐☐☐☐☐☐☐☐☐☐☐☐	

PLAY

Exercise	☐	Laugh	☐	Read	☐
Meditation	☐	Dance	☐	_____	☐
Sex	☐	Sing	☐	_____	☐

CYCLE DAY _____

DATE_____

Sleep Time _____:_____   Wake Time _____:_____   Hours of Sleep _____

DREAMS _____
_____
_____
_____
_____
_____
_____
_____

MORNING   MOOD: Good-Average-Bad   ENERGY LEVEL: High-Average-Low

REASON _____

Strength   Hope   Spirit   Vision

Awakening   Balance   Energy   Faith   Freedom

AFFIRMATION _____

NIGHT   MOOD: Good-Average-Bad   ENERGY LEVEL: High-Average-Low

REASON _____

Strength   Hope   Spirit   Vision

Awakening   Balance   Energy   Faith   Freedom

DAILY DISCOVERIES _____

_____
_____
_____
_____
_____
_____
_____
_____
_____
_____
_____
_____
_____
_____
_____
_____
_____
_____
_____
_____
_____

HEALTH PATTERNS _____

_____
_____
_____
_____
_____
_____
_____

ACHIEVEMENT _____

ACT OF KINDNESS _____

DIET

Meat	☐	☐	☐	☐	☐	☐	☐	☐	☐	☐	☐
Bread	☐	☐	☐	☐	☐	☐	☐	☐	☐	☐	☐
Dairy	☐	☐	☐	☐	☐	☐	☐	☐	☐	☐	☐
Vegetables	☐	☐	☐	☐	☐	☐	☐	☐	☐	☐	☐
Fruit	☐	☐	☐	☐	☐	☐	☐	☐	☐	☐	☐
Water	☐	☐	☐	☐	☐	☐	☐	☐	☐	☐	☐
Vitamins	☐	☐	☐	☐	☐	☐	☐	☐	☐	☐	☐

PHYSICAL DISCOMFORT

PLAY

Exercise	☐	Laugh	☐	Read	☐
Meditation	☐	Dance	☐	_____	☐
Sex	☐	Sing	☐	_____	☐

CYCLE DAY

_____

DATE_____

Sleep Time ____:____ **Wake Time** ____:____ **Hours of Sleep** _____

DREAMS _____
_____
_____
_____
_____
_____
_____
_____

MORNING   **MOOD:** Good-Average-Bad   **ENERGY LEVEL:** High-Average-Low

REASON _____

Strength	Hope	Spirit	Vision

Awakening	Balance	Energy	Faith	Freedom

AFFIRMATION _____

NIGHT   **MOOD:** Good-Average-Bad   **ENERGY LEVEL:** High-Average-Low

REASON _____

Strength	Hope	Spirit	Vision

Awakening	Balance	Energy	Faith	Freedom

DAILY DISCOVERIES _____

_____
_____
_____
_____
_____
_____
_____
_____
_____
_____
_____
_____
_____
_____
_____
_____
_____
_____
_____
_____

HEALTH PATTERNS _____

_____
_____
_____
_____
_____
_____
_____

ACHIEVEMENT _____

ACT OF KINDNESS _____

DIET

Meat	☐☐☐☐☐☐☐☐☐☐☐☐	
Bread	☐☐☐☐☐☐☐☐☐☐☐☐	
Dairy	☐☐☐☐☐☐☐☐☐☐☐☐	
Vegetables	☐☐☐☐☐☐☐☐☐☐☐☐	
Fruit	☐☐☐☐☐☐☐☐☐☐☐☐	
Water	☐☐☐☐☐☐☐☐☐☐☐☐	
Vitamins	☐☐☐☐☐☐☐☐☐☐☐☐	

PHYSICAL DISCOMFORT

PLAY

Exercise	☐	Laugh	☐	Read	☐
Meditation	☐	Dance	☐	_____	☐
Sex	☐	Sing	☐	_____	☐

CYCLE DAY

_____

DATE_____

Sleep Time _____:_____ Wake Time _____:_____ Hours of Sleep _____

DREAMS _____
_____
_____
_____
_____
_____
_____
_____
_____

MORNING   MOOD: Good-Average-Bad   ENERGY LEVEL: High-Average-Low

REASON _____

Strength	Hope	Spirit	Vision

Awakening	Balance	Energy	Faith	Freedom

AFFIRMATION _____

NIGHT   MOOD: Good-Average-Bad   ENERGY LEVEL: High-Average-Low

REASON _____

Strength	Hope	Spirit	Vision

Awakening	Balance	Energy	Faith	Freedom

DAILY DISCOVERIES _____

_____
_____
_____
_____
_____
_____
_____
_____
_____
_____
_____
_____
_____
_____
_____
_____
_____
_____
_____
_____
_____
_____

HEALTH PATTERNS _____

_____
_____
_____
_____
_____
_____
_____

ACHIEVEMENT _____
ACT OF KINDNESS _____

DIET				**PHYSICAL**
Meat	☐☐☐☐☐☐☐☐☐☐☐☐			**DISCOMFORT**
Bread	☐☐☐☐☐☐☐☐☐☐☐☐			
Dairy	☐☐☐☐☐☐☐☐☐☐☐☐			
Vegetables	☐☐☐☐☐☐☐☐☐☐☐☐			
Fruit	☐☐☐☐☐☐☐☐☐☐☐☐			
Water	☐☐☐☐☐☐☐☐☐☐☐☐			
Vitamins	☐☐☐☐☐☐☐☐☐☐☐☐			

PLAY

Exercise	☐	Laugh	☐	Read	☐
Meditation	☐	Dance	☐	_____	☐
Sex	☐	Sing	☐	_____	☐

CYCLE DAY

_____

DATE_____

Sleep Time _____:_____ Wake Time _____:_____ Hours of Sleep _____

DREAMS _____
_____
_____
_____
_____
_____
_____
_____
_____

MORNING MOOD: Good-Average-Bad ENERGY LEVEL: High-Average-Low

REASON _____

Strength   Hope   Spirit   Vision

Awakening   Balance   Energy   Faith   Freedom

AFFIRMATION _____

NIGHT MOOD: Good-Average-Bad ENERGY LEVEL: High-Average-Low

REASON _____

Strength   Hope   Spirit   Vision

Awakening   Balance   Energy   Faith   Freedom

DAILY DISCOVERIES _____

_____
_____
_____
_____
_____
_____
_____
_____
_____
_____
_____
_____
_____
_____
_____
_____
_____
_____
_____
_____
_____

HEALTH PATTERNS _____

_____
_____
_____
_____
_____
_____

ACHIEVEMENT _____

ACT OF KINDNESS _____

DIET		**PHYSICAL**
Meat	☐☐☐☐☐☐☐☐☐☐☐☐	**DISCOMFORT**
Bread	☐☐☐☐☐☐☐☐☐☐☐☐	
Dairy	☐☐☐☐☐☐☐☐☐☐☐☐	
Vegetables	☐☐☐☐☐☐☐☐☐☐☐☐	
Fruit	☐☐☐☐☐☐☐☐☐☐☐☐	
Water	☐☐☐☐☐☐☐☐☐☐☐☐	
Vitamins	☐☐☐☐☐☐☐☐☐☐☐☐	

PLAY

Exercise	☐	Laugh	☐	Read	☐
Meditation	☐	Dance	☐	_____	☐
Sex	☐	Sing	☐	_____	☐

CYCLE DAY

_____

DATE_____

Sleep Time ____:____ Wake Time ____:____ Hours of Sleep _____

DREAMS _____

_____
_____
_____
_____
_____
_____
_____
_____

MORNING   MOOD: Good-Average-Bad   ENERGY LEVEL: High-Average-Low

REASON _____

Strength	Hope	Spirit	Vision

Awakening	Balance	Energy	Faith	Freedom

AFFIRMATION _____

NIGHT   MOOD: Good-Average-Bad   ENERGY LEVEL: High-Average-Low

REASON _____

Strength	Hope	Spirit	Vision

Awakening	Balance	Energy	Faith	Freedom

DAILY DISCOVERIES _____

_____
_____
_____
_____
_____
_____
_____
_____
_____
_____
_____
_____
_____
_____
_____
_____
_____
_____
_____
_____
_____

HEALTH PATTERNS _____

_____
_____
_____
_____
_____
_____
_____

ACHIEVEMENT _____
ACT OF KINDNESS _____

DIET		**PHYSICAL**
Meat	☐☐☐☐☐☐☐☐☐☐☐	**DISCOMFORT**
Bread	☐☐☐☐☐☐☐☐☐☐☐	
Dairy	☐☐☐☐☐☐☐☐☐☐☐	
Vegetables	☐☐☐☐☐☐☐☐☐☐☐	
Fruit	☐☐☐☐☐☐☐☐☐☐☐	
Water	☐☐☐☐☐☐☐☐☐☐☐	
Vitamins	☐☐☐☐☐☐☐☐☐☐☐	

PLAY

Exercise	☐	Laugh	☐	Read	☐	
Meditation	☐	Dance	☐	_____	☐	**CYCLE DAY**
Sex	☐	Sing	☐	_____	☐	_____

DATE_____

Sleep Time ____:____ Wake Time ____:____ Hours of Sleep _____

DREAMS _____
_____
_____
_____
_____
_____
_____
_____
_____

MORNING   MOOD: Good-Average-Bad   ENERGY LEVEL: High-Average-Low

REASON _____

Strength   Hope   Spirit   Vision

Awakening   Balance   Energy   Faith   Freedom

AFFIRMATION _____

NIGHT   MOOD: Good-Average-Bad   ENERGY LEVEL: High-Average-Low

REASON _____

Strength   Hope   Spirit   Vision

Awakening   Balance   Energy   Faith   Freedom

DAILY DISCOVERIES _____

_____
_____
_____
_____
_____
_____
_____
_____
_____
_____
_____
_____
_____
_____
_____
_____
_____
_____
_____
_____
_____
_____
_____

HEALTH PATTERNS _____

_____
_____
_____
_____
_____
_____
_____

ACHIEVEMENT _____
ACT OF KINDNESS _____

DIET

Meat	□	□	□	□	□	□	□	□	□	□	□
Bread	□	□	□	□	□	□	□	□	□	□	□
Dairy	□	□	□	□	□	□	□	□	□	□	□
Vegetables	□	□	□	□	□	□	□	□	□	□	□
Fruit	□	□	□	□	□	□	□	□	□	□	□
Water	□	□	□	□	□	□	□	□	□	□	□
Vitamins	□	□	□	□	□	□	□	□	□	□	□

PHYSICAL DISCOMFORT

PLAY

Exercise	□	Laugh	□	Read	□
Meditation	□	Dance	□	_____	□
Sex	□	Sing	□	_____	□

CYCLE DAY

_____

DATE_____

Sleep Time ____:____   Wake Time ____:____   Hours of Sleep _____

DREAMS _____
_____
_____
_____
_____
_____
_____
_____
_____

MORNING   MOOD: Good-Average-Bad   **ENERGY LEVEL:** High-Average-Low

REASON _____

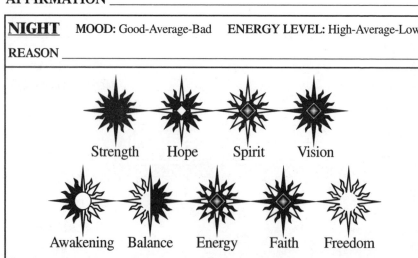

Strength   Hope   Spirit   Vision

Awakening   Balance   Energy   Faith   Freedom

AFFIRMATION _____

NIGHT   MOOD: Good-Average-Bad   **ENERGY LEVEL:** High-Average-Low

REASON _____

Strength   Hope   Spirit   Vision

Awakening   Balance   Energy   Faith   Freedom

DAILY DISCOVERIES _____

_____
_____
_____
_____
_____
_____
_____
_____
_____
_____
_____
_____
_____
_____
_____
_____
_____
_____
_____
_____
_____
_____

HEALTH PATTERNS _____

_____
_____
_____
_____
_____
_____

ACHIEVEMENT _____

ACT OF KINDNESS _____

DIET		**PHYSICAL DISCOMFORT**
Meat	☐☐☐☐☐☐☐☐☐☐☐☐	
Bread	☐☐☐☐☐☐☐☐☐☐☐☐	
Dairy	☐☐☐☐☐☐☐☐☐☐☐☐	
Vegetables	☐☐☐☐☐☐☐☐☐☐☐☐	
Fruit	☐☐☐☐☐☐☐☐☐☐☐☐	
Water	☐☐☐☐☐☐☐☐☐☐☐☐	
Vitamins	☐☐☐☐☐☐☐☐☐☐☐☐	

PLAY

Exercise	☐	Laugh	☐	Read	☐
Meditation	☐	Dance	☐	_____	☐
Sex	☐	Sing	☐	_____	☐

CYCLE DAY

_____

DATE_____

Sleep Time ____:____ Wake Time ____:____ Hours of Sleep _____

DREAMS _____

_____

_____

_____

_____

_____

_____

_____

_____

MORNING   MOOD: Good-Average-Bad   ENERGY LEVEL: High-Average-Low

REASON _____

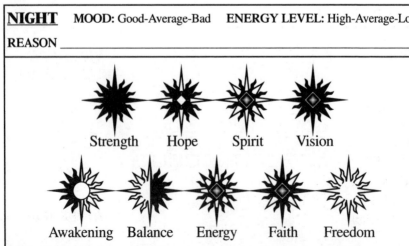

AFFIRMATION _____

NIGHT   MOOD: Good-Average-Bad   ENERGY LEVEL: High-Average-Low

REASON _____

Strength   Hope   Spirit   Vision

Awakening   Balance   Energy   Faith   Freedom

DAILY DISCOVERIES _____

_____
_____
_____
_____
_____
_____
_____
_____
_____
_____
_____
_____
_____
_____
_____
_____
_____
_____
_____
_____

HEALTH PATTERNS _____

_____
_____
_____
_____
_____
_____

ACHIEVEMENT _____
ACT OF KINDNESS _____

DIET

Meat	☐☐☐☐☐☐☐☐☐☐☐
Bread	☐☐☐☐☐☐☐☐☐☐☐
Dairy	☐☐☐☐☐☐☐☐☐☐☐
Vegetables	☐☐☐☐☐☐☐☐☐☐☐
Fruit	☐☐☐☐☐☐☐☐☐☐☐
Water	☐☐☐☐☐☐☐☐☐☐☐
Vitamins	☐☐☐☐☐☐☐☐☐☐☐

PHYSICAL DISCOMFORT

PLAY

Exercise	☐	Laugh	☐	Read	☐
Meditation	☐	Dance	☐	_____	☐
Sex	☐	Sing	☐	_____	☐

CYCLE DAY

_____

DATE_____

Sleep Time _____:_____   Wake Time _____:_____   Hours of Sleep _____

DREAMS _____
_____
_____
_____
_____
_____
_____
_____

<u>**MORNING**</u>   **MOOD:** Good-Average-Bad   **ENERGY LEVEL:** High-Average-Low

REASON _____

Strength	Hope	Spirit	Vision

Awakening	Balance	Energy	Faith	Freedom

AFFIRMATION _____

<u>**NIGHT**</u>   **MOOD:** Good-Average-Bad   **ENERGY LEVEL:** High-Average-Low

REASON _____

Strength	Hope	Spirit	Vision

Awakening	Balance	Energy	Faith	Freedom

DAILY DISCOVERIES _____

_____
_____
_____
_____
_____
_____
_____
_____
_____
_____
_____
_____
_____
_____
_____
_____
_____
_____
_____
_____
_____
_____
_____

HEALTH PATTERNS _____

_____
_____
_____
_____
_____
_____
_____

ACHIEVEMENT _____

ACT OF KINDNESS _____

DIET		**PHYSICAL**
Meat	☐☐☐☐☐☐☐☐☐☐☐	**DISCOMFORT**
Bread	☐☐☐☐☐☐☐☐☐☐☐	
Dairy	☐☐☐☐☐☐☐☐☐☐	
Vegetables	☐☐☐☐☐☐☐☐☐☐	
Fruit	☐☐☐☐☐☐☐☐☐☐	
Water	☐☐☐☐☐☐☐☐☐☐	
Vitamins	☐☐☐☐☐☐☐☐☐☐	

PLAY

Exercise	☐	Laugh	☐	Read	☐
Meditation	☐	Dance	☐	_____	☐
Sex	☐	Sing	☐	_____	☐

CYCLE DAY

_____

DATE_____

Sleep Time ____:____ Wake Time ____:____ Hours of Sleep _____

DREAMS _____
_____
_____
_____
_____
_____
_____
_____

MORNING   MOOD: Good-Average-Bad   ENERGY LEVEL: High-Average-Low

REASON _____

| Strength | Hope | Spirit | Vision |

| Awakening | Balance | Energy | Faith | Freedom |

AFFIRMATION _____

NIGHT   MOOD: Good-Average-Bad   ENERGY LEVEL: High-Average-Low

REASON _____

| Strength | Hope | Spirit | Vision |

| Awakening | Balance | Energy | Faith | Freedom |

DAILY DISCOVERIES _____

_____
_____
_____
_____
_____
_____
_____
_____
_____
_____
_____
_____
_____
_____
_____
_____
_____
_____
_____
_____
_____

HEALTH PATTERNS _____

_____
_____
_____
_____
_____
_____

ACHIEVEMENT _____
ACT OF KINDNESS _____

DIET

Meat	☐	☐	☐	☐	☐	☐	☐	☐	☐	☐	☐	☐	☐
Bread	☐	☐	☐	☐	☐	☐	☐	☐	☐	☐	☐	☐	☐
Dairy	☐	☐	☐	☐	☐	☐	☐	☐	☐	☐	☐	☐	☐
Vegetables	☐	☐	☐	☐	☐	☐	☐	☐	☐	☐	☐	☐	☐
Fruit	☐	☐	☐	☐	☐	☐	☐	☐	☐	☐	☐	☐	☐
Water	☐	☐	☐	☐	☐	☐	☐	☐	☐	☐	☐	☐	☐
Vitamins	☐	☐	☐	☐	☐	☐	☐	☐	☐	☐	☐	☐	☐

PHYSICAL DISCOMFORT

PLAY

Exercise	☐	Laugh	☐	Read	☐
Meditation	☐	Dance	☐	_____	☐
Sex	☐	Sing	☐	_____	☐

CYCLE DAY

_____

DATE_____

Sleep Time ___:___   Wake Time ___:___   Hours of Sleep _____

DREAMS _____
_____
_____
_____
_____
_____
_____
_____

MORNING   MOOD: Good-Average-Bad   ENERGY LEVEL: High-Average-Low

REASON _____

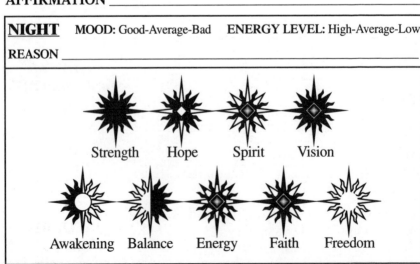

Strength   Hope   Spirit   Vision

Awakening   Balance   Energy   Faith   Freedom

AFFIRMATION _____

NIGHT   MOOD: Good-Average-Bad   ENERGY LEVEL: High-Average-Low

REASON _____

Strength   Hope   Spirit   Vision

Awakening   Balance   Energy   Faith   Freedom

DAILY DISCOVERIES _____

_____
_____
_____
_____
_____
_____
_____
_____
_____
_____
_____
_____
_____
_____
_____
_____
_____
_____
_____
_____

HEALTH PATTERNS _____

_____
_____
_____
_____
_____
_____

ACHIEVEMENT _____

ACT OF KINDNESS _____

DIET

Meat	☐	☐	☐	☐	☐	☐	☐	☐	☐	☐	☐
Bread	☐	☐	☐	☐	☐	☐	☐	☐	☐	☐	☐
Dairy	☐	☐	☐	☐	☐	☐	☐	☐	☐	☐	☐
Vegetables	☐	☐	☐	☐	☐	☐	☐	☐	☐	☐	☐
Fruit	☐	☐	☐	☐	☐	☐	☐	☐	☐	☐	☐
Water	☐	☐	☐	☐	☐	☐	☐	☐	☐	☐	☐
Vitamins	☐	☐	☐	☐	☐	☐	☐	☐	☐	☐	☐

PHYSICAL DISCOMFORT

PLAY

Exercise	☐	Laugh	☐	Read	☐
Meditation	☐	Dance	☐	_____	☐
Sex	☐	Sing	☐	_____	☐

CYCLE DAY

_____

DATE_____

Sleep Time ____:____   Wake Time ____:____   Hours of Sleep _____

DREAMS _____
_____
_____
_____
_____
_____
_____
_____
_____

MORNING   MOOD: Good-Average-Bad   ENERGY LEVEL: High-Average-Low

REASON _____

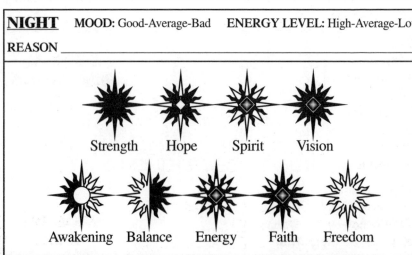

Strength   Hope   Spirit   Vision

Awakening   Balance   Energy   Faith   Freedom

AFFIRMATION _____

NIGHT   MOOD: Good-Average-Bad   ENERGY LEVEL: High-Average-Low

REASON _____

Strength   Hope   Spirit   Vision

Awakening   Balance   Energy   Faith   Freedom

DAILY DISCOVERIES _____
_____
_____
_____
_____
_____
_____
_____
_____
_____
_____
_____
_____
_____
_____
_____
_____
_____
_____
_____
_____
_____
_____

HEALTH PATTERNS _____
_____
_____
_____
_____
_____
_____

ACHIEVEMENT _____
ACT OF KINDNESS _____

DIET

Meat	□□□□□□□□□□□□
Bread	□□□□□□□□□□□□
Dairy	□□□□□□□□□□□
Vegetables	□□□□□□□□□□□
Fruit	□□□□□□□□□□□
Water	□□□□□□□□□□□
Vitamins	□□□□□□□□□□□

PHYSICAL DISCOMFORT

PLAY

Exercise	□	Laugh	□	Read	□
Meditation	□	Dance	□	_____	□
Sex	□	Sing	□	_____	□

CYCLE DAY

_____

DATE_____

Sleep Time ____:____   Wake Time ____:____   Hours of Sleep _____

DREAMS _____

_____

_____

_____

_____

_____

_____

_____

_____

MORNING   MOOD: Good-Average-Bad   ENERGY LEVEL: High-Average-Low

REASON _____

Strength   Hope   Spirit   Vision

Awakening   Balance   Energy   Faith   Freedom

AFFIRMATION _____

NIGHT   MOOD: Good-Average-Bad   ENERGY LEVEL: High-Average-Low

REASON _____

Strength   Hope   Spirit   Vision

Awakening   Balance   Energy   Faith   Freedom

DAILY DISCOVERIES _____

_____
_____
_____
_____
_____
_____
_____
_____
_____
_____
_____
_____
_____
_____
_____
_____
_____
_____
_____
_____
_____

HEALTH PATTERNS _____

_____
_____
_____
_____
_____
_____

ACHIEVEMENT _____

ACT OF KINDNESS _____

DIET			
Meat	□□□□□□□□□□□		**PHYSICAL**
Bread	□□□□□□□□□□□		**DISCOMFORT**
Dairy	□□□□□□□□□□□		
Vegetables	□□□□□□□□□□□		
Fruit	□□□□□□□□□□□		
Water	□□□□□□□□□□□		
Vitamins	□□□□□□□□□□□		

PLAY

Exercise	□	Laugh	□	Read	□
Meditation	□	Dance	□	_____	□
Sex	□	Sing	□	_____	□

CYCLE DAY

_____

DATE_____

Sleep Time ____:____   Wake Time ____:____   Hours of Sleep _____

DREAMS _____
_____
_____
_____
_____
_____
_____
_____
_____

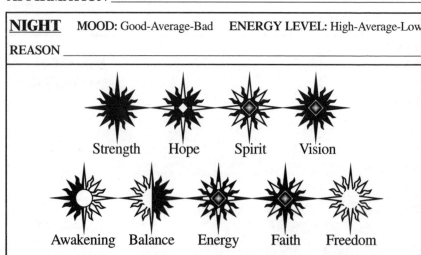

MORNING   MOOD: Good-Average-Bad   ENERGY LEVEL: High-Average-Low

REASON _____

Strength   Hope   Spirit   Vision

Awakening   Balance   Energy   Faith   Freedom

AFFIRMATION _____

NIGHT   MOOD: Good-Average-Bad   ENERGY LEVEL: High-Average-Low

REASON _____

Strength   Hope   Spirit   Vision

Awakening   Balance   Energy   Faith   Freedom

DAILY DISCOVERIES _____
_____
_____
_____
_____
_____
_____
_____
_____
_____
_____
_____
_____
_____
_____
_____
_____
_____
_____
_____
_____
_____

HEALTH PATTERNS _____
_____
_____
_____
_____
_____
_____
_____

ACHIEVEMENT _____
ACT OF KINDNESS _____

DIET
| | | | | | | | | | | | | |
Meat □□□□□□□□□□□□□ **PHYSICAL**
Bread □□□□□□□□□□□□□ **DISCOMFORT**
Dairy □□□□□□□□□□□□□
Vegetables □□□□□□□□□□□□□
Fruit □□□□□□□□□□□□□
Water □□□□□□□□□□□□□
Vitamins □□□□□□□□□□□□□

PLAY
Exercise □ Laugh □ Read □
Meditation □ Dance □ _____ □
Sex □ Sing □ _____ □

CYCLE DAY
_____

DATE_____

Sleep Time ____:____   Wake Time ____:____   Hours of Sleep _____

DREAMS _____
_____
_____
_____
_____
_____
_____
_____

MORNING   MOOD: Good-Average-Bad   ENERGY LEVEL: High-Average-Low

REASON _____

Strength   Hope   Spirit   Vision

Awakening   Balance   Energy   Faith   Freedom

AFFIRMATION _____

NIGHT   MOOD: Good-Average-Bad   ENERGY LEVEL: High-Average-Low

REASON _____

Strength   Hope   Spirit   Vision

Awakening   Balance   Energy   Faith   Freedom

DAILY DISCOVERIES _____

_____
_____
_____
_____
_____
_____
_____
_____
_____
_____
_____
_____
_____
_____
_____
_____
_____
_____
_____
_____

HEALTH PATTERNS _____

_____
_____
_____
_____
_____
_____

ACHIEVEMENT _____

ACT OF KINDNESS _____

DIET

Meat	□	□	□	□	□	□	□	□	□	□	□
Bread	□	□	□	□	□	□	□	□	□	□	□
Dairy	□	□	□	□	□	□	□	□	□	□	□
Vegetables	□	□	□	□	□	□	□	□	□	□	□
Fruit	□	□	□	□	□	□	□	□	□	□	□
Water	□	□	□	□	□	□	□	□	□	□	□
Vitamins	□	□	□	□	□	□	□	□	□	□	□

PHYSICAL DISCOMFORT

PLAY

Exercise	□	Laugh	□	Read	□
Meditation	□	Dance	□	_____	□
Sex	□	Sing	□	_____	□

CYCLE DAY

_____

DATE_____

Sleep Time ____:____   Wake Time ____:____   Hours of Sleep _____

DREAMS _____
_____
_____
_____
_____
_____
_____
_____
_____

MORNING   MOOD: Good-Average-Bad   ENERGY LEVEL: High-Average-Low

REASON _____

Strength   Hope   Spirit   Vision

Awakening   Balance   Energy   Faith   Freedom

AFFIRMATION _____

NIGHT   MOOD: Good-Average-Bad   ENERGY LEVEL: High-Average-Low

REASON _____

Strength   Hope   Spirit   Vision

Awakening   Balance   Energy   Faith   Freedom

DAILY DISCOVERIES _____

_____
_____
_____
_____
_____
_____
_____
_____
_____
_____
_____
_____
_____
_____
_____
_____
_____
_____
_____
_____
_____

HEALTH PATTERNS _____

_____
_____
_____
_____
_____
_____

ACHIEVEMENT _____
ACT OF KINDNESS _____

DIET

Meat	☐☐☐☐☐☐☐☐☐☐☐	
Bread	☐☐☐☐☐☐☐☐☐☐☐	
Dairy	☐☐☐☐☐☐☐☐☐☐☐	
Vegetables	☐☐☐☐☐☐☐☐☐☐☐	
Fruit	☐☐☐☐☐☐☐☐☐☐☐	
Water	☐☐☐☐☐☐☐☐☐☐☐	
Vitamins	☐☐☐☐☐☐☐☐☐☐☐	

PHYSICAL DISCOMFORT

PLAY

Exercise	☐	Laugh	☐	Read	☐
Meditation	☐	Dance	☐	_____	☐
Sex	☐	Sing	☐	_____	☐

CYCLE DAY

_____

DATE_____

Sleep Time ____:____ Wake Time ____:____ Hours of Sleep _____

DREAMS _____
_____
_____
_____
_____
_____
_____
_____
_____

MORNING   **MOOD:** Good-Average-Bad   **ENERGY LEVEL:** High-Average-Low

REASON _____

Strength	Hope	Spirit	Vision	
Awakening	Balance	Energy	Faith	Freedom

AFFIRMATION _____

NIGHT   **MOOD:** Good-Average-Bad   **ENERGY LEVEL:** High-Average-Low

REASON _____

Strength	Hope	Spirit	Vision	
Awakening	Balance	Energy	Faith	Freedom

DAILY DISCOVERIES _____

_____
_____
_____
_____
_____
_____
_____
_____
_____
_____
_____
_____
_____
_____
_____
_____
_____
_____
_____

HEALTH PATTERNS _____

_____
_____
_____
_____
_____
_____
_____

ACHIEVEMENT _____
ACT OF KINDNESS _____

DIET

Meat	☐	☐	☐	☐	☐	☐	☐	☐	☐	☐	☐
Bread	☐	☐	☐	☐	☐	☐	☐	☐	☐	☐	☐
Dairy	☐	☐	☐	☐	☐	☐	☐	☐	☐	☐	☐
Vegetables	☐	☐	☐	☐	☐	☐	☐	☐	☐	☐	☐
Fruit	☐	☐	☐	☐	☐	☐	☐	☐	☐	☐	☐
Water	☐	☐	☐	☐	☐	☐	☐	☐	☐	☐	☐
Vitamins	☐	☐	☐	☐	☐	☐	☐	☐	☐	☐	☐

PHYSICAL DISCOMFORT

PLAY

Exercise	☐	Laugh	☐	Read	☐
Meditation	☐	Dance	☐	_____	☐
Sex	☐	Sing	☐	_____	☐

CYCLE DAY

_____

DATE_____

Sleep Time ____ : ____   **Wake Time** ____ : ____   **Hours of Sleep** _____

DREAMS _____
_____
_____
_____
_____
_____
_____
_____

<u>MORNING</u>   **MOOD:** Good-Average-Bad   **ENERGY LEVEL:** High-Average-Low

REASON _____

Strength	Hope	Spirit	Vision

Awakening	Balance	Energy	Faith	Freedom

AFFIRMATION _____

<u>NIGHT</u>   **MOOD:** Good-Average-Bad   **ENERGY LEVEL:** High-Average-Low

REASON _____

Strength	Hope	Spirit	Vision

Awakening	Balance	Energy	Faith	Freedom

DAILY DISCOVERIES _____

_____
_____
_____
_____
_____
_____
_____
_____
_____
_____
_____
_____
_____
_____
_____
_____
_____
_____
_____
_____
_____
_____

HEALTH PATTERNS _____

_____
_____
_____
_____
_____
_____

ACHIEVEMENT _____

ACT OF KINDNESS _____

DIET		**PHYSICAL**
Meat	☐☐☐☐☐☐☐☐☐☐☐☐	**DISCOMFORT**
Bread	☐☐☐☐☐☐☐☐☐☐☐☐	
Dairy	☐☐☐☐☐☐☐☐☐☐☐☐	
Vegetables	☐☐☐☐☐☐☐☐☐☐☐	
Fruit	☐☐☐☐☐☐☐☐☐☐☐	
Water	☐☐☐☐☐☐☐☐☐☐☐☐	
Vitamins	☐☐☐☐☐☐☐☐☐☐☐☐	

PLAY

Exercise	☐	Laugh	☐	Read	☐	
Meditation	☐	Dance	☐	_____	☐	**CYCLE DAY**
Sex	☐	Sing	☐	_____	☐	_____

DATE_____

Sleep Time ____:____ **Wake Time** ____:____ **Hours of Sleep** _____

DREAMS _____
_____
_____
_____
_____
_____
_____
_____
_____

MORNING   **MOOD:** Good-Average-Bad   **ENERGY LEVEL:** High-Average-Low

REASON _____

Strength   Hope   Spirit   Vision

Awakening   Balance   Energy   Faith   Freedom

AFFIRMATION _____

NIGHT   **MOOD:** Good-Average-Bad   **ENERGY LEVEL:** High-Average-Low

REASON _____

Strength   Hope   Spirit   Vision

Awakening   Balance   Energy   Faith   Freedom

DAILY DISCOVERIES _____

_____
_____
_____
_____
_____
_____
_____
_____
_____
_____
_____
_____
_____
_____
_____
_____
_____
_____
_____
_____
_____

HEALTH PATTERNS _____

_____
_____
_____
_____
_____
_____
_____

ACHIEVEMENT _____

ACT OF KINDNESS _____

DIET													
Meat	□	□	□	□	□	□	□	□	□	□	□	□	
Bread	□	□	□	□	□	□	□	□	□	□	□	□	
Dairy	□	□	□	□	□	□	□	□	□	□	□		
Vegetables	□	□	□	□	□	□	□	□	□	□	□		
Fruit	□	□	□	□	□	□	□	□	□	□	□		
Water	□	□	□	□	□	□	□	□	□	□	□		
Vitamins	□	□	□	□	□	□	□	□	□	□	□		

PHYSICAL DISCOMFORT

PLAY

Exercise	□	Laugh	□	Read	□
Meditation	□	Dance	□	_____	□
Sex	□	Sing	□	_____	□

CYCLE DAY

_____

DATE_____

Sleep Time ____:____   Wake Time ____:____   Hours of Sleep _____

DREAMS _____
_____
_____
_____
_____
_____
_____
_____
_____

MORNING   MOOD: Good-Average-Bad   ENERGY LEVEL: High-Average-Low

REASON _____

Strength	Hope	Spirit	Vision

Awakening	Balance	Energy	Faith	Freedom

AFFIRMATION _____

NIGHT   MOOD: Good-Average-Bad   ENERGY LEVEL: High-Average-Low

REASON _____

Strength	Hope	Spirit	Vision

Awakening	Balance	Energy	Faith	Freedom

DAILY DISCOVERIES _____

_____
_____
_____
_____
_____
_____
_____
_____
_____
_____
_____
_____
_____
_____
_____
_____
_____
_____
_____
_____
_____

HEALTH PATTERNS _____

_____
_____
_____
_____
_____
_____

ACHIEVEMENT _____
ACT OF KINDNESS _____

DIET		PHYSICAL
Meat	☐☐☐☐☐☐☐☐☐☐☐	DISCOMFORT
Bread	☐☐☐☐☐☐☐☐☐☐☐	
Dairy	☐☐☐☐☐☐☐☐☐☐	
Vegetables	☐☐☐☐☐☐☐☐☐☐	
Fruit	☐☐☐☐☐☐☐☐☐☐☐	
Water	☐☐☐☐☐☐☐☐☐☐	
Vitamins	☐☐☐☐☐☐☐☐☐☐	

PLAY

Exercise	☐	Laugh	☐	Read	☐
Meditation	☐	Dance	☐	_____	☐
Sex	☐	Sing	☐	_____	☐

CYCLE DAY

_____

DATE_____

Sleep Time ____:____ Wake Time ____:____ Hours of Sleep _____

DREAMS _____

_____

_____

_____

_____

_____

_____

_____

_____

MORNING   MOOD: Good-Average-Bad   ENERGY LEVEL: High-Average-Low

REASON _____

| Strength | Hope | Spirit | Vision |

| Awakening | Balance | Energy | Faith | Freedom |

AFFIRMATION _____

NIGHT   MOOD: Good-Average-Bad   ENERGY LEVEL: High-Average-Low

REASON _____

| Strength | Hope | Spirit | Vision |

| Awakening | Balance | Energy | Faith | Freedom |

DAILY DISCOVERIES _____

_____
_____
_____
_____
_____
_____
_____
_____
_____
_____
_____
_____
_____
_____
_____
_____
_____
_____
_____
_____

HEALTH PATTERNS _____

_____
_____
_____
_____
_____
_____
_____

ACHIEVEMENT _____
ACT OF KINDNESS _____

DIET		**PHYSICAL**
Meat	☐☐☐☐☐☐☐☐☐☐☐☐	**DISCOMFORT**
Bread	☐☐☐☐☐☐☐☐☐☐☐☐	
Dairy	☐☐☐☐☐☐☐☐☐☐☐☐	
Vegetables	☐☐☐☐☐☐☐☐☐☐☐☐	
Fruit	☐☐☐☐☐☐☐☐☐☐☐☐	
Water	☐☐☐☐☐☐☐☐☐☐☐☐	
Vitamins	☐☐☐☐☐☐☐☐☐☐☐☐	

PLAY

Exercise	☐	Laugh	☐	Read	☐
Meditation	☐	Dance	☐	_____	☐
Sex	☐	Sing	☐	_____	☐

CYCLE DAY

_____

DATE_____

Sleep Time ____:____ **Wake Time** ____:____ **Hours of Sleep** _____

DREAMS _____
_____
_____
_____
_____
_____
_____
_____

<u>**MORNING**</u> **MOOD:** Good-Average-Bad **ENERGY LEVEL:** High-Average-Low

REASON _____

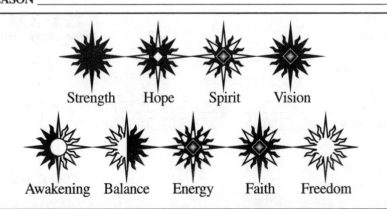

Strength   Hope   Spirit   Vision

Awakening   Balance   Energy   Faith   Freedom

AFFIRMATION _____

<u>**NIGHT**</u> **MOOD:** Good-Average-Bad **ENERGY LEVEL:** High-Average-Low

REASON _____

Strength   Hope   Spirit   Vision

Awakening   Balance   Energy   Faith   Freedom

DAILY DISCOVERIES _____

_____
_____
_____
_____
_____
_____
_____
_____
_____
_____
_____
_____
_____
_____
_____
_____
_____
_____
_____
_____
_____

HEALTH PATTERNS _____

_____
_____
_____
_____
_____
_____
_____

ACHIEVEMENT _____

ACT OF KINDNESS _____

DIET

Meat	☐	☐	☐	☐	☐	☐	☐	☐	☐	☐	☐
Bread	☐	☐	☐	☐	☐	☐	☐	☐	☐	☐	☐
Dairy	☐	☐	☐	☐	☐	☐	☐	☐	☐	☐	
Vegetables	☐	☐	☐	☐	☐	☐	☐	☐	☐	☐	
Fruit	☐	☐	☐	☐	☐	☐	☐	☐	☐	☐	
Water	☐	☐	☐	☐	☐	☐	☐	☐	☐	☐	
Vitamins	☐	☐	☐	☐	☐	☐	☐	☐	☐	☐	

PHYSICAL DISCOMFORT

PLAY

Exercise	☐	Laugh	☐	Read	☐	
Meditation	☐	Dance	☐	_____	☐	
Sex	☐	Sing	☐	_____	☐	

CYCLE DAY

_____

DATE_____

Sleep Time ____:____   Wake Time ____:____   Hours of Sleep _____

DREAMS _____

_____

_____

_____

_____

_____

_____

_____

_____

MORNING   MOOD: Good-Average-Bad   ENERGY LEVEL: High-Average-Low
REASON _____

Strength   Hope   Spirit   Vision

Awakening   Balance   Energy   Faith   Freedom

AFFIRMATION _____

NIGHT   MOOD: Good-Average-Bad   ENERGY LEVEL: High-Average-Low
REASON _____

Strength   Hope   Spirit   Vision

Awakening   Balance   Energy   Faith   Freedom

DAILY DISCOVERIES _____

_____
_____
_____
_____
_____
_____
_____
_____
_____
_____
_____
_____
_____
_____
_____
_____
_____
_____
_____
_____

HEALTH PATTERNS _____

_____
_____
_____
_____
_____
_____
_____

ACHIEVEMENT _____
ACT OF KINDNESS _____

DIET													
Meat	☐	☐	☐	☐	☐	☐	☐	☐	☐	☐	☐	☐	☐
Bread	☐	☐	☐	☐	☐	☐	☐	☐	☐	☐	☐	☐	☐
Dairy	☐	☐	☐	☐	☐	☐	☐	☐	☐	☐	☐	☐	☐
Vegetables	☐	☐	☐	☐	☐	☐	☐	☐	☐	☐	☐	☐	☐
Fruit	☐	☐	☐	☐	☐	☐	☐	☐	☐	☐	☐	☐	☐
Water	☐	☐	☐	☐	☐	☐	☐	☐	☐	☐	☐	☐	☐
Vitamins	☐	☐	☐	☐	☐	☐	☐	☐	☐	☐	☐	☐	☐

PHYSICAL DISCOMFORT

PLAY

Exercise	☐	Laugh	☐	Read	☐
Meditation	☐	Dance	☐	_____	☐
Sex	☐	Sing	☐	_____	☐

CYCLE DAY

_____

DATE_____

Sleep Time ____ : ____   Wake Time ____ : ____   Hours of Sleep _____

DREAMS _____
_____
_____
_____
_____
_____
_____
_____
_____

MORNING   MOOD: Good-Average-Bad   ENERGY LEVEL: High-Average-Low

REASON _____

Strength	Hope	Spirit	Vision

Awakening	Balance	Energy	Faith	Freedom

AFFIRMATION _____

NIGHT   MOOD: Good-Average-Bad   ENERGY LEVEL: High-Average-Low

REASON _____

Strength	Hope	Spirit	Vision

Awakening	Balance	Energy	Faith	Freedom

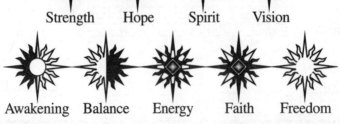

DAILY DISCOVERIES _____

_____
_____
_____
_____
_____
_____
_____
_____
_____
_____
_____
_____
_____
_____
_____
_____
_____
_____
_____
_____

HEALTH PATTERNS _____

_____
_____
_____
_____
_____
_____
_____

ACHIEVEMENT _____

ACT OF KINDNESS _____

DIET

Meat	☐	☐	☐	☐	☐	☐	☐	☐	☐	☐	☐
Bread	☐	☐	☐	☐	☐	☐	☐	☐	☐	☐	☐
Dairy	☐	☐	☐	☐	☐	☐	☐	☐	☐	☐	☐
Vegetables	☐	☐	☐	☐	☐	☐	☐	☐	☐	☐	☐
Fruit	☐	☐	☐	☐	☐	☐	☐	☐	☐	☐	☐
Water	☐	☐	☐	☐	☐	☐	☐	☐	☐	☐	☐
Vitamins	☐	☐	☐	☐	☐	☐	☐	☐	☐	☐	☐

PHYSICAL DISCOMFORT

CYCLE DAY

_____

PLAY

Exercise	☐	Laugh	☐	Read	☐
Meditation	☐	Dance	☐	_____	☐
Sex	☐	Sing	☐	_____	☐

DATE_____

Sleep Time ____:____   Wake Time ____:____   Hours of Sleep _____

DREAMS _____
_____
_____
_____
_____
_____
_____
_____

MORNING   MOOD: Good-Average-Bad   ENERGY LEVEL: High-Average-Low

REASON _____

Strength	Hope	Spirit	Vision

Awakening	Balance	Energy	Faith	Freedom

AFFIRMATION _____

NIGHT   MOOD: Good-Average-Bad   ENERGY LEVEL: High-Average-Low

REASON _____

Strength	Hope	Spirit	Vision

Awakening	Balance	Energy	Faith	Freedom

DAILY DISCOVERIES _____

_____
_____
_____
_____
_____
_____
_____
_____
_____
_____
_____
_____
_____
_____
_____
_____
_____
_____
_____

HEALTH PATTERNS _____

_____
_____
_____
_____
_____
_____

ACHIEVEMENT _____

ACT OF KINDNESS _____

DIET				**PHYSICAL**
Meat	☐☐☐☐☐☐☐☐☐☐☐			**DISCOMFORT**
Bread	☐☐☐☐☐☐☐☐☐☐☐			
Dairy	☐☐☐☐☐☐☐☐☐☐☐			
Vegetables	☐☐☐☐☐☐☐☐☐☐☐			
Fruit	☐☐☐☐☐☐☐☐☐☐☐			
Water	☐☐☐☐☐☐☐☐☐☐☐			
Vitamins	☐☐☐☐☐☐☐☐☐☐☐			

PLAY

Exercise	☐	Laugh	☐	Read	☐	
Meditation	☐	Dance	☐	_____	☐	**CYCLE DAY**
Sex	☐	Sing	☐	_____	☐	_____

DATE_____

Sleep Time ____:____ Wake Time ____:____ Hours of Sleep _____

DREAMS _____
_____
_____
_____
_____
_____
_____
_____

MORNING   MOOD: Good-Average-Bad   ENERGY LEVEL: High-Average-Low

REASON _____

Strength	Hope	Spirit	Vision

Awakening	Balance	Energy	Faith	Freedom

AFFIRMATION _____

NIGHT   MOOD: Good-Average-Bad   ENERGY LEVEL: High-Average-Low

REASON _____

Strength	Hope	Spirit	Vision

Awakening	Balance	Energy	Faith	Freedom

DAILY DISCOVERIES _____

_____
_____
_____
_____
_____
_____
_____
_____
_____
_____
_____
_____
_____
_____
_____
_____
_____
_____
_____
_____
_____

HEALTH PATTERNS _____

_____
_____
_____
_____
_____
_____

ACHIEVEMENT _____
ACT OF KINDNESS _____

DIET		**PHYSICAL**
Meat	☐☐☐☐☐☐☐☐☐☐☐	**DISCOMFORT**
Bread	☐☐☐☐☐☐☐☐☐☐☐	
Dairy	☐☐☐☐☐☐☐☐☐☐☐	
Vegetables	☐☐☐☐☐☐☐☐☐☐☐	
Fruit	☐☐☐☐☐☐☐☐☐☐☐	
Water	☐☐☐☐☐☐☐☐☐☐☐	
Vitamins	☐☐☐☐☐☐☐☐☐☐☐	

PLAY

Exercise	☐	Laugh ☐	Read	☐	
Meditation	☐	Dance ☐	_____	☐	**CYCLE DAY**
Sex	☐	Sing ☐	_____	☐	_____

DATE_____

Sleep Time ____:____ Wake Time ____:____ Hours of Sleep _____

DREAMS _____
_____
_____
_____
_____
_____
_____
_____
_____

MORNING   MOOD: Good-Average-Bad   ENERGY LEVEL: High-Average-Low

REASON _____

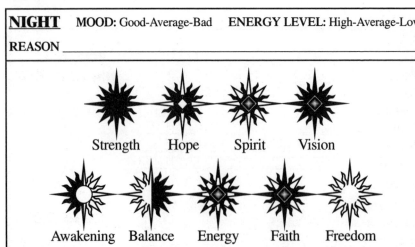

Strength   Hope   Spirit   Vision

Awakening   Balance   Energy   Faith   Freedom

AFFIRMATION _____

NIGHT   MOOD: Good-Average-Bad   ENERGY LEVEL: High-Average-Low

REASON _____

Strength   Hope   Spirit   Vision

Awakening   Balance   Energy   Faith   Freedom

DAILY DISCOVERIES _____

_____
_____
_____
_____
_____
_____
_____
_____
_____
_____
_____
_____
_____
_____
_____
_____
_____
_____
_____
_____
_____

HEALTH PATTERNS _____

_____
_____
_____
_____
_____
_____
_____

ACHIEVEMENT _____
ACT OF KINDNESS _____

DIET

Meat	☐	☐	☐	☐	☐	☐	☐	☐	☐	☐
Bread	☐	☐	☐	☐	☐	☐	☐	☐	☐	☐
Dairy	☐	☐	☐	☐	☐	☐	☐	☐	☐	☐
Vegetables	☐	☐	☐	☐	☐	☐	☐	☐	☐	☐
Fruit	☐	☐	☐	☐	☐	☐	☐	☐	☐	☐
Water	☐	☐	☐	☐	☐	☐	☐	☐	☐	☐
Vitamins	☐	☐	☐	☐	☐	☐	☐	☐	☐	☐

PHYSICAL DISCOMFORT

PLAY

Exercise	☐	Laugh	☐	Read	☐	
Meditation	☐	Dance	☐	_____	☐	
Sex	☐	Sing	☐	_____	☐	

CYCLE DAY

_____

DATE_____

Sleep Time ____:____ Wake Time ____:____ Hours of Sleep _____

DREAMS _____
_____
_____
_____
_____
_____
_____
_____
_____

MORNING   MOOD: Good-Average-Bad   ENERGY LEVEL: High-Average-Low

REASON _____

Strength   Hope   Spirit   Vision

Awakening Balance Energy Faith Freedom

AFFIRMATION _____

NIGHT   MOOD: Good-Average-Bad   ENERGY LEVEL: High-Average-Low

REASON _____

Strength   Hope   Spirit   Vision

Awakening Balance Energy Faith Freedom

DAILY DISCOVERIES _____

_____
_____
_____
_____
_____
_____
_____
_____
_____
_____
_____
_____
_____
_____
_____
_____
_____
_____
_____
_____
_____

HEALTH PATTERNS _____

_____
_____
_____
_____
_____
_____
_____

ACHIEVEMENT _____
ACT OF KINDNESS _____

DIET		**PHYSICAL DISCOMFORT**
Meat	☐☐☐☐☐☐☐☐☐☐☐☐	
Bread	☐☐☐☐☐☐☐☐☐☐☐☐	
Dairy	☐☐☐☐☐☐☐☐☐☐☐☐	
Vegetables	☐☐☐☐☐☐☐☐☐☐☐☐	
Fruit	☐☐☐☐☐☐☐☐☐☐☐☐	
Water	☐☐☐☐☐☐☐☐☐☐☐☐	
Vitamins	☐☐☐☐☐☐☐☐☐☐☐☐	

PLAY

Exercise	☐	Laugh	☐	Read	☐
Meditation	☐	Dance	☐	_____	☐
Sex	☐	Sing	☐	_____	☐

CYCLE DAY

_____

DATE_____

Sleep Time ____:____ Wake Time ____:____ Hours of Sleep _____

DREAMS _____
_____
_____
_____
_____
_____
_____
_____
_____

MORNING   MOOD: Good-Average-Bad   ENERGY LEVEL: High-Average-Low

REASON _____

Strength	Hope	Spirit	Vision

Awakening	Balance	Energy	Faith	Freedom

AFFIRMATION _____

NIGHT   MOOD: Good-Average-Bad   ENERGY LEVEL: High-Average-Low

REASON _____

Strength	Hope	Spirit	Vision

Awakening	Balance	Energy	Faith	Freedom

DAILY DISCOVERIES _____

_____
_____
_____
_____
_____
_____
_____
_____
_____
_____
_____
_____
_____
_____
_____
_____
_____
_____
_____
_____

HEALTH PATTERNS _____

_____
_____
_____
_____
_____
_____
_____

ACHIEVEMENT _____
ACT OF KINDNESS _____

DIET		**PHYSICAL DISCOMFORT**
Meat	□□□□□□□□□□□□	
Bread	□□□□□□□□□□□□	
Dairy	□□□□□□□□□□□□	
Vegetables	□□□□□□□□□□□□	
Fruit	□□□□□□□□□□□□	
Water	□□□□□□□□□□□□	
Vitamins	□□□□□□□□□□□□	

PLAY

Exercise	□	Laugh	□	Read	□
Meditation	□	Dance	□	_____	□
Sex	□	Sing	□	_____	□

CYCLE DAY

_____

DATE_____

Sleep Time ____:____ Wake Time ____:____ Hours of Sleep _____

DREAMS _____

_____

_____

_____

_____

_____

_____

_____

_____

MORNING MOOD: Good-Average-Bad ENERGY LEVEL: High-Average-Low

REASON _____

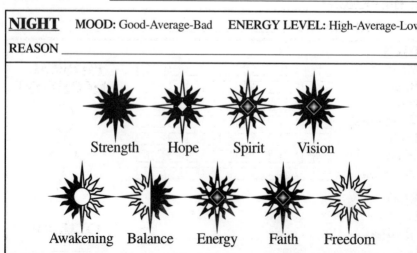

Strength	Hope	Spirit	Vision

| Awakening | Balance | Energy | Faith | Freedom |

AFFIRMATION _____

NIGHT MOOD: Good-Average-Bad ENERGY LEVEL: High-Average-Low

REASON _____

| Strength | Hope | Spirit | Vision |

| Awakening | Balance | Energy | Faith | Freedom |

DAILY DISCOVERIES _____

_____
_____
_____
_____
_____
_____
_____
_____
_____
_____
_____
_____
_____
_____
_____
_____
_____
_____
_____
_____
_____
_____

HEALTH PATTERNS _____

_____
_____
_____
_____
_____
_____
_____

ACHIEVEMENT _____

ACT OF KINDNESS _____

DIET		**PHYSICAL DISCOMFORT**
Meat	☐☐☐☐☐☐☐☐☐☐☐	
Bread	☐☐☐☐☐☐☐☐☐☐☐	
Dairy	☐☐☐☐☐☐☐☐☐☐	
Vegetables	☐☐☐☐☐☐☐☐☐☐☐	
Fruit	☐☐☐☐☐☐☐☐☐☐☐	
Water	☐☐☐☐☐☐☐☐☐☐	
Vitamins	☐☐☐☐☐☐☐☐☐☐	

PLAY

Exercise	☐	Laugh	☐	Read	☐
Meditation	☐	Dance	☐	_____	☐
Sex	☐	Sing	☐	_____	☐

CYCLE DAY

_____

DATE_____

Sleep Time ____:____ Wake Time ____:____ Hours of Sleep _____

DREAMS _____
_____
_____
_____
_____
_____
_____
_____
_____

MORNING   MOOD: Good-Average-Bad   ENERGY LEVEL: High-Average-Low
REASON _____

Strength	Hope	Spirit	Vision

Awakening	Balance	Energy	Faith	Freedom

AFFIRMATION _____

NIGHT   MOOD: Good-Average-Bad   ENERGY LEVEL: High-Average-Low
REASON _____

Strength	Hope	Spirit	Vision

Awakening	Balance	Energy	Faith	Freedom

DAILY DISCOVERIES _____

_____
_____
_____
_____
_____
_____
_____
_____
_____
_____
_____
_____
_____
_____
_____
_____
_____
_____
_____
_____
_____

HEALTH PATTERNS _____

_____
_____
_____
_____
_____
_____
_____

ACHIEVEMENT _____

ACT OF KINDNESS _____

DIET		**PHYSICAL DISCOMFORT**
Meat	☐☐☐☐☐☐☐☐☐☐☐	
Bread	☐☐☐☐☐☐☐☐☐☐☐	
Dairy	☐☐☐☐☐☐☐☐☐☐☐	
Vegetables	☐☐☐☐☐☐☐☐☐☐☐	
Fruit	☐☐☐☐☐☐☐☐☐☐☐	
Water	☐☐☐☐☐☐☐☐☐☐☐	
Vitamins	☐☐☐☐☐☐☐☐☐☐☐	

PLAY

Exercise ☐	Laugh ☐	Read ☐
Meditation ☐	Dance ☐	_____ ☐
Sex ☐	Sing ☐	_____ ☐

CYCLE DAY

_____

DATE_____

Sleep Time ____:____ Wake Time ____:____ Hours of Sleep _____

DREAMS _____
_____
_____
_____
_____
_____
_____
_____

MORNING   MOOD: Good-Average-Bad   ENERGY LEVEL: High-Average-Low

REASON _____

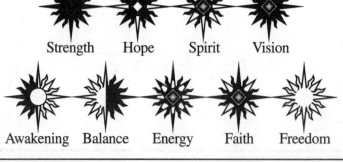

Strength   Hope   Spirit   Vision

Awakening   Balance   Energy   Faith   Freedom

AFFIRMATION _____

NIGHT   MOOD: Good-Average-Bad   ENERGY LEVEL: High-Average-Low

REASON _____

Strength   Hope   Spirit   Vision

Awakening   Balance   Energy   Faith   Freedom

DAILY DISCOVERIES _____

_____
_____
_____
_____
_____
_____
_____
_____
_____
_____
_____
_____
_____
_____
_____
_____
_____
_____
_____
_____
_____
_____

HEALTH PATTERNS _____

_____
_____
_____
_____
_____
_____

ACHIEVEMENT _____

ACT OF KINDNESS _____

DIET			**PHYSICAL DISCOMFORT**
Meat	☐☐☐☐☐☐☐☐☐☐☐		
Bread	☐☐☐☐☐☐☐☐☐☐☐		
Dairy	☐☐☐☐☐☐☐☐☐☐☐		
Vegetables	☐☐☐☐☐☐☐☐☐☐☐		
Fruit	☐☐☐☐☐☐☐☐☐☐☐		
Water	☐☐☐☐☐☐☐☐☐☐☐		
Vitamins	☐☐☐☐☐☐☐☐☐☐☐		

PLAY

Exercise	☐	Laugh	☐	Read	☐	
Meditation	☐	Dance	☐	_____	☐	**CYCLE DAY**
Sex	☐	Sing	☐	_____	☐	_____

DATE_____

Sleep Time _____:_____   Wake Time _____:_____   Hours of Sleep _____

DREAMS _____
_____
_____
_____
_____
_____
_____
_____

MORNING   MOOD: Good-Average-Bad   ENERGY LEVEL: High-Average-Low

REASON _____

| Strength | Hope | Spirit | Vision |

| Awakening | Balance | Energy | Faith | Freedom |

AFFIRMATION _____

NIGHT   MOOD: Good-Average-Bad   ENERGY LEVEL: High-Average-Low

REASON _____

| Strength | Hope | Spirit | Vision |

| Awakening | Balance | Energy | Faith | Freedom |

DAILY DISCOVERIES _____

_____
_____
_____
_____
_____
_____
_____
_____
_____
_____
_____
_____
_____
_____
_____
_____
_____
_____
_____

HEALTH PATTERNS _____

_____
_____
_____
_____
_____
_____

ACHIEVEMENT _____

ACT OF KINDNESS _____

DIET			
Meat	☐☐☐☐☐☐☐☐☐☐☐☐		**PHYSICAL**
Bread	☐☐☐☐☐☐☐☐☐☐☐☐		**DISCOMFORT**
Dairy	☐☐☐☐☐☐☐☐☐☐☐☐		
Vegetables	☐☐☐☐☐☐☐☐☐☐☐☐		
Fruit	☐☐☐☐☐☐☐☐☐☐☐☐		
Water	☐☐☐☐☐☐☐☐☐☐☐☐		
Vitamins	☐☐☐☐☐☐☐☐☐☐☐☐		

PLAY

Exercise	☐	Laugh	☐	Read	☐
Meditation	☐	Dance	☐	_____	☐
Sex	☐	Sing	☐	_____	☐

CYCLE DAY

_____

DATE_____

Sleep Time _____:_____   Wake Time _____:_____   Hours of Sleep _____

DREAMS _____
_____
_____
_____
_____
_____
_____
_____
_____

MORNING   **MOOD:** Good-Average-Bad   **ENERGY LEVEL:** High-Average-Low

REASON _____

Strength   Hope   Spirit   Vision

Awakening   Balance   Energy   Faith   Freedom

AFFIRMATION _____

NIGHT   **MOOD:** Good-Average-Bad   **ENERGY LEVEL:** High-Average-Low

REASON _____

Strength   Hope   Spirit   Vision

Awakening   Balance   Energy   Faith   Freedom

DAILY DISCOVERIES _____
_____
_____
_____
_____
_____
_____
_____
_____
_____
_____
_____
_____
_____
_____
_____
_____
_____
_____
_____
_____
_____

HEALTH PATTERNS _____
_____
_____
_____
_____
_____
_____
_____

ACHIEVEMENT _____
ACT OF KINDNESS _____

DIET		**PHYSICAL**
Meat	☐☐☐☐☐☐☐☐☐☐☐	**DISCOMFORT**
Bread	☐☐☐☐☐☐☐☐☐☐☐	
Dairy	☐☐☐☐☐☐☐☐☐☐☐	
Vegetables	☐☐☐☐☐☐☐☐☐☐☐	
Fruit	☐☐☐☐☐☐☐☐☐☐☐	
Water	☐☐☐☐☐☐☐☐☐☐☐	
Vitamins	☐☐☐☐☐☐☐☐☐☐☐	

PLAY

Exercise	☐	Laugh	☐	Read	☐
Meditation	☐	Dance	☐	_____	☐
Sex	☐	Sing	☐	_____	☐

CYCLE DAY

_____

DATE_____

Sleep Time ____:____ Wake Time ____:____ Hours of Sleep _____

DREAMS _____

_____

_____

_____

_____

_____

_____

_____

MORNING   MOOD: Good-Average-Bad   ENERGY LEVEL: High-Average-Low

REASON _____

Strength   Hope   Spirit   Vision

Awakening   Balance   Energy   Faith   Freedom

AFFIRMATION _____

NIGHT   MOOD: Good-Average-Bad   ENERGY LEVEL: High-Average-Low

REASON _____

Strength   Hope   Spirit   Vision

Awakening   Balance   Energy   Faith   Freedom

DAILY DISCOVERIES _____

_____
_____
_____
_____
_____
_____
_____
_____
_____
_____
_____
_____
_____
_____
_____
_____
_____
_____
_____
_____
_____
_____
_____
_____

HEALTH PATTERNS _____

_____
_____
_____
_____
_____
_____
_____

ACHIEVEMENT _____
ACT OF KINDNESS _____

DIET												
Meat	☐	☐	☐	☐	☐	☐	☐	☐	☐	☐	☐	☐
Bread	☐	☐	☐	☐	☐	☐	☐	☐	☐	☐	☐	☐
Dairy	☐	☐	☐	☐	☐	☐	☐	☐	☐	☐	☐	☐
Vegetables	☐	☐	☐	☐	☐	☐	☐	☐	☐	☐	☐	☐
Fruit	☐	☐	☐	☐	☐	☐	☐	☐	☐	☐	☐	☐
Water	☐	☐	☐	☐	☐	☐	☐	☐	☐	☐	☐	☐
Vitamins	☐	☐	☐	☐	☐	☐	☐	☐	☐	☐	☐	☐

PHYSICAL DISCOMFORT

PLAY

Exercise	☐	Laugh	☐	Read	☐
Meditation	☐	Dance	☐	_____	☐
Sex	☐	Sing	☐	_____	☐

CYCLE DAY

_____

DATE_____

Sleep Time ____ : ____   Wake Time ____ : ____   Hours of Sleep _____

DREAMS _____
_____
_____
_____
_____
_____
_____
_____

MORNING   **MOOD:** Good-Average-Bad   **ENERGY LEVEL:** High-Average-Low

REASON _____

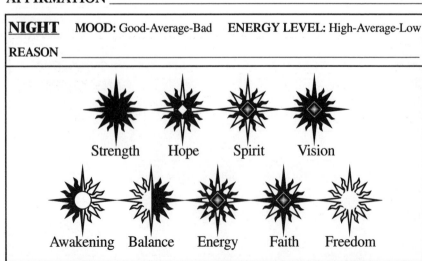

| Strength | Hope | Spirit | Vision |

| Awakening | Balance | Energy | Faith | Freedom |

AFFIRMATION _____

NIGHT   **MOOD:** Good-Average-Bad   **ENERGY LEVEL:** High-Average-Low

REASON _____

| Strength | Hope | Spirit | Vision |

| Awakening | Balance | Energy | Faith | Freedom |

DAILY DISCOVERIES _____

_____
_____
_____
_____
_____
_____
_____
_____
_____
_____
_____
_____
_____
_____
_____
_____
_____
_____
_____
_____
_____
_____

HEALTH PATTERNS _____

_____
_____
_____
_____
_____
_____
_____

ACHIEVEMENT _____

ACT OF KINDNESS _____

DIET		**PHYSICAL DISCOMFORT**
Meat	□□□□□□□□□□□□	
Bread	□□□□□□□□□□□□	
Dairy	□□□□□□□□□□□□	
Vegetables	□□□□□□□□□□□□	
Fruit	□□□□□□□□□□□□	
Water	□□□□□□□□□□□□	
Vitamins	□□□□□□□□□□□□	

PLAY

Exercise	□	Laugh	□	Read	□
Meditation	□	Dance	□	_____	□
Sex	□	Sing	□	_____	□

CYCLE DAY

_____

DATE_____

Sleep Time ____:____   Wake Time ____:____   Hours of Sleep _____

DREAMS _____
_____
_____
_____
_____
_____
_____
_____
_____

MORNING   MOOD: Good-Average-Bad   ENERGY LEVEL: High-Average-Low

REASON _____

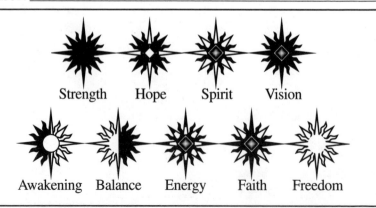

Strength	Hope	Spirit	Vision

Awakening	Balance	Energy	Faith	Freedom

AFFIRMATION _____

NIGHT   MOOD: Good-Average-Bad   ENERGY LEVEL: High-Average-Low

REASON _____

Strength	Hope	Spirit	Vision

Awakening	Balance	Energy	Faith	Freedom

DAILY DISCOVERIES _____

_____
_____
_____
_____
_____
_____
_____
_____
_____
_____
_____
_____
_____
_____
_____
_____
_____
_____
_____
_____

HEALTH PATTERNS _____

_____
_____
_____
_____
_____
_____
_____

ACHIEVEMENT _____

ACT OF KINDNESS _____

DIET

Meat	□	□	□	□	□	□	□	□	□	□	□	□
Bread	□	□	□	□	□	□	□	□	□	□	□	□
Dairy	□	□	□	□	□	□	□	□	□	□	□	
Vegetables	□	□	□	□	□	□	□	□	□	□	□	
Fruit	□	□	□	□	□	□	□	□	□	□	□	
Water	□	□	□	□	□	□	□	□	□	□	□	
Vitamins	□	□	□	□	□	□	□	□	□	□	□	

PHYSICAL DISCOMFORT

PLAY

Exercise	□	Laugh	□	Read	□
Meditation	□	Dance	□	_____	□
Sex	□	Sing	□	_____	□

CYCLE DAY

_____

DATE_____

Sleep Time ____:____ Wake Time ____:____ Hours of Sleep _____

DREAMS _____
_____
_____
_____
_____
_____
_____
_____
_____

MORNING   MOOD: Good-Average-Bad   ENERGY LEVEL: High-Average-Low

REASON _____

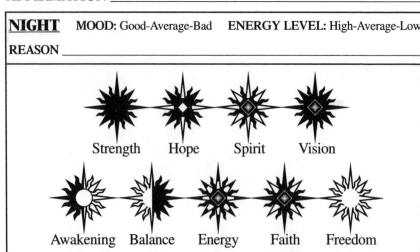

| Strength   Hope   Spirit   Vision

Awakening Balance Energy Faith Freedom

AFFIRMATION _____

NIGHT   MOOD: Good-Average-Bad   ENERGY LEVEL: High-Average-Low

REASON _____

Strength   Hope   Spirit   Vision

Awakening Balance Energy Faith Freedom

DAILY DISCOVERIES _____

_____
_____
_____
_____
_____
_____
_____
_____
_____
_____
_____
_____
_____
_____
_____
_____
_____
_____
_____

HEALTH PATTERNS _____

_____
_____
_____
_____
_____
_____

ACHIEVEMENT _____
ACT OF KINDNESS _____

DIET		**PHYSICAL DISCOMFORT**
Meat	□□□□□□□□□□□□	
Bread	□□□□□□□□□□□□	
Dairy	□□□□□□□□□□□□	
Vegetables	□□□□□□□□□□□□	
Fruit	□□□□□□□□□□□□	
Water	□□□□□□□□□□□□	
Vitamins	□□□□□□□□□□□□	

PLAY

Exercise	□	Laugh	□	Read	□	
Meditation	□	Dance	□	_____	□	**CYCLE DAY**
Sex	□	Sing	□	_____	□	_____

DATE_____

Sleep Time ____:____ Wake Time ____:____ Hours of Sleep _____

DREAMS _____
_____
_____
_____
_____
_____
_____
_____
_____

MORNING   MOOD: Good-Average-Bad   ENERGY LEVEL: High-Average-Low

REASON _____

Strength   Hope   Spirit   Vision

Awakening   Balance   Energy   Faith   Freedom

AFFIRMATION _____

NIGHT   MOOD: Good-Average-Bad   ENERGY LEVEL: High-Average-Low

REASON _____

Strength   Hope   Spirit   Vision

Awakening   Balance   Energy   Faith   Freedom

DAILY DISCOVERIES _____

_____
_____
_____
_____
_____
_____
_____
_____
_____
_____
_____
_____
_____
_____
_____
_____
_____
_____
_____
_____

HEALTH PATTERNS _____

_____
_____
_____
_____
_____
_____

ACHIEVEMENT _____

ACT OF KINDNESS _____

DIET		**PHYSICAL**
Meat	☐☐☐☐☐☐☐☐☐☐☐☐	**DISCOMFORT**
Bread	☐☐☐☐☐☐☐☐☐☐☐☐	
Dairy	☐☐☐☐☐☐☐☐☐☐☐☐	
Vegetables	☐☐☐☐☐☐☐☐☐☐☐☐	
Fruit	☐☐☐☐☐☐☐☐☐☐☐☐	
Water	☐☐☐☐☐☐☐☐☐☐☐☐	
Vitamins	☐☐☐☐☐☐☐☐☐☐☐☐	

PLAY

Exercise	☐	Laugh	☐	Read	☐
Meditation	☐	Dance	☐	_____	☐
Sex	☐	Sing	☐	_____	☐

CYCLE DAY

_____

DATE_____

Sleep Time ____:____ Wake Time ____:____ Hours of Sleep _____

DREAMS _____
_____
_____
_____
_____
_____
_____
_____
_____

MORNING   **MOOD:** Good-Average-Bad   **ENERGY LEVEL:** High-Average-Low

REASON _____

Strength	Hope	Spirit	Vision

Awakening	Balance	Energy	Faith	Freedom

AFFIRMATION _____

NIGHT   **MOOD:** Good-Average-Bad   **ENERGY LEVEL:** High-Average-Low

REASON _____

Strength	Hope	Spirit	Vision

Awakening	Balance	Energy	Faith	Freedom

DAILY DISCOVERIES _____

_____
_____
_____
_____
_____
_____
_____
_____
_____
_____
_____
_____
_____
_____
_____
_____
_____
_____
_____
_____
_____

HEALTH PATTERNS _____

_____
_____
_____
_____
_____
_____

ACHIEVEMENT _____
ACT OF KINDNESS _____

DIET

		PHYSICAL DISCOMFORT
Meat	☐☐☐☐☐☐☐☐☐☐☐☐	
Bread	☐☐☐☐☐☐☐☐☐☐☐☐	
Dairy	☐☐☐☐☐☐☐☐☐☐☐☐	
Vegetables	☐☐☐☐☐☐☐☐☐☐☐☐	
Fruit	☐☐☐☐☐☐☐☐☐☐☐☐	
Water	☐☐☐☐☐☐☐☐☐☐☐☐	
Vitamins	☐☐☐☐☐☐☐☐☐☐☐☐	

PLAY

Exercise	☐	Laugh	☐	Read	☐
Meditation	☐	Dance	☐	_____	☐
Sex	☐	Sing	☐	_____	☐

CYCLE DAY

_____

DATE_____

Sleep Time ____:____ Wake Time ____:____ Hours of Sleep _____

DREAMS _____
_____
_____
_____
_____
_____
_____
_____

MORNING   MOOD: Good-Average-Bad   ENERGY LEVEL: High-Average-Low

REASON _____

Strength   Hope   Spirit   Vision

Awakening   Balance   Energy   Faith   Freedom

AFFIRMATION _____

NIGHT   MOOD: Good-Average-Bad   ENERGY LEVEL: High-Average-Low

REASON _____

Strength   Hope   Spirit   Vision

Awakening   Balance   Energy   Faith   Freedom

DAILY DISCOVERIES _____
_____
_____
_____
_____
_____
_____
_____
_____
_____
_____
_____
_____
_____
_____
_____
_____
_____
_____
_____
_____
_____

HEALTH PATTERNS _____
_____
_____
_____
_____
_____
_____

ACHIEVEMENT _____
ACT OF KINDNESS _____

DIET				
Meat	□□□□□□□□□□□□		**PHYSICAL**	
Bread	□□□□□□□□□□□□		**DISCOMFORT**	
Dairy	□□□□□□□□□□□□			
Vegetables	□□□□□□□□□□□□			
Fruit	□□□□□□□□□□□□			
Water	□□□□□□□□□□□□			
Vitamins	□□□□□□□□□□□□			

PLAY

Exercise	□	Laugh	□	Read	□
Meditation	□	Dance	□	_____	□
Sex	□	Sing	□	_____	□

CYCLE DAY

_____

DATE_____

Sleep Time _____:_____ Wake Time _____:_____ Hours of Sleep _____

DREAMS _____
_____
_____
_____
_____
_____
_____
_____
_____

MORNING   MOOD: Good-Average-Bad   ENERGY LEVEL: High-Average-Low

REASON _____

Strength	Hope	Spirit	Vision

Awakening	Balance	Energy	Faith	Freedom

AFFIRMATION _____

NIGHT   MOOD: Good-Average-Bad   ENERGY LEVEL: High-Average-Low

REASON _____

Strength	Hope	Spirit	Vision

Awakening	Balance	Energy	Faith	Freedom

DAILY DISCOVERIES _____

_____
_____
_____
_____
_____
_____
_____
_____
_____
_____
_____
_____
_____
_____
_____
_____
_____
_____
_____
_____
_____

HEALTH PATTERNS _____

_____
_____
_____
_____
_____
_____

ACHIEVEMENT _____

ACT OF KINDNESS _____

DIET		**PHYSICAL DISCOMFORT**
Meat	☐☐☐☐☐☐☐☐☐☐☐☐	
Bread	☐☐☐☐☐☐☐☐☐☐☐☐	
Dairy	☐☐☐☐☐☐☐☐☐☐☐☐	
Vegetables	☐☐☐☐☐☐☐☐☐☐☐☐	
Fruit	☐☐☐☐☐☐☐☐☐☐☐☐	
Water	☐☐☐☐☐☐☐☐☐☐☐☐	
Vitamins	☐☐☐☐☐☐☐☐☐☐☐☐	

PLAY

Exercise	☐	Laugh	☐	Read	☐
Meditation	☐	Dance	☐	_____	☐
Sex	☐	Sing	☐	_____	☐

CYCLE DAY

_____

DATE_____

Sleep Time ____:____   Wake Time ____:____   Hours of Sleep _____

DREAMS _____

_____
_____
_____
_____
_____
_____
_____
_____
_____

MORNING   **MOOD:** Good-Average-Bad   **ENERGY LEVEL:** High-Average-Low

REASON _____

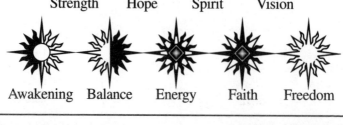

Strength   Hope   Spirit   Vision

Awakening   Balance   Energy   Faith   Freedom

AFFIRMATION _____

NIGHT   **MOOD:** Good-Average-Bad   **ENERGY LEVEL:** High-Average-Low

REASON _____

Strength   Hope   Spirit   Vision

Awakening   Balance   Energy   Faith   Freedom

DAILY DISCOVERIES _____

_____
_____
_____
_____
_____
_____
_____
_____
_____
_____
_____
_____
_____
_____
_____
_____
_____
_____
_____
_____

HEALTH PATTERNS _____

_____
_____
_____
_____
_____
_____

ACHIEVEMENT _____
ACT OF KINDNESS _____

DIET

Meat	☐	☐	☐	☐	☐	☐	☐	☐	☐	☐	☐
Bread	☐	☐	☐	☐	☐	☐	☐	☐	☐	☐	☐
Dairy	☐	☐	☐	☐	☐	☐	☐	☐	☐	☐	☐
Vegetables	☐	☐	☐	☐	☐	☐	☐	☐	☐	☐	☐
Fruit	☐	☐	☐	☐	☐	☐	☐	☐	☐	☐	☐
Water	☐	☐	☐	☐	☐	☐	☐	☐	☐	☐	☐
Vitamins	☐	☐	☐	☐	☐	☐	☐	☐	☐	☐	☐

PHYSICAL DISCOMFORT

PLAY

Exercise	☐	Laugh	☐	Read	☐
Meditation	☐	Dance	☐	_____	☐
Sex	☐	Sing	☐	_____	☐

CYCLE DAY

_____

DATE_____

Sleep Time ____:____ Wake Time ____:____ Hours of Sleep _____

DREAMS _____
_____
_____
_____
_____
_____
_____
_____
_____

MORNING   MOOD: Good-Average-Bad   ENERGY LEVEL: High-Average-Low

REASON _____

Strength   Hope   Spirit   Vision

Awakening   Balance   Energy   Faith   Freedom

AFFIRMATION _____

NIGHT   MOOD: Good-Average-Bad   ENERGY LEVEL: High-Average-Low

REASON _____

Strength   Hope   Spirit   Vision

Awakening   Balance   Energy   Faith   Freedom

DAILY DISCOVERIES _____

_____
_____
_____
_____
_____
_____
_____
_____
_____
_____
_____
_____
_____
_____
_____
_____
_____
_____
_____
_____
_____

HEALTH PATTERNS _____

_____
_____
_____
_____
_____
_____
_____

ACHIEVEMENT _____
ACT OF KINDNESS _____

DIET

Meat	☐	☐	☐	☐	☐	☐	☐	☐	☐	☐	☐
Bread	☐	☐	☐	☐	☐	☐	☐	☐	☐	☐	☐
Dairy	☐	☐	☐	☐	☐	☐	☐	☐	☐	☐	☐
Vegetables	☐	☐	☐	☐	☐	☐	☐	☐	☐	☐	☐
Fruit	☐	☐	☐	☐	☐	☐	☐	☐	☐	☐	☐
Water	☐	☐	☐	☐	☐	☐	☐	☐	☐	☐	☐
Vitamins	☐	☐	☐	☐	☐	☐	☐	☐	☐	☐	☐

PHYSICAL DISCOMFORT

PLAY

Exercise	☐	Laugh	☐	Read	☐
Meditation	☐	Dance	☐	_____	☐
Sex	☐	Sing	☐	_____	☐

CYCLE DAY

_____

DATE_____

Sleep Time _____:_____   Wake Time _____:_____   Hours of Sleep _____

DREAMS _____
_____
_____
_____
_____
_____
_____
_____
_____

<u>**MORNING**</u>   **MOOD:** Good-Average-Bad   **ENERGY LEVEL:** High-Average-Low

REASON _____

| Strength | Hope | Spirit | Vision |

| Awakening | Balance | Energy | Faith | Freedom |

AFFIRMATION _____

<u>**NIGHT**</u>   **MOOD:** Good-Average-Bad   **ENERGY LEVEL:** High-Average-Low

REASON _____

| Strength | Hope | Spirit | Vision |

| Awakening | Balance | Energy | Faith | Freedom |

DAILY DISCOVERIES _____
_____
_____
_____
_____
_____
_____
_____
_____
_____
_____
_____
_____
_____
_____
_____
_____
_____
_____
_____
_____
_____

HEALTH PATTERNS _____
_____
_____
_____
_____
_____
_____
_____

ACHIEVEMENT _____
ACT OF KINDNESS _____

DIET												
Meat	☐	☐	☐	☐	☐	☐	☐	☐	☐	☐	☐	☐
Bread	☐	☐	☐	☐	☐	☐	☐	☐	☐	☐	☐	☐
Dairy	☐	☐	☐	☐	☐	☐	☐	☐	☐	☐	☐	☐
Vegetables	☐	☐	☐	☐	☐	☐	☐	☐	☐	☐	☐	☐
Fruit	☐	☐	☐	☐	☐	☐	☐	☐	☐	☐	☐	☐
Water	☐	☐	☐	☐	☐	☐	☐	☐	☐	☐	☐	☐
Vitamins	☐	☐	☐	☐	☐	☐	☐	☐	☐	☐	☐	☐

PHYSICAL DISCOMFORT

PLAY

Exercise ☐   Laugh ☐   Read ☐

Meditation ☐   Dance ☐   _____ ☐

Sex ☐   Sing ☐   _____ ☐

CYCLE DAY

_____

DATE_____

Sleep Time ____:____ Wake Time ____:____ Hours of Sleep _____

DREAMS _____
_____
_____
_____
_____
_____
_____
_____
_____

MORNING   MOOD: Good-Average-Bad   ENERGY LEVEL: High-Average-Low

REASON _____

Strength	Hope	Spirit	Vision

Awakening	Balance	Energy	Faith	Freedom

AFFIRMATION _____

NIGHT   MOOD: Good-Average-Bad   ENERGY LEVEL: High-Average-Low

REASON _____

Strength	Hope	Spirit	Vision

Awakening	Balance	Energy	Faith	Freedom

DAILY DISCOVERIES _____

_____
_____
_____
_____
_____
_____
_____
_____
_____
_____
_____
_____
_____
_____
_____
_____
_____
_____
_____
_____

HEALTH PATTERNS _____

_____
_____
_____
_____
_____
_____
_____

ACHIEVEMENT _____

ACT OF KINDNESS _____

DIET

Meat	□□□□□□□□□□□□		
Bread	□□□□□□□□□□□□		
Dairy	□□□□□□□□□□□		
Vegetables	□□□□□□□□□□□		
Fruit	□□□□□□□□□□□		
Water	□□□□□□□□□□□		
Vitamins	□□□□□□□□□□□		

PHYSICAL DISCOMFORT

PLAY

Exercise	□	Laugh	□	Read	□
Meditation	□	Dance	□	_____	□
Sex	□	Sing	□	_____	□

CYCLE DAY _____

DATE_____

Sleep Time ____:____   Wake Time ____:____   Hours of Sleep _____

DREAMS _____
_____
_____
_____
_____
_____
_____
_____
_____

MORNING   MOOD: Good-Average-Bad   ENERGY LEVEL: High-Average-Low

REASON _____

Strength	Hope	Spirit	Vision

Awakening	Balance	Energy	Faith	Freedom

AFFIRMATION _____

NIGHT   MOOD: Good-Average-Bad   ENERGY LEVEL: High-Average-Low

REASON _____

Strength	Hope	Spirit	Vision

Awakening	Balance	Energy	Faith	Freedom

DAILY DISCOVERIES _____

_____
_____
_____
_____
_____
_____
_____
_____
_____
_____
_____
_____
_____
_____
_____
_____
_____
_____
_____
_____
_____

HEALTH PATTERNS _____

_____
_____
_____
_____
_____
_____
_____

ACHIEVEMENT _____

ACT OF KINDNESS _____

DIET		**PHYSICAL DISCOMFORT**
Meat	☐☐☐☐☐☐☐☐☐☐☐☐	
Bread	☐☐☐☐☐☐☐☐☐☐☐☐	
Dairy	☐☐☐☐☐☐☐☐☐☐☐	
Vegetables	☐☐☐☐☐☐☐☐☐☐☐	
Fruit	☐☐☐☐☐☐☐☐☐☐☐	
Water	☐☐☐☐☐☐☐☐☐☐☐	
Vitamins	☐☐☐☐☐☐☐☐☐☐☐	

PLAY

Exercise	☐	Laugh	☐	Read	☐
Meditation	☐	Dance	☐	_____	☐
Sex	☐	Sing	☐	_____	☐

CYCLE DAY

_____

DATE_____

Sleep Time ____:____ Wake Time ____:____ Hours of Sleep _____

DREAMS _____
_____
_____
_____
_____
_____
_____
_____
_____

MORNING   MOOD: Good-Average-Bad   ENERGY LEVEL: High-Average-Low

REASON _____

Strength	Hope	Spirit	Vision

Awakening	Balance	Energy	Faith	Freedom

AFFIRMATION _____

NIGHT   MOOD: Good-Average-Bad   ENERGY LEVEL: High-Average-Low

REASON _____

Strength	Hope	Spirit	Vision

Awakening	Balance	Energy	Faith	Freedom

DAILY DISCOVERIES _____

_____
_____
_____
_____
_____
_____
_____
_____
_____
_____
_____
_____
_____
_____
_____
_____
_____
_____
_____
_____
_____

HEALTH PATTERNS _____

_____
_____
_____
_____
_____
_____
_____

ACHIEVEMENT _____
ACT OF KINDNESS _____

DIET

Meat	☐☐☐☐☐☐☐☐☐☐☐☐
Bread	☐☐☐☐☐☐☐☐☐☐☐☐
Dairy	☐☐☐☐☐☐☐☐☐☐☐☐
Vegetables	☐☐☐☐☐☐☐☐☐☐☐☐
Fruit	☐☐☐☐☐☐☐☐☐☐☐☐
Water	☐☐☐☐☐☐☐☐☐☐☐☐
Vitamins	☐☐☐☐☐☐☐☐☐☐☐☐

PHYSICAL DISCOMFORT

PLAY

Exercise	☐	Laugh	☐	Read	☐
Meditation	☐	Dance	☐	_____	☐
Sex	☐	Sing	☐	_____	☐

CYCLE DAY

_____

DATE_____

Sleep Time ____:____ Wake Time ____:____ Hours of Sleep _____

DREAMS _____

_____
_____
_____
_____
_____
_____
_____
_____

MORNING **MOOD:** Good-Average-Bad **ENERGY LEVEL:** High-Average-Low

REASON _____

Strength	Hope	Spirit	Vision

Awakening	Balance	Energy	Faith	Freedom

AFFIRMATION _____

NIGHT **MOOD:** Good-Average-Bad **ENERGY LEVEL:** High-Average-Low

REASON _____

Strength	Hope	Spirit	Vision

Awakening	Balance	Energy	Faith	Freedom

DAILY DISCOVERIES _____

_____
_____
_____
_____
_____
_____
_____
_____
_____
_____
_____
_____
_____
_____
_____
_____
_____
_____
_____
_____

HEALTH PATTERNS _____

_____
_____
_____
_____
_____
_____
_____

ACHIEVEMENT _____

ACT OF KINDNESS _____

DIET		**PHYSICAL**
Meat	☐☐☐☐☐☐☐☐☐☐☐☐	**DISCOMFORT**
Bread	☐☐☐☐☐☐☐☐☐☐☐☐	
Dairy	☐☐☐☐☐☐☐☐☐☐☐☐	
Vegetables	☐☐☐☐☐☐☐☐☐☐☐☐	
Fruit	☐☐☐☐☐☐☐☐☐☐☐☐	
Water	☐☐☐☐☐☐☐☐☐☐☐☐	
Vitamins	☐☐☐☐☐☐☐☐☐☐☐☐	

PLAY

Exercise	☐	Laugh	☐	Read	☐
Meditation	☐	Dance	☐	_____	☐
Sex	☐	Sing	☐	_____	☐

CYCLE DAY

_____

DATE_____

Sleep Time ____:____   Wake Time ____:____   Hours of Sleep _____

DREAMS _____
_____
_____
_____
_____
_____
_____
_____
_____

<u>MORNING</u>   MOOD: Good-Average-Bad   **ENERGY LEVEL:** High-Average-Low

REASON _____

Strength	Hope	Spirit	Vision

Awakening	Balance	Energy	Faith	Freedom

AFFIRMATION _____

<u>NIGHT</u>   MOOD: Good-Average-Bad   **ENERGY LEVEL:** High-Average-Low

REASON _____

Strength	Hope	Spirit	Vision

Awakening	Balance	Energy	Faith	Freedom

DAILY DISCOVERIES _____

_____
_____
_____
_____
_____
_____
_____
_____
_____
_____
_____
_____
_____
_____
_____
_____
_____
_____
_____
_____

HEALTH PATTERNS _____

_____
_____
_____
_____
_____
_____
_____

ACHIEVEMENT _____
ACT OF KINDNESS _____

DIET

Meat	☐	☐	☐	☐	☐	☐	☐	☐	☐	☐
Bread	☐	☐	☐	☐	☐	☐	☐	☐	☐	☐
Dairy	☐	☐	☐	☐	☐	☐	☐	☐	☐	☐
Vegetables	☐	☐	☐	☐	☐	☐	☐	☐	☐	☐
Fruit	☐	☐	☐	☐	☐	☐	☐	☐	☐	☐
Water	☐	☐	☐	☐	☐	☐	☐	☐	☐	☐
Vitamins	☐	☐	☐	☐	☐	☐	☐	☐	☐	☐

PHYSICAL DISCOMFORT

PLAY

Exercise	☐	Laugh	☐	Read	☐
Meditation	☐	Dance	☐	_____	☐
Sex	☐	Sing	☐	_____	☐

CYCLE DAY

_____

DATE_____

Sleep Time ____:____   Wake Time ____:____   Hours of Sleep _____

DREAMS _____
_____
_____
_____
_____
_____
_____
_____
_____

MORNING   MOOD: Good-Average-Bad   ENERGY LEVEL: High-Average-Low

REASON _____

Strength	Hope	Spirit	Vision

Awakening	Balance	Energy	Faith	Freedom

AFFIRMATION _____

NIGHT   MOOD: Good-Average-Bad   ENERGY LEVEL: High-Average-Low

REASON _____

Strength	Hope	Spirit	Vision

Awakening	Balance	Energy	Faith	Freedom

DAILY DISCOVERIES _____

_____
_____
_____
_____
_____
_____
_____
_____
_____
_____
_____
_____
_____
_____
_____
_____
_____
_____
_____
_____
_____
_____
_____

HEALTH PATTERNS _____

_____
_____
_____
_____
_____
_____
_____

ACHIEVEMENT _____

ACT OF KINDNESS _____

DIET		**PHYSICAL**
Meat	□□□□□□□□□□□	**DISCOMFORT**
Bread	□□□□□□□□□□□	
Dairy	□□□□□□□□□□□	
Vegetables	□□□□□□□□□□□	
Fruit	□□□□□□□□□□□	
Water	□□□□□□□□□□□	
Vitamins	□□□□□□□□□□□	

PLAY

Exercise	□	Laugh	□	Read	□	
Meditation	□	Dance	□	_____	□	
Sex	□	Sing	□	_____	□	

CYCLE DAY

_____

DATE_____

Sleep Time ____:____ Wake Time ____:____ Hours of Sleep _____

DREAMS _____
_____
_____
_____
_____
_____
_____
_____
_____

MORNING   MOOD: Good-Average-Bad   ENERGY LEVEL: High-Average-Low

REASON _____

Strength   Hope   Spirit   Vision

Awakening   Balance   Energy   Faith   Freedom

AFFIRMATION _____

NIGHT   MOOD: Good-Average-Bad   ENERGY LEVEL: High-Average-Low

REASON _____

Strength   Hope   Spirit   Vision

Awakening   Balance   Energy   Faith   Freedom

DAILY DISCOVERIES _____

_____
_____
_____
_____
_____
_____
_____
_____
_____
_____
_____
_____
_____
_____
_____
_____
_____
_____
_____
_____

HEALTH PATTERNS _____

_____
_____
_____
_____
_____
_____
_____

ACHIEVEMENT _____

ACT OF KINDNESS _____

DIET		**PHYSICAL**
Meat	☐☐☐☐☐☐☐☐☐☐☐☐	**DISCOMFORT**
Bread	☐☐☐☐☐☐☐☐☐☐☐☐	
Dairy	☐☐☐☐☐☐☐☐☐☐☐☐	
Vegetables	☐☐☐☐☐☐☐☐☐☐☐☐	
Fruit	☐☐☐☐☐☐☐☐☐☐☐☐	
Water	☐☐☐☐☐☐☐☐☐☐☐☐	
Vitamins	☐☐☐☐☐☐☐☐☐☐☐☐	

PLAY

Exercise	☐	Laugh	☐	Read	☐
Meditation	☐	Dance	☐	_____	☐
Sex	☐	Sing	☐	_____	☐

CYCLE DAY

_____

DATE_____

Sleep Time ____:____   Wake Time ____:____   Hours of Sleep _____

DREAMS _____
_____
_____
_____
_____
_____
_____
_____

MORNING   MOOD: Good-Average-Bad   ENERGY LEVEL: High-Average-Low

REASON _____

Strength   Hope   Spirit   Vision

Awakening   Balance   Energy   Faith   Freedom

AFFIRMATION _____

NIGHT   MOOD: Good-Average-Bad   ENERGY LEVEL: High-Average-Low

REASON _____

Strength   Hope   Spirit   Vision

Awakening   Balance   Energy   Faith   Freedom

DAILY DISCOVERIES _____

_____
_____
_____
_____
_____
_____
_____
_____
_____
_____
_____
_____
_____
_____
_____
_____
_____
_____
_____
_____

HEALTH PATTERNS _____

_____
_____
_____
_____
_____
_____
_____

ACHIEVEMENT _____

ACT OF KINDNESS _____

DIET

Meat	☐	☐	☐	☐	☐	☐	☐	☐	☐	☐	☐
Bread	☐	☐	☐	☐	☐	☐	☐	☐	☐	☐	☐
Dairy	☐	☐	☐	☐	☐	☐	☐	☐	☐	☐	☐
Vegetables	☐	☐	☐	☐	☐	☐	☐	☐	☐	☐	☐
Fruit	☐	☐	☐	☐	☐	☐	☐	☐	☐	☐	☐
Water	☐	☐	☐	☐	☐	☐	☐	☐	☐	☐	☐
Vitamins	☐	☐	☐	☐	☐	☐	☐	☐	☐	☐	☐

PHYSICAL DISCOMFORT

PLAY

Exercise	☐	Laugh	☐	Read	☐	
Meditation	☐	Dance	☐	_____	☐	
Sex	☐	Sing	☐	_____	☐	

CYCLE DAY

_____

DATE_____

Sleep Time ____ : ____   Wake Time ____ : ____   Hours of Sleep _____

DREAMS _____
_____
_____
_____
_____
_____
_____
_____

MORNING   MOOD: Good-Average-Bad   **ENERGY LEVEL:** High-Average-Low

REASON _____

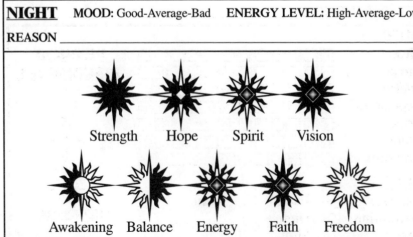

Strength   Hope   Spirit   Vision

Awakening   Balance   Energy   Faith   Freedom

AFFIRMATION _____

NIGHT   MOOD: Good-Average-Bad   **ENERGY LEVEL:** High-Average-Low

REASON _____

Strength   Hope   Spirit   Vision

Awakening   Balance   Energy   Faith   Freedom

DAILY DISCOVERIES _____

_____
_____
_____
_____
_____
_____
_____
_____
_____
_____
_____
_____
_____
_____
_____
_____
_____
_____
_____

HEALTH PATTERNS _____

_____
_____
_____
_____
_____
_____
_____

ACHIEVEMENT _____
ACT OF KINDNESS _____

DIET
Meat ☐☐☐☐☐☐☐☐☐☐☐☐☐ **PHYSICAL**
Bread ☐☐☐☐☐☐☐☐☐☐☐☐☐ **DISCOMFORT**
Dairy ☐☐☐☐☐☐☐☐☐☐☐☐☐
Vegetables ☐☐☐☐☐☐☐☐☐☐☐☐☐
Fruit ☐☐☐☐☐☐☐☐☐☐☐☐☐
Water ☐☐☐☐☐☐☐☐☐☐☐☐☐
Vitamins ☐☐☐☐☐☐☐☐☐☐☐☐☐

PLAY
Exercise ☐ Laugh ☐ Read ☐
Meditation ☐ Dance ☐ _____ ☐   **CYCLE DAY**
Sex ☐ Sing ☐ _____ ☐   _____

DATE_____

Sleep Time ____:____ Wake Time ____:____ Hours of Sleep _____

DREAMS _____
_____
_____
_____
_____
_____
_____
_____

MORNING   MOOD: Good-Average-Bad   ENERGY LEVEL: High-Average-Low

REASON _____

Strength	Hope	Spirit	Vision

Awakening	Balance	Energy	Faith	Freedom

AFFIRMATION _____

NIGHT   MOOD: Good-Average-Bad   ENERGY LEVEL: High-Average-Low

REASON _____

Strength	Hope	Spirit	Vision

Awakening	Balance	Energy	Faith	Freedom

DAILY DISCOVERIES _____

_____
_____
_____
_____
_____
_____
_____
_____
_____
_____
_____
_____
_____
_____
_____
_____
_____
_____
_____

HEALTH PATTERNS _____

_____
_____
_____
_____
_____
_____

ACHIEVEMENT _____

ACT OF KINDNESS _____

DIET			**PHYSICAL**
Meat	□□□□□□□□□□□□		**DISCOMFORT**
Bread	□□□□□□□□□□□□		
Dairy	□□□□□□□□□□□		
Vegetables	□□□□□□□□□□□		
Fruit	□□□□□□□□□□□		
Water	□□□□□□□□□□□		
Vitamins	□□□□□□□□□□□		

PLAY

Exercise	□	Laugh	□	Read	□
Meditation	□	Dance	□	_____	□
Sex	□	Sing	□	_____	□

CYCLE DAY

_____

DATE_____

Sleep Time ____:____ Wake Time ____:____ Hours of Sleep _____

DREAMS _____
_____
_____
_____
_____
_____
_____
_____
_____

MORNING   MOOD: Good-Average-Bad   ENERGY LEVEL: High-Average-Low

REASON _____

Strength   Hope   Spirit   Vision

Awakening   Balance   Energy   Faith   Freedom

AFFIRMATION _____

NIGHT   MOOD: Good-Average-Bad   ENERGY LEVEL: High-Average-Low

REASON _____

Strength   Hope   Spirit   Vision

Awakening   Balance   Energy   Faith   Freedom

DAILY DISCOVERIES _____

_____
_____
_____
_____
_____
_____
_____
_____
_____
_____
_____
_____
_____
_____
_____
_____
_____
_____
_____
_____

HEALTH PATTERNS _____

_____
_____
_____
_____
_____
_____
_____

ACHIEVEMENT _____
ACT OF KINDNESS _____

DIET			**PHYSICAL DISCOMFORT**
Meat	☐☐☐☐☐☐☐☐☐☐☐☐		
Bread	☐☐☐☐☐☐☐☐☐☐☐☐		
Dairy	☐☐☐☐☐☐☐☐☐☐☐☐		
Vegetables	☐☐☐☐☐☐☐☐☐☐☐☐		
Fruit	☐☐☐☐☐☐☐☐☐☐☐☐		
Water	☐☐☐☐☐☐☐☐☐☐☐☐		
Vitamins	☐☐☐☐☐☐☐☐☐☐☐☐		

PLAY

Exercise	☐	Laugh	☐	Read	☐
Meditation	☐	Dance	☐	_____	☐
Sex	☐	Sing	☐	_____	☐

CYCLE DAY
_____

DATE_____

Sleep Time ____:____ Wake Time ____:____ Hours of Sleep _____

DREAMS _____
_____
_____
_____
_____
_____
_____
_____
_____

MORNING   MOOD: Good-Average-Bad   ENERGY LEVEL: High-Average-Low

REASON _____

Strength   Hope   Spirit   Vision

Awakening   Balance   Energy   Faith   Freedom

AFFIRMATION _____

NIGHT   MOOD: Good-Average-Bad   ENERGY LEVEL: High-Average-Low

REASON _____

Strength   Hope   Spirit   Vision

Awakening   Balance   Energy   Faith   Freedom

DAILY DISCOVERIES _____

_____
_____
_____
_____
_____
_____
_____
_____
_____
_____
_____
_____
_____
_____
_____
_____
_____
_____
_____
_____

HEALTH PATTERNS _____

_____
_____
_____
_____
_____
_____

ACHIEVEMENT _____
ACT OF KINDNESS _____

DIET

Meat	□ □ □ □ □ □ □ □ □ □ □
Bread	□ □ □ □ □ □ □ □ □ □ □
Dairy	□ □ □ □ □ □ □ □ □ □ □
Vegetables	□ □ □ □ □ □ □ □ □ □ □
Fruit	□ □ □ □ □ □ □ □ □ □ □
Water	□ □ □ □ □ □ □ □ □ □ □
Vitamins	□ □ □ □ □ □ □ □ □ □ □

PHYSICAL DISCOMFORT

PLAY

Exercise	□	Laugh	□	Read	□
Meditation	□	Dance	□	_____	□
Sex	□	Sing	□	_____	□

CYCLE DAY

_____

DATE_____

Sleep Time ____:____   Wake Time ____:____   Hours of Sleep _____

DREAMS _____

_____

_____

_____

_____

_____

_____

_____

_____

MORNING   MOOD: Good-Average-Bad   ENERGY LEVEL: High-Average-Low

REASON _____

Strength	Hope	Spirit	Vision

Awakening	Balance	Energy	Faith	Freedom

AFFIRMATION _____

NIGHT   MOOD: Good-Average-Bad   ENERGY LEVEL: High-Average-Low

REASON _____

Strength	Hope	Spirit	Vision

Awakening	Balance	Energy	Faith	Freedom

DAILY DISCOVERIES _____

_____
_____
_____
_____
_____
_____
_____
_____
_____
_____
_____
_____
_____
_____
_____
_____
_____
_____
_____
_____
_____
_____

HEALTH PATTERNS _____

_____
_____
_____
_____
_____
_____
_____

ACHIEVEMENT _____
ACT OF KINDNESS _____

DIET		**PHYSICAL**
Meat	☐☐☐☐☐☐☐☐☐☐☐☐	**DISCOMFORT**
Bread	☐☐☐☐☐☐☐☐☐☐☐☐	
Dairy	☐☐☐☐☐☐☐☐☐☐☐☐	
Vegetables	☐☐☐☐☐☐☐☐☐☐☐☐	
Fruit	☐☐☐☐☐☐☐☐☐☐☐☐	
Water	☐☐☐☐☐☐☐☐☐☐☐☐	
Vitamins	☐☐☐☐☐☐☐☐☐☐☐☐	

PLAY

Exercise	☐	Laugh	☐	Read	☐
Meditation	☐	Dance	☐	_____	☐
Sex	☐	Sing	☐	_____	☐

CYCLE DAY

_____

DATE_____

Sleep Time ____:____   Wake Time ____:____   Hours of Sleep _____

DREAMS _____
_____
_____
_____
_____
_____
_____
_____

MORNING   MOOD: Good-Average-Bad   ENERGY LEVEL: High-Average-Low

REASON _____

Strength	Hope	Spirit	Vision

Awakening	Balance	Energy	Faith	Freedom

AFFIRMATION _____

NIGHT   MOOD: Good-Average-Bad   ENERGY LEVEL: High-Average-Low

REASON _____

Strength	Hope	Spirit	Vision

Awakening	Balance	Energy	Faith	Freedom

DAILY DISCOVERIES _____

_____
_____
_____
_____
_____
_____
_____
_____
_____
_____
_____
_____
_____
_____
_____
_____
_____
_____
_____

HEALTH PATTERNS _____

_____
_____
_____
_____
_____
_____

ACHIEVEMENT _____
ACT OF KINDNESS _____

DIET

Meat	☐	☐	☐	☐	☐	☐	☐	☐	☐	☐	☐	☐
Bread	☐	☐	☐	☐	☐	☐	☐	☐	☐	☐	☐	☐
Dairy	☐	☐	☐	☐	☐	☐	☐	☐	☐	☐	☐	☐
Vegetables	☐	☐	☐	☐	☐	☐	☐	☐	☐	☐	☐	☐
Fruit	☐	☐	☐	☐	☐	☐	☐	☐	☐	☐	☐	☐
Water	☐	☐	☐	☐	☐	☐	☐	☐	☐	☐	☐	☐
Vitamins	☐	☐	☐	☐	☐	☐	☐	☐	☐	☐	☐	☐

PHYSICAL DISCOMFORT

PLAY

Exercise	☐	Laugh	☐	Read	☐
Meditation	☐	Dance	☐	_____	☐
Sex	☐	Sing	☐	_____	☐

CYCLE DAY

_____

DATE_____

Sleep Time ____:____ Wake Time ____:____ Hours of Sleep _____

DREAMS _____
_____
_____
_____
_____
_____
_____
_____
_____

MORNING   MOOD: Good-Average-Bad   ENERGY LEVEL: High-Average-Low

REASON _____

Strength   Hope   Spirit   Vision

Awakening   Balance   Energy   Faith   Freedom

AFFIRMATION _____

NIGHT   MOOD: Good-Average-Bad   ENERGY LEVEL: High-Average-Low

REASON _____

Strength   Hope   Spirit   Vision

Awakening   Balance   Energy   Faith   Freedom

DAILY DISCOVERIES _____

_____
_____
_____
_____
_____
_____
_____
_____
_____
_____
_____
_____
_____
_____
_____
_____
_____
_____
_____
_____
_____

HEALTH PATTERNS _____

_____
_____
_____
_____
_____
_____

ACHIEVEMENT _____

ACT OF KINDNESS _____

DIET

Meat	☐	☐	☐	☐	☐	☐	☐	☐	☐	☐	☐	☐	☐
Bread	☐	☐	☐	☐	☐	☐	☐	☐	☐	☐	☐	☐	☐
Dairy	☐	☐	☐	☐	☐	☐	☐	☐	☐	☐	☐	☐	☐
Vegetables	☐	☐	☐	☐	☐	☐	☐	☐	☐	☐	☐	☐	☐
Fruit	☐	☐	☐	☐	☐	☐	☐	☐	☐	☐	☐	☐	☐
Water	☐	☐	☐	☐	☐	☐	☐	☐	☐	☐	☐	☐	☐
Vitamins	☐	☐	☐	☐	☐	☐	☐	☐	☐	☐	☐	☐	☐

PHYSICAL DISCOMFORT

PLAY

Exercise	☐	Laugh	☐	Read	☐
Meditation	☐	Dance	☐	_____	☐
Sex	☐	Sing	☐	_____	☐

CYCLE DAY

_____

DATE_____

Sleep Time ____:____   Wake Time ____:____   Hours of Sleep _____

DREAMS _____
_____
_____
_____
_____
_____
_____
_____
_____

MORNING   MOOD: Good-Average-Bad   ENERGY LEVEL: High-Average-Low

REASON _____

Strength	Hope	Spirit	Vision	
Awakening	Balance	Energy	Faith	Freedom

AFFIRMATION _____

NIGHT   MOOD: Good-Average-Bad   ENERGY LEVEL: High-Average-Low

REASON _____

Strength	Hope	Spirit	Vision	
Awakening	Balance	Energy	Faith	Freedom

DAILY DISCOVERIES _____

_____
_____
_____
_____
_____
_____
_____
_____
_____
_____
_____
_____
_____
_____
_____
_____
_____
_____
_____
_____

HEALTH PATTERNS _____

_____
_____
_____
_____
_____
_____

ACHIEVEMENT _____
ACT OF KINDNESS _____

DIET		**PHYSICAL**
Meat	☐☐☐☐☐☐☐☐☐☐☐	**DISCOMFORT**
Bread	☐☐☐☐☐☐☐☐☐☐☐	
Dairy	☐☐☐☐☐☐☐☐☐☐☐	
Vegetables	☐☐☐☐☐☐☐☐☐☐☐	
Fruit	☐☐☐☐☐☐☐☐☐☐☐	
Water	☐☐☐☐☐☐☐☐☐☐☐	
Vitamins	☐☐☐☐☐☐☐☐☐☐☐	

PLAY

Exercise	☐	Laugh	☐	Read	☐	
Meditation	☐	Dance	☐	_____	☐	**CYCLE DAY**
Sex	☐	Sing	☐	_____	☐	_____

DATE_____

Sleep Time ____:____   Wake Time ____:____   Hours of Sleep _____

DREAMS _____

_____

_____

_____

_____

_____

_____

_____

<u>**MORNING**</u>   MOOD: Good-Average-Bad   ENERGY LEVEL: High-Average-Low

REASON _____

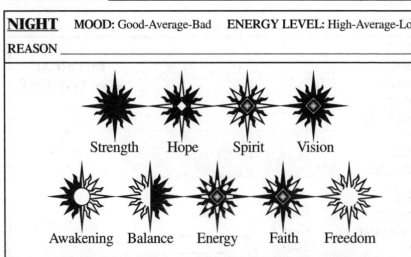

Strength   Hope   Spirit   Vision

Awakening   Balance   Energy   Faith   Freedom

AFFIRMATION _____

<u>**NIGHT**</u>   MOOD: Good-Average-Bad   ENERGY LEVEL: High-Average-Low

REASON _____

Strength   Hope   Spirit   Vision

Awakening   Balance   Energy   Faith   Freedom

DAILY DISCOVERIES _____

_____
_____
_____
_____
_____
_____
_____
_____
_____
_____
_____
_____
_____
_____
_____
_____
_____
_____
_____
_____

HEALTH PATTERNS _____

_____
_____
_____
_____
_____
_____

ACHIEVEMENT _____
ACT OF KINDNESS _____

DIET		**PHYSICAL**
Meat	☐☐☐☐☐☐☐☐☐☐☐☐	**DISCOMFORT**
Bread	☐☐☐☐☐☐☐☐☐☐☐☐	
Dairy	☐☐☐☐☐☐☐☐☐☐☐☐	
Vegetables	☐☐☐☐☐☐☐☐☐☐☐☐	
Fruit	☐☐☐☐☐☐☐☐☐☐☐☐	
Water	☐☐☐☐☐☐☐☐☐☐☐☐	
Vitamins	☐☐☐☐☐☐☐☐☐☐☐☐	

PLAY

Exercise	☐	Laugh	☐	Read	☐
Meditation	☐	Dance	☐	_____	☐
Sex	☐	Sing	☐	_____	☐

CYCLE DAY

_____

DATE_____

Sleep Time ____:____ Wake Time ____:____ Hours of Sleep _____

DREAMS _____
_____
_____
_____
_____
_____
_____
_____

MORNING   MOOD: Good-Average-Bad   ENERGY LEVEL: High-Average-Low

REASON _____

| Strength | Hope | Spirit | Vision |

| Awakening | Balance | Energy | Faith | Freedom |

AFFIRMATION _____

NIGHT   MOOD: Good-Average-Bad   ENERGY LEVEL: High-Average-Low

REASON _____

| Strength | Hope | Spirit | Vision |

| Awakening | Balance | Energy | Faith | Freedom |

DAILY DISCOVERIES _____

_____
_____
_____
_____
_____
_____
_____
_____
_____
_____
_____
_____
_____
_____
_____
_____
_____
_____
_____
_____

HEALTH PATTERNS _____

_____
_____
_____
_____
_____
_____
_____

ACHIEVEMENT _____

ACT OF KINDNESS _____

DIET

Meat	☐	☐	☐	☐	☐	☐	☐	☐	☐	☐	☐
Bread	☐	☐	☐	☐	☐	☐	☐	☐	☐	☐	☐
Dairy	☐	☐	☐	☐	☐	☐	☐	☐	☐	☐	☐
Vegetables	☐	☐	☐	☐	☐	☐	☐	☐	☐	☐	☐
Fruit	☐	☐	☐	☐	☐	☐	☐	☐	☐	☐	☐
Water	☐	☐	☐	☐	☐	☐	☐	☐	☐	☐	☐
Vitamins	☐	☐	☐	☐	☐	☐	☐	☐	☐	☐	☐

PHYSICAL DISCOMFORT

PLAY

Exercise	☐	Laugh	☐	Read	☐	
Meditation	☐	Dance	☐	_____	☐	
Sex	☐	Sing	☐	_____	☐	

CYCLE DAY

_____

DATE_____

Sleep Time ____:____ Wake Time ____:____ Hours of Sleep _____

DREAMS _____
_____
_____
_____
_____
_____
_____
_____
_____

MORNING MOOD: Good-Average-Bad ENERGY LEVEL: High-Average-Low

REASON _____

Strength   Hope   Spirit   Vision

Awakening Balance Energy Faith Freedom

AFFIRMATION _____

NIGHT MOOD: Good-Average-Bad ENERGY LEVEL: High-Average-Low

REASON _____

Strength   Hope   Spirit   Vision

Awakening Balance Energy Faith Freedom

DAILY DISCOVERIES _____

_____
_____
_____
_____
_____
_____
_____
_____
_____
_____
_____
_____
_____
_____
_____
_____
_____
_____
_____
_____

HEALTH PATTERNS _____

_____
_____
_____
_____
_____
_____

ACHIEVEMENT _____
ACT OF KINDNESS _____

DIET		**PHYSICAL DISCOMFORT**
Meat	☐☐☐☐☐☐☐☐☐☐☐☐	
Bread	☐☐☐☐☐☐☐☐☐☐☐☐	
Dairy	☐☐☐☐☐☐☐☐☐☐☐☐	
Vegetables	☐☐☐☐☐☐☐☐☐☐☐☐	
Fruit	☐☐☐☐☐☐☐☐☐☐☐☐	
Water	☐☐☐☐☐☐☐☐☐☐☐☐	
Vitamins	☐☐☐☐☐☐☐☐☐☐☐☐	

PLAY

Exercise ☐	Laugh ☐	Read ☐	
Meditation ☐	Dance ☐	_____ ☐	**CYCLE DAY**
Sex ☐	Sing ☐	_____ ☐	_____

DATE_____

Sleep Time ____:____ **Wake Time** ____:____ **Hours of Sleep** _____

DREAMS _____
_____
_____
_____
_____
_____
_____
_____
_____

MORNING   MOOD: Good-Average-Bad ENERGY LEVEL: High-Average-Low

REASON _____

| Strength | Hope | Spirit | Vision |

| Awakening | Balance | Energy | Faith | Freedom |

AFFIRMATION _____

NIGHT   MOOD: Good-Average-Bad   ENERGY LEVEL: High-Average-Low

REASON _____

| Strength | Hope | Spirit | Vision |

| Awakening | Balance | Energy | Faith | Freedom |

DAILY DISCOVERIES _____

_____
_____
_____
_____
_____
_____
_____
_____
_____
_____
_____
_____
_____
_____
_____
_____
_____
_____
_____
_____

HEALTH PATTERNS _____

_____
_____
_____
_____
_____
_____

ACHIEVEMENT _____

ACT OF KINDNESS _____

DIET		**PHYSICAL DISCOMFORT**
Meat	☐☐☐☐☐☐☐☐☐☐☐☐	
Bread	☐☐☐☐☐☐☐☐☐☐☐☐	
Dairy	☐☐☐☐☐☐☐☐☐☐☐☐	
Vegetables	☐☐☐☐☐☐☐☐☐☐☐☐	
Fruit	☐☐☐☐☐☐☐☐☐☐☐☐	
Water	☐☐☐☐☐☐☐☐☐☐☐☐	
Vitamins	☐☐☐☐☐☐☐☐☐☐☐☐	

PLAY

Exercise	☐	Laugh	☐	Read	☐
Meditation	☐	Dance	☐	_____	☐
Sex	☐	Sing	☐	_____	☐

CYCLE DAY

_____

DATE_____

Sleep Time ____:____ Wake Time ____:____ Hours of Sleep _____

DREAMS _____
_____
_____
_____
_____
_____
_____
_____
_____

MORNING   **MOOD:** Good-Average-Bad   **ENERGY LEVEL:** High-Average-Low

REASON _____

Strength	Hope	Spirit	Vision

Awakening	Balance	Energy	Faith	Freedom

AFFIRMATION _____

NIGHT   **MOOD:** Good-Average-Bad   **ENERGY LEVEL:** High-Average-Low

REASON _____

Strength	Hope	Spirit	Vision

Awakening	Balance	Energy	Faith	Freedom

DAILY DISCOVERIES _____

_____
_____
_____
_____
_____
_____
_____
_____
_____
_____
_____
_____
_____
_____
_____
_____
_____
_____
_____
_____
_____

HEALTH PATTERNS _____

_____
_____
_____
_____
_____
_____
_____

ACHIEVEMENT _____

ACT OF KINDNESS _____

DIET		
Meat	☐☐☐☐☐☐☐☐☐☐☐☐	**PHYSICAL**
Bread	☐☐☐☐☐☐☐☐☐☐☐☐	**DISCOMFORT**
Dairy	☐☐☐☐☐☐☐☐☐☐☐☐	
Vegetables	☐☐☐☐☐☐☐☐☐☐☐☐	
Fruit	☐☐☐☐☐☐☐☐☐☐☐☐	
Water	☐☐☐☐☐☐☐☐☐☐☐☐	
Vitamins	☐☐☐☐☐☐☐☐☐☐☐☐	

PLAY

Exercise	☐	Laugh	☐	Read	☐
Meditation	☐	Dance	☐	_____	☐
Sex	☐	Sing	☐	_____	☐

CYCLE DAY

_____

DATE_____

Sleep Time ____:____   Wake Time ____:____   Hours of Sleep _____

DREAMS _____
_____
_____
_____
_____
_____
_____
_____
_____

<u>MORNING</u>   MOOD: Good-Average-Bad   ENERGY LEVEL: High-Average-Low

REASON _____

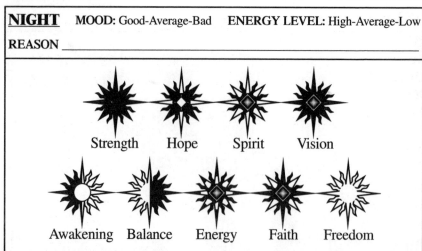

| Strength | Hope | Spirit | Vision | |
| Awakening | Balance | Energy | Faith | Freedom |

AFFIRMATION _____

<u>NIGHT</u>   MOOD: Good-Average-Bad   ENERGY LEVEL: High-Average-Low

REASON _____

| Strength | Hope | Spirit | Vision | |
| Awakening | Balance | Energy | Faith | Freedom |

DAILY DISCOVERIES _____

_____
_____
_____
_____
_____
_____
_____
_____
_____
_____
_____
_____
_____
_____
_____
_____
_____
_____
_____

HEALTH PATTERNS _____

_____
_____
_____
_____
_____
_____

ACHIEVEMENT _____

ACT OF KINDNESS _____

DIET			
Meat	☐☐☐☐☐☐☐☐☐☐☐☐☐		**PHYSICAL**
Bread	☐☐☐☐☐☐☐☐☐☐☐☐☐		**DISCOMFORT**
Dairy	☐☐☐☐☐☐☐☐☐☐☐☐		
Vegetables	☐☐☐☐☐☐☐☐☐☐☐☐		
Fruit	☐☐☐☐☐☐☐☐☐☐☐☐		
Water	☐☐☐☐☐☐☐☐☐☐☐☐☐		
Vitamins	☐☐☐☐☐☐☐☐☐☐☐☐		

PLAY

Exercise	☐	Laugh	☐	Read	☐
Meditation	☐	Dance	☐	_____	☐
Sex	☐	Sing	☐	_____	☐

CYCLE DAY

_____

DATE_____

Sleep Time ____:____ Wake Time ____:____ Hours of Sleep _____

DREAMS _____
_____
_____
_____
_____
_____
_____
_____
_____

MORNING   MOOD: Good-Average-Bad   ENERGY LEVEL: High-Average-Low

REASON _____

Strength	Hope	Spirit	Vision

Awakening	Balance	Energy	Faith	Freedom

AFFIRMATION _____

NIGHT   MOOD: Good-Average-Bad   ENERGY LEVEL: High-Average-Low

REASON _____

Strength	Hope	Spirit	Vision

Awakening	Balance	Energy	Faith	Freedom

DAILY DISCOVERIES _____

_____
_____
_____
_____
_____
_____
_____
_____
_____
_____
_____
_____
_____
_____
_____
_____
_____
_____
_____
_____
_____

HEALTH PATTERNS _____

_____
_____
_____
_____
_____
_____

ACHIEVEMENT _____

ACT OF KINDNESS _____

DIET

			PHYSICAL DISCOMFORT
Meat	☐☐☐☐☐☐☐☐☐☐☐☐		
Bread	☐☐☐☐☐☐☐☐☐☐☐☐		
Dairy	☐☐☐☐☐☐☐☐☐☐☐☐		
Vegetables	☐☐☐☐☐☐☐☐☐☐☐☐		
Fruit	☐☐☐☐☐☐☐☐☐☐☐☐		
Water	☐☐☐☐☐☐☐☐☐☐☐☐		
Vitamins	☐☐☐☐☐☐☐☐☐☐☐☐		

PLAY

Exercise	☐	Laugh	☐	Read	☐
Meditation	☐	Dance	☐	_____	☐
Sex	☐	Sing	☐	_____	☐

CYCLE DAY

_____

DATE_____

Sleep Time ____:____ Wake Time ____:____ Hours of Sleep _____

DREAMS _____
_____
_____
_____
_____
_____
_____
_____
_____

MORNING   MOOD: Good-Average-Bad   ENERGY LEVEL: High-Average-Low

REASON _____

| Strength | Hope | Spirit | Vision |

| Awakening | Balance | Energy | Faith | Freedom |

AFFIRMATION _____

NIGHT   MOOD: Good-Average-Bad   ENERGY LEVEL: High-Average-Low

REASON _____

| Strength | Hope | Spirit | Vision |

| Awakening | Balance | Energy | Faith | Freedom |

DAILY DISCOVERIES _____

_____
_____
_____
_____
_____
_____
_____
_____
_____
_____
_____
_____
_____
_____
_____
_____
_____
_____
_____

HEALTH PATTERNS _____

_____
_____
_____
_____
_____
_____
_____

ACHIEVEMENT _____

ACT OF KINDNESS _____

DIET

		PHYSICAL DISCOMFORT
Meat	☐☐☐☐☐☐☐☐☐☐☐☐	
Bread	☐☐☐☐☐☐☐☐☐☐☐☐	
Dairy	☐☐☐☐☐☐☐☐☐☐☐☐	
Vegetables	☐☐☐☐☐☐☐☐☐☐☐☐	
Fruit	☐☐☐☐☐☐☐☐☐☐☐☐	
Water	☐☐☐☐☐☐☐☐☐☐☐☐	
Vitamins	☐☐☐☐☐☐☐☐☐☐☐☐	

PLAY

Exercise	☐	Laugh	☐	Read	☐
Meditation	☐	Dance	☐	_____	☐
Sex	☐	Sing	☐	_____	☐

CYCLE DAY _____

DATE_____

Sleep Time ____:____ Wake Time ____:____ Hours of Sleep _____

DREAMS _____
_____
_____
_____
_____
_____
_____
_____
_____

<u>**MORNING**</u>   MOOD: Good-Average-Bad   **ENERGY LEVEL:** High-Average-Low

REASON _____

Strength	Hope	Spirit	Vision	

Awakening	Balance	Energy	Faith	Freedom

AFFIRMATION _____

<u>**NIGHT**</u>   MOOD: Good-Average-Bad   **ENERGY LEVEL:** High-Average-Low

REASON _____

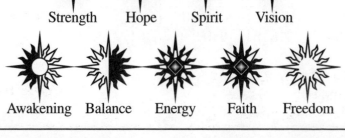

Strength	Hope	Spirit	Vision	

Awakening	Balance	Energy	Faith	Freedom

DAILY DISCOVERIES _____

_____
_____
_____
_____
_____
_____
_____
_____
_____
_____
_____
_____
_____
_____
_____
_____
_____
_____
_____
_____
_____

HEALTH PATTERNS _____

_____
_____
_____
_____
_____
_____

ACHIEVEMENT _____

ACT OF KINDNESS _____

DIET

Meat	☐	☐	☐	☐	☐	☐	☐	☐	☐	☐	☐
Bread	☐	☐	☐	☐	☐	☐	☐	☐	☐	☐	☐
Dairy	☐	☐	☐	☐	☐	☐	☐	☐	☐	☐	☐
Vegetables	☐	☐	☐	☐	☐	☐	☐	☐	☐	☐	☐
Fruit	☐	☐	☐	☐	☐	☐	☐	☐	☐	☐	☐
Water	☐	☐	☐	☐	☐	☐	☐	☐	☐	☐	☐
Vitamins	☐	☐	☐	☐	☐	☐	☐	☐	☐	☐	☐

PHYSICAL DISCOMFORT

PLAY

Exercise	☐	Laugh	☐	Read	☐
Meditation	☐	Dance	☐	_____	☐
Sex	☐	Sing	☐	_____	☐

CYCLE DAY

_____

DATE_____

Sleep Time ____:____ Wake Time ____:____ Hours of Sleep _____

DREAMS _____
_____
_____
_____
_____
_____
_____
_____
_____

MORNING   MOOD: Good-Average-Bad   ENERGY LEVEL: High-Average-Low

REASON _____

Strength	Hope	Spirit	Vision

Awakening	Balance	Energy	Faith	Freedom

AFFIRMATION _____

NIGHT   MOOD: Good-Average-Bad   ENERGY LEVEL: High-Average-Low

REASON _____

Strength	Hope	Spirit	Vision

Awakening	Balance	Energy	Faith	Freedom

DAILY DISCOVERIES _____

_____
_____
_____
_____
_____
_____
_____
_____
_____
_____
_____
_____
_____
_____
_____
_____
_____
_____
_____
_____
_____
_____

HEALTH PATTERNS _____

_____
_____
_____
_____
_____
_____

ACHIEVEMENT _____

ACT OF KINDNESS _____

DIET

Meat	☐☐☐☐☐☐☐☐☐☐☐	**PHYSICAL**
Bread	☐☐☐☐☐☐☐☐☐☐☐	**DISCOMFORT**
Dairy	☐☐☐☐☐☐☐☐☐☐☐	
Vegetables	☐☐☐☐☐☐☐☐☐☐☐	
Fruit	☐☐☐☐☐☐☐☐☐☐☐	
Water	☐☐☐☐☐☐☐☐☐☐☐	
Vitamins	☐☐☐☐☐☐☐☐☐☐☐	

PLAY

Exercise	☐	Laugh	☐	Read	☐
Meditation	☐	Dance	☐	_____	☐
Sex	☐	Sing	☐	_____	☐

CYCLE DAY

_____

DATE_____

Sleep Time _____:_____ Wake Time _____:_____ Hours of Sleep _____

DREAMS _____
_____
_____
_____
_____
_____
_____
_____

MORNING   MOOD: Good-Average-Bad   ENERGY LEVEL: High-Average-Low

REASON _____

Strength   Hope   Spirit   Vision

Awakening   Balance   Energy   Faith   Freedom

AFFIRMATION _____

NIGHT   MOOD: Good-Average-Bad   ENERGY LEVEL: High-Average-Low

REASON _____

Strength   Hope   Spirit   Vision

Awakening   Balance   Energy   Faith   Freedom

DAILY DISCOVERIES _____

_____
_____
_____
_____
_____
_____
_____
_____
_____
_____
_____
_____
_____
_____
_____
_____
_____
_____
_____
_____
_____

HEALTH PATTERNS _____

_____
_____
_____
_____
_____
_____

ACHIEVEMENT _____

ACT OF KINDNESS _____

DIET		**PHYSICAL**
Meat	☐☐☐☐☐☐☐☐☐☐☐☐	**DISCOMFORT**
Bread	☐☐☐☐☐☐☐☐☐☐☐☐	
Dairy	☐☐☐☐☐☐☐☐☐☐☐☐	
Vegetables	☐☐☐☐☐☐☐☐☐☐☐☐	
Fruit	☐☐☐☐☐☐☐☐☐☐☐☐	
Water	☐☐☐☐☐☐☐☐☐☐☐☐	
Vitamins	☐☐☐☐☐☐☐☐☐☐☐☐	

PLAY

Exercise	☐	Laugh	☐	Read	☐
Meditation	☐	Dance	☐	_____	☐
Sex	☐	Sing	☐	_____	☐

CYCLE DAY

_____

DATE_____

Sleep Time ____:____ Wake Time ____:____ Hours of Sleep _____

DREAMS _____

_____

_____

_____

_____

_____

_____

_____

MORNING   MOOD: Good-Average-Bad   ENERGY LEVEL: High-Average-Low

REASON _____

Strength	Hope	Spirit	Vision

Awakening	Balance	Energy	Faith	Freedom

AFFIRMATION _____

NIGHT   MOOD: Good-Average-Bad   ENERGY LEVEL: High-Average-Low

REASON _____

Strength	Hope	Spirit	Vision

Awakening	Balance	Energy	Faith	Freedom

DAILY DISCOVERIES _____

_____
_____
_____
_____
_____
_____
_____
_____
_____
_____
_____
_____
_____
_____
_____
_____
_____
_____
_____
_____
_____
_____

HEALTH PATTERNS _____

_____
_____
_____
_____
_____
_____
_____

ACHIEVEMENT _____

ACT OF KINDNESS _____

DIET		
Meat	□□□□□□□□□□□□□	**PHYSICAL**
Bread	□□□□□□□□□□□□□	**DISCOMFORT**
Dairy	□□□□□□□□□□□□□	
Vegetables	□□□□□□□□□□□□□	
Fruit	□□□□□□□□□□□□□	
Water	□□□□□□□□□□□□□	
Vitamins	□□□□□□□□□□□□□	

PLAY

Exercise	□	Laugh	□	Read	□
Meditation	□	Dance	□	_____	□
Sex	□	Sing	□	_____	□

CYCLE DAY

_____

DATE_____

Sleep Time ____:____ Wake Time ____:____ Hours of Sleep _____

DREAMS _____
_____
_____
_____
_____
_____
_____
_____
_____

MORNING   MOOD: Good-Average-Bad   ENERGY LEVEL: High-Average-Low

REASON _____

| Strength | Hope | Spirit | Vision |

| Awakening | Balance | Energy | Faith | Freedom |

AFFIRMATION _____

NIGHT   MOOD: Good-Average-Bad   ENERGY LEVEL: High-Average-Low

REASON _____

| Strength | Hope | Spirit | Vision |

| Awakening | Balance | Energy | Faith | Freedom |

DAILY DISCOVERIES _____

_____
_____
_____
_____
_____
_____
_____
_____
_____
_____
_____
_____
_____
_____
_____
_____
_____
_____
_____
_____
_____

HEALTH PATTERNS _____

_____
_____
_____
_____
_____
_____

ACHIEVEMENT _____

ACT OF KINDNESS _____

DIET

		PHYSICAL
Meat	☐☐☐☐☐☐☐☐☐☐☐☐	**DISCOMFORT**
Bread	☐☐☐☐☐☐☐☐☐☐☐☐	
Dairy	☐☐☐☐☐☐☐☐☐☐☐☐	
Vegetables	☐☐☐☐☐☐☐☐☐☐☐☐	
Fruit	☐☐☐☐☐☐☐☐☐☐☐☐	
Water	☐☐☐☐☐☐☐☐☐☐☐☐	
Vitamins	☐☐☐☐☐☐☐☐☐☐☐☐	

PLAY

Exercise	☐	Laugh	☐	Read	☐
Meditation	☐	Dance	☐	_____	☐
Sex	☐	Sing	☐	_____	☐

CYCLE DAY

_____

DATE_____

Sleep Time ____:____ Wake Time ____:____ Hours of Sleep _____

DREAMS _____
_____
_____
_____
_____
_____
_____
_____
_____

MORNING MOOD: Good-Average-Bad ENERGY LEVEL: High-Average-Low

REASON _____

Strength	Hope	Spirit	Vision

Awakening	Balance	Energy	Faith	Freedom

AFFIRMATION _____

NIGHT MOOD: Good-Average-Bad ENERGY LEVEL: High-Average-Low

REASON _____

Strength	Hope	Spirit	Vision

Awakening	Balance	Energy	Faith	Freedom

DAILY DISCOVERIES _____
_____
_____
_____
_____
_____
_____
_____
_____
_____
_____
_____
_____
_____
_____
_____
_____
_____
_____
_____
_____
_____

HEALTH PATTERNS _____
_____
_____
_____
_____
_____
_____
_____

ACHIEVEMENT _____
ACT OF KINDNESS _____

DIET		**PHYSICAL**
Meat	□□□□□□□□□□□□	**DISCOMFORT**
Bread	□□□□□□□□□□□□	
Dairy	□□□□□□□□□□□□	
Vegetables	□□□□□□□□□□□□	
Fruit	□□□□□□□□□□□□	
Water	□□□□□□□□□□□□	
Vitamins	□□□□□□□□□□□□	

PLAY

Exercise	□	Laugh	□	Read	□
Meditation	□	Dance	□	_____	□
Sex	□	Sing	□	_____	□

CYCLE DAY

_____

DATE_____

Sleep Time ____:____ Wake Time ____:____ Hours of Sleep _____

DREAMS _____
_____
_____
_____
_____
_____
_____
_____
_____

MORNING   MOOD: Good-Average-Bad   ENERGY LEVEL: High-Average-Low

REASON _____

Strength	Hope	Spirit	Vision	
Awakening	Balance	Energy	Faith	Freedom

AFFIRMATION _____

NIGHT   MOOD: Good-Average-Bad   ENERGY LEVEL: High-Average-Low

REASON _____

Strength	Hope	Spirit	Vision	
Awakening	Balance	Energy	Faith	Freedom

DAILY DISCOVERIES _____

_____
_____
_____
_____
_____
_____
_____
_____
_____
_____
_____
_____
_____
_____
_____
_____
_____
_____
_____
_____
_____

HEALTH PATTERNS _____

_____
_____
_____
_____
_____
_____

ACHIEVEMENT _____

ACT OF KINDNESS _____

DIET		**PHYSICAL DISCOMFORT**
Meat	☐☐☐☐☐☐☐☐☐☐☐☐	
Bread	☐☐☐☐☐☐☐☐☐☐☐☐	
Dairy	☐☐☐☐☐☐☐☐☐☐☐☐	
Vegetables	☐☐☐☐☐☐☐☐☐☐☐☐	
Fruit	☐☐☐☐☐☐☐☐☐☐☐☐	
Water	☐☐☐☐☐☐☐☐☐☐☐☐	
Vitamins	☐☐☐☐☐☐☐☐☐☐☐☐	

PLAY

Exercise ☐	Laugh ☐	Read ☐	
Meditation ☐	Dance ☐	_____ ☐	**CYCLE DAY**
Sex ☐	Sing ☐	_____ ☐	_____

DATE_____

Sleep Time ____:____   Wake Time ____:____   Hours of Sleep _____

DREAMS _____
_____
_____
_____
_____
_____
_____
_____
_____

MORNING   MOOD: Good-Average-Bad   **ENERGY LEVEL:** High-Average-Low

REASON _____

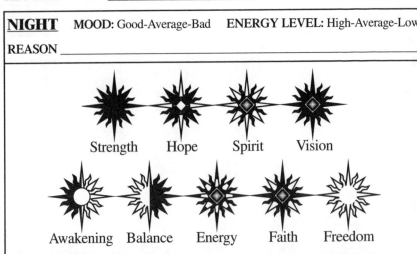

Strength	Hope	Spirit	Vision

Awakening	Balance	Energy	Faith	Freedom

AFFIRMATION _____

NIGHT   MOOD: Good-Average-Bad   **ENERGY LEVEL:** High-Average-Low

REASON _____

Strength	Hope	Spirit	Vision

Awakening	Balance	Energy	Faith	Freedom

DAILY DISCOVERIES _____

_____
_____
_____
_____
_____
_____
_____
_____
_____
_____
_____
_____
_____
_____
_____
_____
_____
_____
_____
_____
_____

HEALTH PATTERNS _____

_____
_____
_____
_____
_____
_____
_____

ACHIEVEMENT _____

ACT OF KINDNESS _____

DIET		**PHYSICAL**
Meat	☐☐☐☐☐☐☐☐☐☐☐☐	**DISCOMFORT**
Bread	☐☐☐☐☐☐☐☐☐☐☐☐	
Dairy	☐☐☐☐☐☐☐☐☐☐☐☐	
Vegetables	☐☐☐☐☐☐☐☐☐☐☐☐	
Fruit	☐☐☐☐☐☐☐☐☐☐☐☐	
Water	☐☐☐☐☐☐☐☐☐☐☐☐	
Vitamins	☐☐☐☐☐☐☐☐☐☐☐☐	

PLAY

Exercise	☐	Laugh	☐	Read	☐
Meditation	☐	Dance	☐	_____	☐
Sex	☐	Sing	☐	_____	☐

CYCLE DAY

_____

DATE_____

Sleep Time ____:____   Wake Time ____:____   Hours of Sleep _____

DREAMS _____

_____

_____

_____

_____

_____

_____

_____

_____

MORNING   MOOD: Good-Average-Bad   ENERGY LEVEL: High-Average-Low

REASON _____

Strength	Hope	Spirit	Vision	
Awakening	Balance	Energy	Faith	Freedom

AFFIRMATION _____

NIGHT   MOOD: Good-Average-Bad   ENERGY LEVEL: High-Average-Low

REASON _____

Strength	Hope	Spirit	Vision	
Awakening	Balance	Energy	Faith	Freedom

DAILY DISCOVERIES _____

_____
_____
_____
_____
_____
_____
_____
_____
_____
_____
_____
_____
_____
_____
_____
_____
_____
_____
_____
_____
_____

HEALTH PATTERNS _____

_____
_____
_____
_____
_____
_____
_____

ACHIEVEMENT _____

ACT OF KINDNESS _____

DIET

Meat	☐	☐	☐	☐	☐	☐	☐	☐	☐	☐	☐
Bread	☐	☐	☐	☐	☐	☐	☐	☐	☐	☐	☐
Dairy	☐	☐	☐	☐	☐	☐	☐	☐	☐	☐	☐
Vegetables	☐	☐	☐	☐	☐	☐	☐	☐	☐	☐	☐
Fruit	☐	☐	☐	☐	☐	☐	☐	☐	☐	☐	☐
Water	☐	☐	☐	☐	☐	☐	☐	☐	☐	☐	☐
Vitamins	☐	☐	☐	☐	☐	☐	☐	☐	☐	☐	☐

PHYSICAL DISCOMFORT

PLAY

Exercise ☐   Laugh ☐   Read ☐
Meditation ☐   Dance ☐   _____ ☐
Sex ☐   Sing ☐   _____ ☐

CYCLE DAY

_____

DATE_____

Sleep Time ____:____ Wake Time ____:____ Hours of Sleep _____

DREAMS _____

_____

_____

_____

_____

_____

_____

_____

_____

MORNING   MOOD: Good-Average-Bad   ENERGY LEVEL: High-Average-Low

REASON _____

Strength   Hope   Spirit   Vision

Awakening   Balance   Energy   Faith   Freedom

AFFIRMATION _____

NIGHT   MOOD: Good-Average-Bad   ENERGY LEVEL: High-Average-Low

REASON _____

Strength   Hope   Spirit   Vision

Awakening   Balance   Energy   Faith   Freedom

DAILY DISCOVERIES _____

_____
_____
_____
_____
_____
_____
_____
_____
_____
_____
_____
_____
_____
_____
_____
_____
_____
_____
_____
_____
_____

HEALTH PATTERNS _____

_____
_____
_____
_____
_____
_____
_____

ACHIEVEMENT _____
ACT OF KINDNESS _____

DIET

Meat	☐☐☐☐☐☐☐☐☐☐☐☐
Bread	☐☐☐☐☐☐☐☐☐☐☐☐
Dairy	☐☐☐☐☐☐☐☐☐☐☐
Vegetables	☐☐☐☐☐☐☐☐☐☐☐
Fruit	☐☐☐☐☐☐☐☐☐☐☐
Water	☐☐☐☐☐☐☐☐☐☐☐
Vitamins	☐☐☐☐☐☐☐☐☐☐☐

PHYSICAL DISCOMFORT

PLAY

Exercise	☐	Laugh	☐	Read	☐
Meditation	☐	Dance	☐	_____	☐
Sex	☐	Sing	☐	_____	☐

CYCLE DAY
_____

DATE_____

Sleep Time ____:____ Wake Time ____:____ Hours of Sleep _____

DREAMS _____
_____
_____
_____
_____
_____
_____
_____
_____

MORNING   MOOD: Good-Average-Bad   ENERGY LEVEL: High-Average-Low

REASON _____

Strength   Hope   Spirit   Vision

Awakening   Balance   Energy   Faith   Freedom

AFFIRMATION _____

NIGHT   MOOD: Good-Average-Bad   ENERGY LEVEL: High-Average-Low

REASON _____

Strength   Hope   Spirit   Vision

Awakening   Balance   Energy   Faith   Freedom

DAILY DISCOVERIES _____

_____
_____
_____
_____
_____
_____
_____
_____
_____
_____
_____
_____
_____
_____
_____
_____
_____
_____
_____
_____
_____

HEALTH PATTERNS _____

_____
_____
_____
_____
_____
_____
_____

ACHIEVEMENT _____

ACT OF KINDNESS _____

DIET

		PHYSICAL DISCOMFORT
Meat	☐☐☐☐☐☐☐☐☐☐☐	
Bread	☐☐☐☐☐☐☐☐☐☐☐	
Dairy	☐☐☐☐☐☐☐☐☐☐	
Vegetables	☐☐☐☐☐☐☐☐☐☐	
Fruit	☐☐☐☐☐☐☐☐☐☐	
Water	☐☐☐☐☐☐☐☐☐☐	
Vitamins	☐☐☐☐☐☐☐☐☐☐	

PLAY

Exercise	☐	Laugh	☐	Read	☐
Meditation	☐	Dance	☐	_____	☐
Sex	☐	Sing	☐	_____	☐

CYCLE DAY

_____

DATE_____

Sleep Time ____ : ____ Wake Time ____ : ____ Hours of Sleep _____

DREAMS _____
_____
_____
_____
_____
_____
_____
_____
_____

MORNING   MOOD: Good-Average-Bad   ENERGY LEVEL: High-Average-Low

REASON _____

Strength   Hope   Spirit   Vision

Awakening   Balance   Energy   Faith   Freedom

AFFIRMATION _____

NIGHT   MOOD: Good-Average-Bad   ENERGY LEVEL: High-Average-Low

REASON _____

Strength   Hope   Spirit   Vision

Awakening   Balance   Energy   Faith   Freedom

DAILY DISCOVERIES _____

_____
_____
_____
_____
_____
_____
_____
_____
_____
_____
_____
_____
_____
_____
_____
_____
_____
_____
_____
_____

HEALTH PATTERNS _____

_____
_____
_____
_____
_____
_____

ACHIEVEMENT _____
ACT OF KINDNESS _____

DIET		**PHYSICAL DISCOMFORT**
Meat	□□□□□□□□□□□	
Bread	□□□□□□□□□□□	
Dairy	□□□□□□□□□□□	
Vegetables	□□□□□□□□□□□	
Fruit	□□□□□□□□□□□	
Water	□□□□□□□□□□□	
Vitamins	□□□□□□□□□□□	

PLAY

Exercise	□	Laugh	□	Read	□
Meditation	□	Dance	□	_____	□
Sex	□	Sing	□	_____	□

CYCLE DAY _____

DATE_____

Sleep Time ____:____   Wake Time ____:____   Hours of Sleep _____

DREAMS _____
_____
_____
_____
_____
_____
_____
_____
_____

MORNING   MOOD: Good-Average-Bad   ENERGY LEVEL: High-Average-Low

REASON _____

Strength   Hope   Spirit   Vision

Awakening   Balance   Energy   Faith   Freedom

AFFIRMATION _____

NIGHT   MOOD: Good-Average-Bad   ENERGY LEVEL: High-Average-Low

REASON _____

Strength   Hope   Spirit   Vision

Awakening   Balance   Energy   Faith   Freedom

DAILY DISCOVERIES _____

_____
_____
_____
_____
_____
_____
_____
_____
_____
_____
_____
_____
_____
_____
_____
_____
_____
_____
_____
_____
_____

HEALTH PATTERNS _____

_____
_____
_____
_____
_____
_____
_____

ACHIEVEMENT _____

ACT OF KINDNESS _____

DIET

Meat	☐	☐	☐	☐	☐	☐	☐	☐	☐	☐	☐	☐
Bread	☐	☐	☐	☐	☐	☐	☐	☐	☐	☐	☐	☐
Dairy	☐	☐	☐	☐	☐	☐	☐	☐	☐	☐	☐	☐
Vegetables	☐	☐	☐	☐	☐	☐	☐	☐	☐	☐	☐	☐
Fruit	☐	☐	☐	☐	☐	☐	☐	☐	☐	☐	☐	☐
Water	☐	☐	☐	☐	☐	☐	☐	☐	☐	☐	☐	☐
Vitamins	☐	☐	☐	☐	☐	☐	☐	☐	☐	☐	☐	☐

PHYSICAL DISCOMFORT

PLAY

Exercise	☐	Laugh	☐	Read	☐
Meditation	☐	Dance	☐	_____	☐
Sex	☐	Sing	☐	_____	☐

CYCLE DAY

_____

DATE_____

Sleep Time ____:____ Wake Time ____:____ Hours of Sleep _____

DREAMS _____
_____
_____
_____
_____
_____
_____
_____
_____

MORNING   MOOD: Good-Average-Bad   ENERGY LEVEL: High-Average-Low

REASON _____

Strength   Hope   Spirit   Vision

Awakening   Balance   Energy   Faith   Freedom

AFFIRMATION _____

NIGHT   MOOD: Good-Average-Bad   ENERGY LEVEL: High-Average-Low

REASON _____

Strength   Hope   Spirit   Vision

Awakening   Balance   Energy   Faith   Freedom

DAILY DISCOVERIES _____

_____
_____
_____
_____
_____
_____
_____
_____
_____
_____
_____
_____
_____
_____
_____
_____
_____
_____
_____
_____

HEALTH PATTERNS _____

_____
_____
_____
_____
_____
_____

ACHIEVEMENT _____
ACT OF KINDNESS _____

DIET

Meat	☐	☐	☐	☐	☐	☐	☐	☐	☐	☐	☐	☐
Bread	☐	☐	☐	☐	☐	☐	☐	☐	☐	☐	☐	☐
Dairy	☐	☐	☐	☐	☐	☐	☐	☐	☐	☐	☐	☐
Vegetables	☐	☐	☐	☐	☐	☐	☐	☐	☐	☐	☐	☐
Fruit	☐	☐	☐	☐	☐	☐	☐	☐	☐	☐	☐	☐
Water	☐	☐	☐	☐	☐	☐	☐	☐	☐	☐	☐	☐
Vitamins	☐	☐	☐	☐	☐	☐	☐	☐	☐	☐	☐	☐

PHYSICAL DISCOMFORT

PLAY

Exercise	☐	Laugh	☐	Read	☐
Meditation	☐	Dance	☐	_____	☐
Sex	☐	Sing	☐	_____	☐

CYCLE DAY

_____

DATE_____

Sleep Time ____:____ Wake Time ____:____ Hours of Sleep _____

DREAMS _____
_____
_____
_____
_____
_____
_____
_____
_____

MORNING   MOOD: Good-Average-Bad   ENERGY LEVEL: High-Average-Low

REASON _____

Strength	Hope	Spirit	Vision	
Awakening	Balance	Energy	Faith	Freedom

AFFIRMATION _____

NIGHT   MOOD: Good-Average-Bad   ENERGY LEVEL: High-Average-Low

REASON _____

Strength	Hope	Spirit	Vision	
Awakening	Balance	Energy	Faith	Freedom

DAILY DISCOVERIES _____

_____
_____
_____
_____
_____
_____
_____
_____
_____
_____
_____
_____
_____
_____
_____
_____
_____
_____
_____
_____

HEALTH PATTERNS _____

_____
_____
_____
_____
_____
_____

ACHIEVEMENT _____

ACT OF KINDNESS _____

DIET

Meat	☐☐☐☐☐☐☐☐☐☐☐☐☐		**PHYSICAL**
Bread	☐☐☐☐☐☐☐☐☐☐☐☐☐		**DISCOMFORT**
Dairy	☐☐☐☐☐☐☐☐☐☐☐☐☐		
Vegetables	☐☐☐☐☐☐☐☐☐☐☐☐☐		
Fruit	☐☐☐☐☐☐☐☐☐☐☐☐☐		
Water	☐☐☐☐☐☐☐☐☐☐☐☐☐		
Vitamins	☐☐☐☐☐☐☐☐☐☐☐☐☐		

PLAY

Exercise	☐	Laugh	☐	Read	☐
Meditation	☐	Dance	☐	_____	☐
Sex	☐	Sing	☐	_____	☐

CYCLE DAY

_____

DATE_____

Sleep Time ____ : ____ Wake Time ____ : ____ Hours of Sleep _____

DREAMS _____
_____
_____
_____
_____
_____
_____
_____
_____
_____

<u>**MORNING**</u>   **MOOD:** Good-Average-Bad   **ENERGY LEVEL:** High-Average-Low

REASON _____

Strength	Hope	Spirit	Vision	
Awakening	Balance	Energy	Faith	Freedom

AFFIRMATION _____

<u>**NIGHT**</u>   **MOOD:** Good-Average-Bad   **ENERGY LEVEL:** High-Average-Low

REASON _____

Strength	Hope	Spirit	Vision	
Awakening	Balance	Energy	Faith	Freedom

DAILY DISCOVERIES _____

_____
_____
_____
_____
_____
_____
_____
_____
_____
_____
_____
_____
_____
_____
_____
_____
_____
_____
_____
_____
_____
_____

HEALTH PATTERNS _____

_____
_____
_____
_____
_____
_____
_____

ACHIEVEMENT _____

ACT OF KINDNESS _____

DIET

Meat	☐☐☐☐☐☐☐☐☐☐☐☐☐	**PHYSICAL**
Bread	☐☐☐☐☐☐☐☐☐☐☐☐☐	**DISCOMFORT**
Dairy	☐☐☐☐☐☐☐☐☐☐☐☐	
Vegetables	☐☐☐☐☐☐☐☐☐☐☐☐	
Fruit	☐☐☐☐☐☐☐☐☐☐☐☐	
Water	☐☐☐☐☐☐☐☐☐☐☐☐	
Vitamins	☐☐☐☐☐☐☐☐☐☐☐☐	

PLAY

Exercise	☐	Laugh	☐	Read	☐
Meditation	☐	Dance	☐	_____	☐
Sex	☐	Sing	☐	_____	☐

CYCLE DAY

_____

DATE_____

Sleep Time _____:_____ Wake Time _____:_____ Hours of Sleep _____

DREAMS _____
_____
_____
_____
_____
_____
_____
_____
_____

MORNING   MOOD: Good-Average-Bad   ENERGY LEVEL: High-Average-Low

REASON _____

Strength   Hope   Spirit   Vision

Awakening   Balance   Energy   Faith   Freedom

AFFIRMATION _____

NIGHT   MOOD: Good-Average-Bad   ENERGY LEVEL: High-Average-Low

REASON _____

Strength   Hope   Spirit   Vision

Awakening   Balance   Energy   Faith   Freedom

DAILY DISCOVERIES _____

_____
_____
_____
_____
_____
_____
_____
_____
_____
_____
_____
_____
_____
_____
_____
_____
_____
_____
_____
_____

HEALTH PATTERNS _____

_____
_____
_____
_____
_____
_____

ACHIEVEMENT _____
ACT OF KINDNESS _____

DIET		**PHYSICAL DISCOMFORT**
Meat	□□□□□□□□□□□	
Bread	□□□□□□□□□□□	
Dairy	□□□□□□□□□□□	
Vegetables	□□□□□□□□□□□	
Fruit	□□□□□□□□□□□	
Water	□□□□□□□□□□□	
Vitamins	□□□□□□□□□□□	

PLAY

Exercise	□	Laugh	□	Read	□
Meditation	□	Dance	□	_____	□
Sex	□	Sing	□	_____	□

CYCLE DAY

_____

DATE_____

Sleep Time ____:____ Wake Time ____:____ Hours of Sleep _____

DREAMS _____
_____
_____
_____
_____
_____
_____
_____

MORNING   MOOD: Good-Average-Bad   ENERGY LEVEL: High-Average-Low

REASON _____

| Strength | Hope | Spirit | Vision |

| Awakening | Balance | Energy | Faith | Freedom |

AFFIRMATION _____

NIGHT   MOOD: Good-Average-Bad   ENERGY LEVEL: High-Average-Low

REASON _____

| Strength | Hope | Spirit | Vision |

| Awakening | Balance | Energy | Faith | Freedom |

DAILY DISCOVERIES _____

_____
_____
_____
_____
_____
_____
_____
_____
_____
_____
_____
_____
_____
_____
_____
_____
_____
_____
_____
_____

HEALTH PATTERNS _____

_____
_____
_____
_____
_____
_____
_____

ACHIEVEMENT _____

ACT OF KINDNESS _____

DIET
Meat
Bread
Dairy
Vegetables
Fruit
Water
Vitamins

PHYSICAL DISCOMFORT

PLAY
Exercise	☐	Laugh	☐	Read	☐
Meditation	☐	Dance	☐	_____	☐
Sex	☐	Sing	☐	_____	☐

CYCLE DAY

_____

DATE_____

Sleep Time ____:____   Wake Time ____:____   Hours of Sleep _____

DREAMS _____
_____
_____
_____
_____
_____
_____
_____
_____

MORNING   MOOD: Good-Average-Bad   ENERGY LEVEL: High-Average-Low

REASON _____

| Strength | Hope | Spirit | Vision |

| Awakening | Balance | Energy | Faith | Freedom |

AFFIRMATION _____

NIGHT   MOOD: Good-Average-Bad   ENERGY LEVEL: High-Average-Low

REASON _____

| Strength | Hope | Spirit | Vision |

| Awakening | Balance | Energy | Faith | Freedom |

DAILY DISCOVERIES _____

_____
_____
_____
_____
_____
_____
_____
_____
_____
_____
_____
_____
_____
_____
_____
_____
_____
_____
_____
_____

HEALTH PATTERNS _____

_____
_____
_____
_____
_____
_____
_____

ACHIEVEMENT _____

ACT OF KINDNESS _____

DIET

Meat	☐	☐	☐	☐	☐	☐	☐	☐	☐	☐	☐	☐
Bread	☐	☐	☐	☐	☐	☐	☐	☐	☐	☐	☐	☐
Dairy	☐	☐	☐	☐	☐	☐	☐	☐	☐	☐	☐	☐
Vegetables	☐	☐	☐	☐	☐	☐	☐	☐	☐	☐	☐	☐
Fruit	☐	☐	☐	☐	☐	☐	☐	☐	☐	☐	☐	☐
Water	☐	☐	☐	☐	☐	☐	☐	☐	☐	☐	☐	☐
Vitamins	☐	☐	☐	☐	☐	☐	☐	☐	☐	☐	☐	☐

PHYSICAL DISCOMFORT

PLAY

Exercise	☐	Laugh	☐	Read	☐	
Meditation	☐	Dance	☐	_____	☐	
Sex	☐	Sing	☐	_____	☐	

CYCLE DAY

_____

DATE_____

Sleep Time ____:____ Wake Time ____:____ Hours of Sleep _____

DREAMS _____

_____
_____
_____
_____
_____
_____
_____
_____

MORNING   MOOD: Good-Average-Bad   ENERGY LEVEL: High-Average-Low

REASON _____

Strength   Hope   Spirit   Vision

Awakening Balance Energy Faith Freedom

AFFIRMATION _____

NIGHT   MOOD: Good-Average-Bad   ENERGY LEVEL: High-Average-Low

REASON _____

Strength   Hope   Spirit   Vision

Awakening Balance Energy Faith Freedom

DAILY DISCOVERIES _____

_____
_____
_____
_____
_____
_____
_____
_____
_____
_____
_____
_____
_____
_____
_____
_____
_____
_____
_____
_____
_____
_____
_____

HEALTH PATTERNS _____

_____
_____
_____
_____
_____
_____
_____

ACHIEVEMENT _____

ACT OF KINDNESS _____

DIET		**PHYSICAL**
Meat	☐☐☐☐☐☐☐☐☐☐☐☐	**DISCOMFORT**
Bread	☐☐☐☐☐☐☐☐☐☐☐☐	
Dairy	☐☐☐☐☐☐☐☐☐☐☐☐	
Vegetables	☐☐☐☐☐☐☐☐☐☐☐☐	
Fruit	☐☐☐☐☐☐☐☐☐☐☐☐	
Water	☐☐☐☐☐☐☐☐☐☐☐☐	
Vitamins	☐☐☐☐☐☐☐☐☐☐☐☐	

PLAY

Exercise	☐	Laugh	☐	Read	☐
Meditation	☐	Dance	☐	_____	☐
Sex	☐	Sing	☐	_____	☐

CYCLE DAY

_____

DATE_____

Sleep Time ____:____ Wake Time ____:____ Hours of Sleep _____

DREAMS _____
_____
_____
_____
_____
_____
_____
_____
_____

MORNING   MOOD: Good-Average-Bad   ENERGY LEVEL: High-Average-Low

REASON _____

Strength	Hope	Spirit	Vision

Awakening	Balance	Energy	Faith	Freedom

AFFIRMATION _____

NIGHT   MOOD: Good-Average-Bad   ENERGY LEVEL: High-Average-Low

REASON _____

Strength	Hope	Spirit	Vision

Awakening	Balance	Energy	Faith	Freedom

DAILY DISCOVERIES _____

_____
_____
_____
_____
_____
_____
_____
_____
_____
_____
_____
_____
_____
_____
_____
_____
_____
_____
_____

HEALTH PATTERNS _____

_____
_____
_____
_____
_____
_____
_____

ACHIEVEMENT _____
ACT OF KINDNESS _____

DIET

Meat	☐	☐	☐	☐	☐	☐	☐	☐	☐	☐	☐	☐	☐
Bread	☐	☐	☐	☐	☐	☐	☐	☐	☐	☐	☐	☐	☐
Dairy	☐	☐	☐	☐	☐	☐	☐	☐	☐	☐	☐	☐	
Vegetables	☐	☐	☐	☐	☐	☐	☐	☐	☐	☐	☐	☐	
Fruit	☐	☐	☐	☐	☐	☐	☐	☐	☐	☐	☐	☐	
Water	☐	☐	☐	☐	☐	☐	☐	☐	☐	☐	☐	☐	
Vitamins	☐	☐	☐	☐	☐	☐	☐	☐	☐	☐	☐	☐	

PHYSICAL DISCOMFORT

PLAY

Exercise	☐	Laugh	☐	Read	☐	
Meditation	☐	Dance	☐	_____	☐	
Sex	☐	Sing	☐	_____	☐	

CYCLE DAY

_____

DATE_____

Sleep Time ____:____ Wake Time ____:____ Hours of Sleep _____

DREAMS _____
_____
_____
_____
_____
_____
_____
_____
_____

<u>**MORNING**</u>   MOOD: Good-Average-Bad   ENERGY LEVEL: High-Average-Low

REASON _____

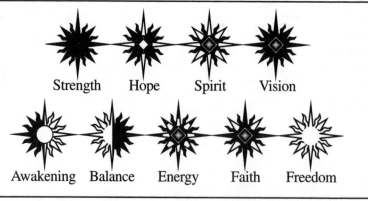

Strength   Hope   Spirit   Vision

Awakening   Balance   Energy   Faith   Freedom

AFFIRMATION _____

<u>**NIGHT**</u>   MOOD: Good-Average-Bad   ENERGY LEVEL: High-Average-Low

REASON _____

Strength   Hope   Spirit   Vision

Awakening   Balance   Energy   Faith   Freedom

DAILY DISCOVERIES _____

_____
_____
_____
_____
_____
_____
_____
_____
_____
_____
_____
_____
_____
_____
_____
_____
_____
_____
_____
_____

HEALTH PATTERNS _____

_____
_____
_____
_____
_____
_____
_____

ACHIEVEMENT _____

ACT OF KINDNESS _____

DIET

Meat	□	□	□	□	□	□	□	□	□	□	□	□
Bread	□	□	□	□	□	□	□	□	□	□	□	□
Dairy	□	□	□	□	□	□	□	□	□	□	□	□
Vegetables	□	□	□	□	□	□	□	□	□	□	□	□
Fruit	□	□	□	□	□	□	□	□	□	□	□	□
Water	□	□	□	□	□	□	□	□	□	□	□	□
Vitamins	□	□	□	□	□	□	□	□	□	□	□	□

PHYSICAL DISCOMFORT

PLAY

Exercise	□	Laugh	□	Read	□	
Meditation	□	Dance	□	_____	□	
Sex	□	Sing	□	_____	□	

CYCLE DAY

_____

DATE_____

Sleep Time ____:____   **Wake Time** ____:____   **Hours of Sleep** _____

DREAMS _____
_____
_____
_____
_____
_____
_____
_____

MORNING   **MOOD:** Good-Average-Bad   **ENERGY LEVEL:** High-Average-Low

REASON _____

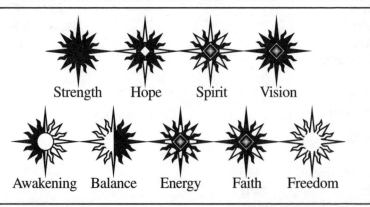

Strength	Hope	Spirit	Vision

Awakening	Balance	Energy	Faith	Freedom

AFFIRMATION _____

NIGHT   **MOOD:** Good-Average-Bad   **ENERGY LEVEL:** High-Average-Low

REASON _____

Strength	Hope	Spirit	Vision

Awakening	Balance	Energy	Faith	Freedom

DAILY DISCOVERIES _____
_____
_____
_____
_____
_____
_____
_____
_____
_____
_____
_____
_____
_____
_____
_____
_____
_____
_____
_____
_____
_____
_____

HEALTH PATTERNS _____
_____
_____
_____
_____
_____
_____

ACHIEVEMENT _____
ACT OF KINDNESS _____

DIET		
Meat	☐☐☐☐☐☐☐☐☐☐☐☐	**PHYSICAL**
Bread	☐☐☐☐☐☐☐☐☐☐☐☐	**DISCOMFORT**
Dairy	☐☐☐☐☐☐☐☐☐☐☐☐	
Vegetables	☐☐☐☐☐☐☐☐☐☐☐☐	
Fruit	☐☐☐☐☐☐☐☐☐☐☐☐	
Water	☐☐☐☐☐☐☐☐☐☐☐☐	
Vitamins	☐☐☐☐☐☐☐☐☐☐☐	

PLAY

Exercise	☐	Laugh	☐	Read	☐
Meditation	☐	Dance	☐	_____	☐
Sex	☐	Sing	☐	_____	☐

CYCLE DAY

_____

DATE_____

Sleep Time ____ : ____ **Wake Time** ____ : ____ **Hours of Sleep** _____

DREAMS _____

_____

_____

_____

_____

_____

_____

_____

_____

<u>MORNING</u>   **MOOD:** Good-Average-Bad   **ENERGY LEVEL:** High-Average-Low

REASON _____

Strength   Hope   Spirit   Vision

Awakening   Balance   Energy   Faith   Freedom

AFFIRMATION _____

<u>NIGHT</u>   **MOOD:** Good-Average-Bad   **ENERGY LEVEL:** High-Average-Low

REASON _____

Strength   Hope   Spirit   Vision

Awakening   Balance   Energy   Faith   Freedom

DAILY DISCOVERIES _____

_____
_____
_____
_____
_____
_____
_____
_____
_____
_____
_____
_____
_____
_____
_____
_____
_____
_____
_____
_____

HEALTH PATTERNS _____

_____
_____
_____
_____
_____
_____

ACHIEVEMENT _____

ACT OF KINDNESS _____

DIET		**PHYSICAL**
Meat	☐☐☐☐☐☐☐☐☐☐☐☐	**DISCOMFORT**
Bread	☐☐☐☐☐☐☐☐☐☐☐☐	
Dairy	☐☐☐☐☐☐☐☐☐☐☐☐	
Vegetables	☐☐☐☐☐☐☐☐☐☐☐☐	
Fruit	☐☐☐☐☐☐☐☐☐☐☐☐	
Water	☐☐☐☐☐☐☐☐☐☐☐☐	
Vitamins	☐☐☐☐☐☐☐☐☐☐☐☐	

PLAY

Exercise	☐	Laugh	☐	Read	☐
Meditation	☐	Dance	☐	_____	☐
Sex	☐	Sing	☐	_____	☐

CYCLE DAY

_____

DATE_____

Sleep Time ____:____ Wake Time ____:____ Hours of Sleep _____

DREAMS _____
_____
_____
_____
_____
_____
_____
_____
_____

MORNING   MOOD: Good-Average-Bad   ENERGY LEVEL: High-Average-Low

REASON _____

Strength	Hope	Spirit	Vision

Awakening	Balance	Energy	Faith	Freedom

AFFIRMATION _____

NIGHT   MOOD: Good-Average-Bad   ENERGY LEVEL: High-Average-Low

REASON _____

Strength	Hope	Spirit	Vision

Awakening	Balance	Energy	Faith	Freedom

DAILY DISCOVERIES _____
_____
_____
_____
_____
_____
_____
_____
_____
_____
_____
_____
_____
_____
_____
_____
_____
_____
_____
_____
_____
_____

HEALTH PATTERNS _____
_____
_____
_____
_____
_____
_____

ACHIEVEMENT _____
ACT OF KINDNESS _____

DIET		**PHYSICAL**
Meat	☐☐☐☐☐☐☐☐☐☐☐	**DISCOMFORT**
Bread	☐☐☐☐☐☐☐☐☐☐☐	
Dairy	☐☐☐☐☐☐☐☐☐☐☐	
Vegetables	☐☐☐☐☐☐☐☐☐☐☐	
Fruit	☐☐☐☐☐☐☐☐☐☐☐	
Water	☐☐☐☐☐☐☐☐☐☐☐	
Vitamins	☐☐☐☐☐☐☐☐☐☐☐	

PLAY

Exercise	☐	Laugh	☐	Read	☐
Meditation	☐	Dance	☐	_____	☐
Sex	☐	Sing	☐	_____	☐

CYCLE DAY

_____

DATE_____

Sleep Time ____:____   Wake Time ____:____   Hours of Sleep _____

DREAMS _____
_____
_____
_____
_____
_____
_____
_____
_____

MORNING   MOOD: Good-Average-Bad   ENERGY LEVEL: High-Average-Low

REASON _____

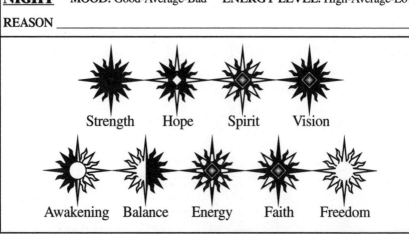

Strength	Hope	Spirit	Vision

Awakening	Balance	Energy	Faith	Freedom

AFFIRMATION _____

NIGHT   MOOD: Good-Average-Bad   ENERGY LEVEL: High-Average-Low

REASON _____

Strength	Hope	Spirit	Vision

Awakening	Balance	Energy	Faith	Freedom

DAILY DISCOVERIES _____

_____
_____
_____
_____
_____
_____
_____
_____
_____
_____
_____
_____
_____
_____
_____
_____
_____
_____
_____
_____
_____

HEALTH PATTERNS _____

_____
_____
_____
_____
_____
_____
_____

ACHIEVEMENT _____
ACT OF KINDNESS _____

DIET

Meat	□	□	□	□	□	□	□	□	□	□	□	□
Bread	□	□	□	□	□	□	□	□	□	□	□	□
Dairy	□	□	□	□	□	□	□	□	□	□	□	□
Vegetables	□	□	□	□	□	□	□	□	□	□	□	□
Fruit	□	□	□	□	□	□	□	□	□	□	□	□
Water	□	□	□	□	□	□	□	□	□	□	□	□
Vitamins	□	□	□	□	□	□	□	□	□	□	□	□

PHYSICAL DISCOMFORT

PLAY

Exercise	□	Laugh	□	Read	□	
Meditation	□	Dance	□	_____	□	
Sex	□	Sing	□	_____	□	

CYCLE DAY

_____

DATE_____

Sleep Time _____:_____ Wake Time _____:_____ Hours of Sleep _____

DREAMS _____
_____
_____
_____
_____
_____
_____
_____
_____

MORNING   MOOD: Good-Average-Bad   ENERGY LEVEL: High-Average-Low

REASON _____

Strength	Hope	Spirit	Vision	
Awakening	Balance	Energy	Faith	Freedom

AFFIRMATION _____

NIGHT   MOOD: Good-Average-Bad   ENERGY LEVEL: High-Average-Low

REASON _____

Strength	Hope	Spirit	Vision	
Awakening	Balance	Energy	Faith	Freedom

DAILY DISCOVERIES _____

_____
_____
_____
_____
_____
_____
_____
_____
_____
_____
_____
_____
_____
_____
_____
_____
_____
_____
_____
_____

HEALTH PATTERNS _____

_____
_____
_____
_____
_____
_____

ACHIEVEMENT _____

ACT OF KINDNESS _____

DIET		
Meat	☐☐☐☐☐☐☐☐☐☐☐	**PHYSICAL**
Bread	☐☐☐☐☐☐☐☐☐☐☐	**DISCOMFORT**
Dairy	☐☐☐☐☐☐☐☐☐☐☐	
Vegetables	☐☐☐☐☐☐☐☐☐☐☐	
Fruit	☐☐☐☐☐☐☐☐☐☐☐	
Water	☐☐☐☐☐☐☐☐☐☐☐	
Vitamins	☐☐☐☐☐☐☐☐☐☐☐	

PLAY

Exercise	☐	Laugh	☐	Read	☐
Meditation	☐	Dance	☐	_____	☐
Sex	☐	Sing	☐	_____	☐

CYCLE DAY

_____

DATE_____

Sleep Time _____ : _____   Wake Time _____ : _____   Hours of Sleep _____

DREAMS _____

_____

_____

_____

_____

_____

_____

_____

_____

MORNING   MOOD: Good-Average-Bad   ENERGY LEVEL: High-Average-Low

REASON _____

Strength   Hope   Spirit   Vision

Awakening   Balance   Energy   Faith   Freedom

AFFIRMATION _____

NIGHT   MOOD: Good-Average-Bad   ENERGY LEVEL: High-Average-Low

REASON _____

Strength   Hope   Spirit   Vision

Awakening   Balance   Energy   Faith   Freedom

DAILY DISCOVERIES _____

_____
_____
_____
_____
_____
_____
_____
_____
_____
_____
_____
_____
_____
_____
_____
_____
_____
_____
_____
_____
_____
_____
_____

HEALTH PATTERNS _____

_____
_____
_____
_____
_____
_____
_____

ACHIEVEMENT _____

ACT OF KINDNESS _____

DIET		**PHYSICAL DISCOMFORT**
Meat	☐☐☐☐☐☐☐☐☐☐☐☐	
Bread	☐☐☐☐☐☐☐☐☐☐☐☐	
Dairy	☐☐☐☐☐☐☐☐☐☐☐☐	
Vegetables	☐☐☐☐☐☐☐☐☐☐☐☐	
Fruit	☐☐☐☐☐☐☐☐☐☐☐☐	
Water	☐☐☐☐☐☐☐☐☐☐☐☐	
Vitamins	☐☐☐☐☐☐☐☐☐☐☐☐	

PLAY

Exercise	☐	Laugh	☐	Read	☐
Meditation	☐	Dance	☐	_____	☐
Sex	☐	Sing	☐	_____	☐

CYCLE DAY

_____

DATE_____

Sleep Time ____:____   Wake Time ____:____   Hours of Sleep _____

DREAMS _____

_____

_____

_____

_____

_____

_____

_____

_____

_____

MORNING   MOOD: Good-Average-Bad   ENERGY LEVEL: High-Average-Low

REASON _____

Strength   Hope   Spirit   Vision

Awakening   Balance   Energy   Faith   Freedom

AFFIRMATION _____

NIGHT   MOOD: Good-Average-Bad   ENERGY LEVEL: High-Average-Low

REASON _____

Strength   Hope   Spirit   Vision

Awakening   Balance   Energy   Faith   Freedom

DAILY DISCOVERIES _____

_____
_____
_____
_____
_____
_____
_____
_____
_____
_____
_____
_____
_____
_____
_____
_____
_____
_____
_____
_____
_____

HEALTH PATTERNS _____

_____
_____
_____
_____
_____
_____

ACHIEVEMENT _____
ACT OF KINDNESS _____

DIET

		PHYSICAL
Meat	☐☐☐☐☐☐☐☐☐☐☐☐	**PHYSICAL**
Bread	☐☐☐☐☐☐☐☐☐☐☐☐	**DISCOMFORT**
Dairy	☐☐☐☐☐☐☐☐☐☐☐☐	
Vegetables	☐☐☐☐☐☐☐☐☐☐☐☐	
Fruit	☐☐☐☐☐☐☐☐☐☐☐☐	
Water	☐☐☐☐☐☐☐☐☐☐☐☐	
Vitamins	☐☐☐☐☐☐☐☐☐☐☐☐	

PLAY

Exercise	☐	Laugh	☐	Read	☐
Meditation	☐	Dance	☐	_____	☐
Sex	☐	Sing	☐	_____	☐

CYCLE DAY
_____

DATE_____

Sleep Time ____:____ Wake Time ____:____ Hours of Sleep _____

DREAMS _____
_____
_____
_____
_____
_____
_____
_____
_____
_____

MORNING   MOOD: Good-Average-Bad   ENERGY LEVEL: High-Average-Low

REASON _____

Strength	Hope	Spirit	Vision	

Awakening	Balance	Energy	Faith	Freedom

AFFIRMATION _____

NIGHT   MOOD: Good-Average-Bad   ENERGY LEVEL: High-Average-Low

REASON _____

Strength	Hope	Spirit	Vision	

Awakening	Balance	Energy	Faith	Freedom

DAILY DISCOVERIES _____

_____
_____
_____
_____
_____
_____
_____
_____
_____
_____
_____
_____
_____
_____
_____
_____
_____
_____
_____

HEALTH PATTERNS _____

_____
_____
_____
_____
_____
_____

ACHIEVEMENT _____
ACT OF KINDNESS _____

DIET

Meat	□	□	□	□	□	□	□	□	□	□	□
Bread	□	□	□	□	□	□	□	□	□	□	□
Dairy	□	□	□	□	□	□	□	□	□	□	
Vegetables	□	□	□	□	□	□	□	□	□	□	
Fruit	□	□	□	□	□	□	□	□	□	□	
Water	□	□	□	□	□	□	□	□	□	□	
Vitamins	□	□	□	□	□	□	□	□	□	□	

PHYSICAL DISCOMFORT

PLAY

Exercise	□	Laugh	□	Read	□	
Meditation	□	Dance	□	_____	□	
Sex	□	Sing	□	_____	□	

CYCLE DAY

_____

DATE_____

Sleep Time ____ : ____   Wake Time ____ : ____   Hours of Sleep _____

DREAMS _____

_____

_____

_____

_____

_____

_____

_____

_____

MORNING   MOOD: Good-Average-Bad   ENERGY LEVEL: High-Average-Low

REASON _____

Strength	Hope	Spirit	Vision	
Awakening	Balance	Energy	Faith	Freedom

AFFIRMATION _____

NIGHT   MOOD: Good-Average-Bad   ENERGY LEVEL: High-Average-Low

REASON _____

Strength	Hope	Spirit	Vision	
Awakening	Balance	Energy	Faith	Freedom

DAILY DISCOVERIES _____

_____
_____
_____
_____
_____
_____
_____
_____
_____
_____
_____
_____
_____
_____
_____
_____
_____
_____
_____
_____

HEALTH PATTERNS _____

_____
_____
_____
_____
_____
_____
_____

ACHIEVEMENT _____
ACT OF KINDNESS _____

DIET

Meat	☐	☐	☐	☐	☐	☐	☐	☐	☐	☐	☐
Bread	☐	☐	☐	☐	☐	☐	☐	☐	☐	☐	☐
Dairy	☐	☐	☐	☐	☐	☐	☐	☐	☐	☐	☐
Vegetables	☐	☐	☐	☐	☐	☐	☐	☐	☐	☐	☐
Fruit	☐	☐	☐	☐	☐	☐	☐	☐	☐	☐	☐
Water	☐	☐	☐	☐	☐	☐	☐	☐	☐	☐	☐
Vitamins	☐	☐	☐	☐	☐	☐	☐	☐	☐	☐	☐

PHYSICAL DISCOMFORT

PLAY

Exercise	☐	Laugh	☐	Read	☐
Meditation	☐	Dance	☐	_____	☐
Sex	☐	Sing	☐	_____	☐

CYCLE DAY

_____

DATE_____

Sleep Time ____:____ Wake Time ____:____ Hours of Sleep _____

DREAMS _____
_____
_____
_____
_____
_____
_____
_____

MORNING   MOOD: Good-Average-Bad ENERGY LEVEL: High-Average-Low

REASON _____

Strength	Hope	Spirit	Vision	
Awakening	Balance	Energy	Faith	Freedom

AFFIRMATION _____

NIGHT   MOOD: Good-Average-Bad ENERGY LEVEL: High-Average-Low

REASON _____

Strength	Hope	Spirit	Vision	
Awakening	Balance	Energy	Faith	Freedom

DAILY DISCOVERIES _____

_____
_____
_____
_____
_____
_____
_____
_____
_____
_____
_____
_____
_____
_____
_____
_____
_____
_____
_____
_____

HEALTH PATTERNS _____

_____
_____
_____
_____
_____
_____

ACHIEVEMENT _____
ACT OF KINDNESS _____

DIET														
Meat	☐	☐	☐	☐	☐	☐	☐	☐	☐	☐	☐	☐	☐	
Bread	☐	☐	☐	☐	☐	☐	☐	☐	☐	☐	☐	☐	☐	
Dairy	☐	☐	☐	☐	☐	☐	☐	☐	☐	☐	☐	☐	☐	
Vegetables	☐	☐	☐	☐	☐	☐	☐	☐	☐	☐	☐	☐	☐	
Fruit	☐	☐	☐	☐	☐	☐	☐	☐	☐	☐	☐	☐	☐	
Water	☐	☐	☐	☐	☐	☐	☐	☐	☐	☐	☐	☐	☐	
Vitamins	☐	☐	☐	☐	☐	☐	☐	☐	☐	☐	☐	☐	☐	

PHYSICAL DISCOMFORT

PLAY

Exercise	☐	Laugh	☐	Read	☐
Meditation	☐	Dance	☐	_____	☐
Sex	☐	Sing	☐	_____	☐

CYCLE DAY

_____

DATE_____

Sleep Time ____:____   Wake Time ____:____   Hours of Sleep _____

DREAMS _____

_____

_____

_____

_____

_____

_____

_____

MORNING   MOOD: Good-Average-Bad   ENERGY LEVEL: High-Average-Low

REASON _____

Strength   Hope   Spirit   Vision

Awakening   Balance   Energy   Faith   Freedom

AFFIRMATION _____

NIGHT   MOOD: Good-Average-Bad   ENERGY LEVEL: High-Average-Low

REASON _____

Strength   Hope   Spirit   Vision

Awakening   Balance   Energy   Faith   Freedom

DAILY DISCOVERIES _____

_____
_____
_____
_____
_____
_____
_____
_____
_____
_____
_____
_____
_____
_____
_____
_____
_____
_____
_____

HEALTH PATTERNS _____

_____
_____
_____
_____
_____
_____

ACHIEVEMENT _____

ACT OF KINDNESS _____

DIET
Meat
Bread
Dairy
Vegetables
Fruit
Water
Vitamins

PHYSICAL DISCOMFORT

PLAY

Exercise	☐	Laugh	☐	Read	☐
Meditation	☐	Dance	☐	_____	☐
Sex	☐	Sing	☐	_____	☐

CYCLE DAY

_____

DATE_____

Sleep Time ____:____ Wake Time ____:____ Hours of Sleep _____

DREAMS _____
_____
_____
_____
_____
_____
_____
_____
_____

MORNING   MOOD: Good-Average-Bad   ENERGY LEVEL: High-Average-Low

REASON _____

Strength   Hope   Spirit   Vision

Awakening   Balance   Energy   Faith   Freedom

AFFIRMATION _____

NIGHT   MOOD: Good-Average-Bad   ENERGY LEVEL: High-Average-Low

REASON _____

Strength   Hope   Spirit   Vision

Awakening   Balance   Energy   Faith   Freedom

DAILY DISCOVERIES _____

_____
_____
_____
_____
_____
_____
_____
_____
_____
_____
_____
_____
_____
_____
_____
_____
_____
_____
_____

HEALTH PATTERNS _____

_____
_____
_____
_____
_____
_____
_____

ACHIEVEMENT _____
ACT OF KINDNESS _____

DIET		**PHYSICAL**
Meat	□□□□□□□□□□□□	**DISCOMFORT**
Bread	□□□□□□□□□□□□	
Dairy	□□□□□□□□□□□□	
Vegetables	□□□□□□□□□□□□	
Fruit	□□□□□□□□□□□□	
Water	□□□□□□□□□□□□	
Vitamins	□□□□□□□□□□□□	

PLAY

Exercise	□	Laugh	□	Read	□	
Meditation	□	Dance	□	_____	□	**CYCLE DAY**
Sex	□	Sing	□	_____	□	_____

DATE_____

Sleep Time ____:____   Wake Time ____:____   Hours of Sleep _____

DREAMS _____

_____

_____

_____

_____

_____

_____

_____

_____

MORNING   MOOD: Good-Average-Bad   ENERGY LEVEL: High-Average-Low

REASON _____

Strength	Hope	Spirit	Vision

Awakening	Balance	Energy	Faith	Freedom

AFFIRMATION _____

NIGHT   MOOD: Good-Average-Bad   ENERGY LEVEL: High-Average-Low

REASON _____

Strength	Hope	Spirit	Vision

Awakening	Balance	Energy	Faith	Freedom

DAILY DISCOVERIES _____

_____
_____
_____
_____
_____
_____
_____
_____
_____
_____
_____
_____
_____
_____
_____
_____
_____
_____
_____

HEALTH PATTERNS _____

_____
_____
_____
_____
_____
_____
_____

ACHIEVEMENT _____

ACT OF KINDNESS _____

DIET

Meat	□	□	□	□	□	□	□	□	□	□	□
Bread	□	□	□	□	□	□	□	□	□	□	□
Dairy	□	□	□	□	□	□	□	□	□	□	□
Vegetables	□	□	□	□	□	□	□	□	□	□	□
Fruit	□	□	□	□	□	□	□	□	□	□	□
Water	□	□	□	□	□	□	□	□	□	□	□
Vitamins	□	□	□	□	□	□	□	□	□	□	□

PHYSICAL DISCOMFORT

PLAY

Exercise	□	Laugh	□	Read	□
Meditation	□	Dance	□	_____	□
Sex	□	Sing	□	_____	□

CYCLE DAY

_____

DATE_____

Sleep Time ____:____ Wake Time ____:____ Hours of Sleep _____

DREAMS _____
_____
_____
_____
_____
_____
_____
_____

MORNING   MOOD: Good-Average-Bad   ENERGY LEVEL: High-Average-Low

REASON _____

Strength	Hope	Spirit	Vision	
Awakening	Balance	Energy	Faith	Freedom

AFFIRMATION _____

NIGHT   MOOD: Good-Average-Bad   ENERGY LEVEL: High-Average-Low

REASON _____

Strength	Hope	Spirit	Vision	
Awakening	Balance	Energy	Faith	Freedom

DAILY DISCOVERIES _____

_____
_____
_____
_____
_____
_____
_____
_____
_____
_____
_____
_____
_____
_____
_____
_____
_____
_____
_____
_____
_____
_____

HEALTH PATTERNS _____

_____
_____
_____
_____
_____
_____

ACHIEVEMENT _____
ACT OF KINDNESS _____

DIET		**PHYSICAL DISCOMFORT**
Meat	☐☐☐☐☐☐☐☐☐☐☐	
Bread	☐☐☐☐☐☐☐☐☐☐☐	
Dairy	☐☐☐☐☐☐☐☐☐☐☐	
Vegetables	☐☐☐☐☐☐☐☐☐☐☐	
Fruit	☐☐☐☐☐☐☐☐☐☐☐	
Water	☐☐☐☐☐☐☐☐☐☐☐	
Vitamins	☐☐☐☐☐☐☐☐☐☐☐	

PLAY

Exercise	☐	Laugh	☐	Read	☐
Meditation	☐	Dance	☐	_____	☐
Sex	☐	Sing	☐	_____	☐

CYCLE DAY

_____

DATE_____

Sleep Time ____:____ Wake Time ____:____ Hours of Sleep _____

DREAMS _____
_____
_____
_____
_____
_____
_____
_____
_____

MORNING   MOOD: Good-Average-Bad   ENERGY LEVEL: High-Average-Low

REASON _____

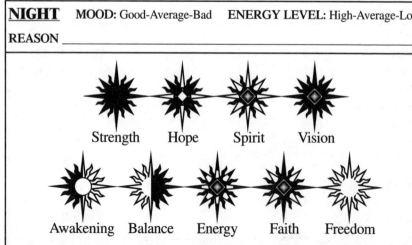

| Strength | Hope | Spirit | Vision |

| Awakening | Balance | Energy | Faith | Freedom |

AFFIRMATION _____

NIGHT   MOOD: Good-Average-Bad   ENERGY LEVEL: High-Average-Low

REASON _____

| Strength | Hope | Spirit | Vision |

| Awakening | Balance | Energy | Faith | Freedom |

DAILY DISCOVERIES _____

_____
_____
_____
_____
_____
_____
_____
_____
_____
_____
_____
_____
_____
_____
_____
_____
_____
_____
_____
_____
_____
_____

HEALTH PATTERNS _____

_____
_____
_____
_____
_____
_____
_____

ACHIEVEMENT _____

ACT OF KINDNESS _____

DIET

		PHYSICAL DISCOMFORT
Meat	☐☐☐☐☐☐☐☐☐☐☐☐	
Bread	☐☐☐☐☐☐☐☐☐☐☐☐	
Dairy	☐☐☐☐☐☐☐☐☐☐☐☐	
Vegetables	☐☐☐☐☐☐☐☐☐☐☐☐	
Fruit	☐☐☐☐☐☐☐☐☐☐☐☐	
Water	☐☐☐☐☐☐☐☐☐☐☐☐	
Vitamins	☐☐☐☐☐☐☐☐☐☐☐☐	

PLAY

Exercise ☐   Laugh ☐   Read ☐

Meditation ☐   Dance ☐   _____ ☐

Sex ☐   Sing ☐   _____ ☐

CYCLE DAY

_____

DATE_____

Sleep Time ____ : ____   Wake Time ____ : ____   Hours of Sleep _____

DREAMS _____
_____
_____
_____
_____
_____
_____
_____
_____

MORNING   MOOD: Good-Average-Bad   ENERGY LEVEL: High-Average-Low

REASON _____

Strength   Hope   Spirit   Vision

Awakening   Balance   Energy   Faith   Freedom

AFFIRMATION _____

NIGHT   MOOD: Good-Average-Bad   ENERGY LEVEL: High-Average-Low

REASON _____

Strength   Hope   Spirit   Vision

Awakening   Balance   Energy   Faith   Freedom

DAILY DISCOVERIES _____

_____
_____
_____
_____
_____
_____
_____
_____
_____
_____
_____
_____
_____
_____
_____
_____
_____
_____
_____
_____
_____

HEALTH PATTERNS _____

_____
_____
_____
_____
_____
_____
_____

ACHIEVEMENT _____

ACT OF KINDNESS _____

DIET		**PHYSICAL**
Meat	□□□□□□□□□□□□	**DISCOMFORT**
Bread	□□□□□□□□□□□□	
Dairy	□□□□□□□□□□□□	
Vegetables	□□□□□□□□□□□□	
Fruit	□□□□□□□□□□□□	
Water	□□□□□□□□□□□□	
Vitamins	□□□□□□□□□□□□	

PLAY

Exercise	□	Laugh	□	Read	□
Meditation	□	Dance	□	_____	□
Sex	□	Sing	□	_____	□

CYCLE DAY

_____

DATE_____

Sleep Time ____:____   Wake Time ____:____   Hours of Sleep _____

DREAMS _____
_____
_____
_____
_____
_____
_____
_____
_____

MORNING   MOOD: Good-Average-Bad   ENERGY LEVEL: High-Average-Low

REASON _____

Strength	Hope	Spirit	Vision

Awakening	Balance	Energy	Faith	Freedom

AFFIRMATION _____

NIGHT   MOOD: Good-Average-Bad   ENERGY LEVEL: High-Average-Low

REASON _____

Strength	Hope	Spirit	Vision

Awakening	Balance	Energy	Faith	Freedom

DAILY DISCOVERIES _____

_____
_____
_____
_____
_____
_____
_____
_____
_____
_____
_____
_____
_____
_____
_____
_____
_____
_____
_____
_____

HEALTH PATTERNS _____

_____
_____
_____
_____
_____
_____
_____

ACHIEVEMENT _____
ACT OF KINDNESS _____

DIET		**PHYSICAL**
Meat	☐☐☐☐☐☐☐☐☐☐☐☐	**DISCOMFORT**
Bread	☐☐☐☐☐☐☐☐☐☐☐☐	
Dairy	☐☐☐☐☐☐☐☐☐☐☐☐	
Vegetables	☐☐☐☐☐☐☐☐☐☐☐☐	
Fruit	☐☐☐☐☐☐☐☐☐☐☐☐	
Water	☐☐☐☐☐☐☐☐☐☐☐☐	
Vitamins	☐☐☐☐☐☐☐☐☐☐☐☐	

PLAY

Exercise ☐	Laugh ☐	Read ☐	
Meditation ☐	Dance ☐	_____ ☐	**CYCLE DAY**
Sex ☐	Sing ☐	_____ ☐	_____

DATE_____

Sleep Time ____:____ Wake Time ____:____ Hours of Sleep _____

DREAMS _____
_____
_____
_____
_____
_____
_____
_____
_____

MORNING MOOD: Good-Average-Bad ENERGY LEVEL: High-Average-Low

REASON _____

Strength	Hope	Spirit	Vision

Awakening	Balance	Energy	Faith	Freedom

AFFIRMATION _____

NIGHT MOOD: Good-Average-Bad ENERGY LEVEL: High-Average-Low

REASON _____

Strength	Hope	Spirit	Vision

Awakening	Balance	Energy	Faith	Freedom

DAILY DISCOVERIES _____
_____
_____
_____
_____
_____
_____
_____
_____
_____
_____
_____
_____
_____
_____
_____
_____
_____
_____
_____
_____
_____

HEALTH PATTERNS _____
_____
_____
_____
_____
_____
_____

ACHIEVEMENT _____
ACT OF KINDNESS _____

DIET													**PHYSICAL DISCOMFORT**
Meat	☐	☐	☐	☐	☐	☐	☐	☐	☐	☐	☐	☐	
Bread	☐	☐	☐	☐	☐	☐	☐	☐	☐	☐	☐	☐	
Dairy	☐	☐	☐	☐	☐	☐	☐	☐	☐	☐	☐	☐	
Vegetables	☐	☐	☐	☐	☐	☐	☐	☐	☐	☐	☐	☐	
Fruit	☐	☐	☐	☐	☐	☐	☐	☐	☐	☐	☐	☐	
Water	☐	☐	☐	☐	☐	☐	☐	☐	☐	☐	☐	☐	
Vitamins	☐	☐	☐	☐	☐	☐	☐	☐	☐	☐	☐	☐	

PLAY

Exercise	☐	Laugh	☐	Read	☐	
Meditation	☐	Dance	☐	_____	☐	**CYCLE DAY**
Sex	☐	Sing	☐	_____	☐	_____

DATE_____

Sleep Time ____:____   Wake Time ____:____   Hours of Sleep _____

DREAMS _____
_____
_____
_____
_____
_____
_____
_____
_____
_____

MORNING   MOOD: Good-Average-Bad   ENERGY LEVEL: High-Average-Low

REASON _____

Strength	Hope	Spirit	Vision	
Awakening	Balance	Energy	Faith	Freedom

AFFIRMATION _____

NIGHT   MOOD: Good-Average-Bad   ENERGY LEVEL: High-Average-Low

REASON _____

Strength	Hope	Spirit	Vision	
Awakening	Balance	Energy	Faith	Freedom

DAILY DISCOVERIES _____

_____
_____
_____
_____
_____
_____
_____
_____
_____
_____
_____
_____
_____
_____
_____
_____
_____
_____
_____

HEALTH PATTERNS _____

_____
_____
_____
_____
_____
_____

ACHIEVEMENT _____

ACT OF KINDNESS _____

DIET
Meat   ☐☐☐☐☐☐☐☐☐☐☐   **PHYSICAL**
Bread   ☐☐☐☐☐☐☐☐☐☐☐   **DISCOMFORT**
Dairy   ☐☐☐☐☐☐☐☐☐☐
Vegetables   ☐☐☐☐☐☐☐☐☐☐
Fruit   ☐☐☐☐☐☐☐☐☐☐☐
Water   ☐☐☐☐☐☐☐☐☐☐☐
Vitamins   ☐☐☐☐☐☐☐☐☐☐

PLAY

Exercise	☐	Laugh	☐	Read	☐
Meditation	☐	Dance	☐	_____	☐
Sex	☐	Sing	☐	_____	☐

CYCLE DAY

_____

DATE_____

Sleep Time ____:____ Wake Time ____:____ Hours of Sleep _____

DREAMS _____
_____
_____
_____
_____
_____
_____
_____
_____

MORNING MOOD: Good-Average-Bad ENERGY LEVEL: High-Average-Low

REASON _____

Strength   Hope   Spirit   Vision

Awakening Balance Energy Faith Freedom

AFFIRMATION _____

NIGHT MOOD: Good-Average-Bad ENERGY LEVEL: High-Average-Low

REASON _____

Strength   Hope   Spirit   Vision

Awakening Balance Energy Faith Freedom

DAILY DISCOVERIES _____

_____
_____
_____
_____
_____
_____
_____
_____
_____
_____
_____
_____
_____
_____
_____
_____
_____
_____
_____
_____

HEALTH PATTERNS _____

_____
_____
_____
_____
_____
_____

ACHIEVEMENT _____
ACT OF KINDNESS _____

DIET												
Meat	□	□	□	□	□	□	□	□	□	□	□	□
Bread	□	□	□	□	□	□	□	□	□	□	□	□
Dairy	□	□	□	□	□	□	□	□	□	□	□	□
Vegetables	□	□	□	□	□	□	□	□	□	□	□	□
Fruit	□	□	□	□	□	□	□	□	□	□	□	□
Water	□	□	□	□	□	□	□	□	□	□	□	□
Vitamins	□	□	□	□	□	□	□	□	□	□	□	□

PHYSICAL DISCOMFORT

PLAY

Exercise	□	Laugh	□	Read	□
Meditation	□	Dance	□	_____	□
Sex	□	Sing	□	_____	□

CYCLE DAY

_____

DATE_____

Sleep Time _____:_____ Wake Time _____:_____ Hours of Sleep _____

DREAMS _____
_____
_____
_____
_____
_____
_____
_____
_____

MORNING   **MOOD:** Good-Average-Bad   **ENERGY LEVEL:** High-Average-Low

REASON _____

Strength	Hope	Spirit	Vision

Awakening	Balance	Energy	Faith	Freedom

AFFIRMATION _____

NIGHT   **MOOD:** Good-Average-Bad   **ENERGY LEVEL:** High-Average-Low

REASON _____

Strength	Hope	Spirit	Vision

Awakening	Balance	Energy	Faith	Freedom

DAILY DISCOVERIES _____

_____
_____
_____
_____
_____
_____
_____
_____
_____
_____
_____
_____
_____
_____
_____
_____
_____
_____
_____
_____
_____

HEALTH PATTERNS _____

_____
_____
_____
_____
_____
_____

ACHIEVEMENT _____
ACT OF KINDNESS _____

DIET

		PHYSICAL DISCOMFORT
Meat	☐☐☐☐☐☐☐☐☐☐☐☐	
Bread	☐☐☐☐☐☐☐☐☐☐☐☐	
Dairy	☐☐☐☐☐☐☐☐☐☐☐☐	
Vegetables	☐☐☐☐☐☐☐☐☐☐☐☐	
Fruit	☐☐☐☐☐☐☐☐☐☐☐☐	
Water	☐☐☐☐☐☐☐☐☐☐☐☐	
Vitamins	☐☐☐☐☐☐☐☐☐☐☐☐	

PLAY

Exercise ☐   Laugh ☐   Read ☐
Meditation ☐   Dance ☐   _____ ☐
Sex ☐   Sing ☐   _____ ☐

CYCLE DAY

_____

DATE_____

Sleep Time _____:_____   Wake Time _____:_____   Hours of Sleep _____

DREAMS _____
_____
_____
_____
_____
_____
_____
_____
_____

MORNING   MOOD: Good-Average-Bad   ENERGY LEVEL: High-Average-Low

REASON _____

Strength	Hope	Spirit	Vision	
Awakening	Balance	Energy	Faith	Freedom

AFFIRMATION _____

NIGHT   MOOD: Good-Average-Bad   ENERGY LEVEL: High-Average-Low

REASON _____

Strength	Hope	Spirit	Vision	
Awakening	Balance	Energy	Faith	Freedom

DAILY DISCOVERIES _____

_____
_____
_____
_____
_____
_____
_____
_____
_____
_____
_____
_____
_____
_____
_____
_____
_____
_____
_____
_____

HEALTH PATTERNS _____

_____
_____
_____
_____
_____
_____

ACHIEVEMENT _____

ACT OF KINDNESS _____

DIET		**PHYSICAL**
Meat	☐☐☐☐☐☐☐☐☐☐☐☐	**DISCOMFORT**
Bread	☐☐☐☐☐☐☐☐☐☐☐☐	
Dairy	☐☐☐☐☐☐☐☐☐☐☐☐	
Vegetables	☐☐☐☐☐☐☐☐☐☐☐☐	
Fruit	☐☐☐☐☐☐☐☐☐☐☐☐	
Water	☐☐☐☐☐☐☐☐☐☐☐☐	
Vitamins	☐☐☐☐☐☐☐☐☐☐☐☐	

PLAY

Exercise	☐	Laugh	☐	Read	☐
Meditation	☐	Dance	☐	_____	☐
Sex	☐	Sing	☐	_____	☐

CYCLE DAY

_____

DATE_____

Sleep Time _____:_____ Wake Time _____:_____ Hours of Sleep _____

DREAMS _____
_____
_____
_____
_____
_____
_____
_____
_____

MORNING   MOOD: Good-Average-Bad   ENERGY LEVEL: High-Average-Low

REASON _____

Strength   Hope   Spirit   Vision

Awakening   Balance   Energy   Faith   Freedom

AFFIRMATION _____

NIGHT   MOOD: Good-Average-Bad   ENERGY LEVEL: High-Average-Low

REASON _____

Strength   Hope   Spirit   Vision

Awakening   Balance   Energy   Faith   Freedom

DAILY DISCOVERIES _____

_____
_____
_____
_____
_____
_____
_____
_____
_____
_____
_____
_____
_____
_____
_____
_____
_____
_____
_____
_____
_____

HEALTH PATTERNS _____

_____
_____
_____
_____
_____
_____
_____

ACHIEVEMENT _____

ACT OF KINDNESS _____

DIET		**PHYSICAL DISCOMFORT**
Meat	☐☐☐☐☐☐☐☐☐☐☐	
Bread	☐☐☐☐☐☐☐☐☐☐☐	
Dairy	☐☐☐☐☐☐☐☐☐☐☐	
Vegetables	☐☐☐☐☐☐☐☐☐☐☐	
Fruit	☐☐☐☐☐☐☐☐☐☐☐	
Water	☐☐☐☐☐☐☐☐☐☐☐	
Vitamins	☐☐☐☐☐☐☐☐☐☐☐	

PLAY

Exercise	☐	Laugh	☐	Read	☐
Meditation	☐	Dance	☐	_____	☐
Sex	☐	Sing	☐	_____	☐

CYCLE DAY

_____

DATE_____

Sleep Time ____:____ Wake Time ____:____ Hours of Sleep _____

DREAMS _____

_____

_____

_____

_____

_____

_____

_____

_____

MORNING   MOOD: Good-Average-Bad   ENERGY LEVEL: High-Average-Low

REASON _____

Strength	Hope	Spirit	Vision

Awakening	Balance	Energy	Faith	Freedom

AFFIRMATION _____

NIGHT   MOOD: Good-Average-Bad   ENERGY LEVEL: High-Average-Low

REASON _____

Strength	Hope	Spirit	Vision

Awakening	Balance	Energy	Faith	Freedom

DAILY DISCOVERIES _____

_____
_____
_____
_____
_____
_____
_____
_____
_____
_____
_____
_____
_____
_____
_____
_____
_____
_____
_____
_____

HEALTH PATTERNS _____

_____
_____
_____
_____
_____
_____

ACHIEVEMENT _____

ACT OF KINDNESS _____

DIET		**PHYSICAL DISCOMFORT**
Meat	☐☐☐☐☐☐☐☐☐☐☐☐	
Bread	☐☐☐☐☐☐☐☐☐☐☐☐	
Dairy	☐☐☐☐☐☐☐☐☐☐☐☐	
Vegetables	☐☐☐☐☐☐☐☐☐☐☐	
Fruit	☐☐☐☐☐☐☐☐☐☐☐☐	
Water	☐☐☐☐☐☐☐☐☐☐☐	
Vitamins	☐☐☐☐☐☐☐☐☐☐☐☐	

PLAY

Exercise ☐	Laugh ☐	Read ☐
Meditation ☐	Dance ☐	_____ ☐
Sex ☐	Sing ☐	_____ ☐

CYCLE DAY
_____

DATE_____

Sleep Time ____:____   Wake Time ____:____   Hours of Sleep _____

DREAMS _____
_____
_____
_____
_____
_____
_____
_____
_____

MORNING   MOOD: Good-Average-Bad   ENERGY LEVEL: High-Average-Low

REASON _____

Strength   Hope   Spirit   Vision

Awakening   Balance   Energy   Faith   Freedom

AFFIRMATION _____

NIGHT   MOOD: Good-Average-Bad   ENERGY LEVEL: High-Average-Low

REASON _____

Strength   Hope   Spirit   Vision

Awakening   Balance   Energy   Faith   Freedom

DAILY DISCOVERIES _____

_____
_____
_____
_____
_____
_____
_____
_____
_____
_____
_____
_____
_____
_____
_____
_____
_____
_____
_____

HEALTH PATTERNS _____

_____
_____
_____
_____
_____
_____

ACHIEVEMENT _____
ACT OF KINDNESS _____

DIET

Meat	☐☐☐☐☐☐☐☐☐☐☐
Bread	☐☐☐☐☐☐☐☐☐☐☐☐
Dairy	☐☐☐☐☐☐☐☐☐☐☐
Vegetables	☐☐☐☐☐☐☐☐☐☐☐
Fruit	☐☐☐☐☐☐☐☐☐☐☐
Water	☐☐☐☐☐☐☐☐☐☐☐
Vitamins	☐☐☐☐☐☐☐☐☐☐☐

PHYSICAL DISCOMFORT

PLAY

Exercise	☐	Laugh	☐	Read	☐
Meditation	☐	Dance	☐	_____	☐
Sex	☐	Sing	☐	_____	☐

CYCLE DAY

_____

DATE_____

Sleep Time _____:_____ Wake Time _____:_____ Hours of Sleep _____

DREAMS _____
_____
_____
_____
_____
_____
_____
_____
_____

MORNING   MOOD: Good-Average-Bad ENERGY LEVEL: High-Average-Low

REASON _____

Strength	Hope	Spirit	Vision

Awakening	Balance	Energy	Faith	Freedom

AFFIRMATION _____

NIGHT   MOOD: Good-Average-Bad ENERGY LEVEL: High-Average-Low

REASON _____

Strength	Hope	Spirit	Vision

Awakening	Balance	Energy	Faith	Freedom

DAILY DISCOVERIES _____

_____
_____
_____
_____
_____
_____
_____
_____
_____
_____
_____
_____
_____
_____
_____
_____
_____
_____
_____
_____
_____
_____
_____

HEALTH PATTERNS _____

_____
_____
_____
_____
_____
_____
_____

ACHIEVEMENT _____

ACT OF KINDNESS _____

DIET

Meat	☐	☐	☐	☐	☐	☐	☐	☐	☐	☐	☐
Bread	☐	☐	☐	☐	☐	☐	☐	☐	☐	☐	☐
Dairy	☐	☐	☐	☐	☐	☐	☐	☐	☐	☐	
Vegetables	☐	☐	☐	☐	☐	☐	☐	☐	☐	☐	
Fruit	☐	☐	☐	☐	☐	☐	☐	☐	☐	☐	
Water	☐	☐	☐	☐	☐	☐	☐	☐	☐	☐	
Vitamins	☐	☐	☐	☐	☐	☐	☐	☐	☐	☐	

PHYSICAL DISCOMFORT

PLAY

Exercise	☐	Laugh	☐	Read	☐	
Meditation	☐	Dance	☐	_____	☐	
Sex	☐	Sing	☐	_____	☐	

CYCLE DAY

_____

DATE_____

Sleep Time ____:____ Wake Time ____:____ Hours of Sleep _____

DREAMS _____
_____
_____
_____
_____
_____
_____
_____

MORNING   MOOD: Good-Average-Bad   ENERGY LEVEL: High-Average-Low

REASON _____

| Strength | Hope | Spirit | Vision |

| Awakening | Balance | Energy | Faith | Freedom |

AFFIRMATION _____

NIGHT   MOOD: Good-Average-Bad   ENERGY LEVEL: High-Average-Low

REASON _____

| Strength | Hope | Spirit | Vision |

| Awakening | Balance | Energy | Faith | Freedom |

DAILY DISCOVERIES _____

_____
_____
_____
_____
_____
_____
_____
_____
_____
_____
_____
_____
_____
_____
_____
_____
_____
_____
_____
_____
_____
_____

HEALTH PATTERNS _____

_____
_____
_____
_____
_____
_____
_____

ACHIEVEMENT _____

ACT OF KINDNESS _____

DIET
Meat ☐☐☐☐☐☐☐☐☐☐☐☐   **PHYSICAL**
Bread ☐☐☐☐☐☐☐☐☐☐☐☐   **DISCOMFORT**
Dairy ☐☐☐☐☐☐☐☐☐☐☐
Vegetables ☐☐☐☐☐☐☐☐☐☐☐
Fruit ☐☐☐☐☐☐☐☐☐☐☐
Water ☐☐☐☐☐☐☐☐☐☐☐
Vitamins ☐☐☐☐☐☐☐☐☐☐☐

PLAY
Exercise ☐   Laugh ☐   Read ☐
Meditation ☐   Dance ☐   _____ ☐   **CYCLE DAY**
Sex ☐   Sing ☐   _____ ☐   _____

DATE_____

Sleep Time ____:____ Wake Time ____:____ Hours of Sleep _____

DREAMS _____
_____
_____
_____
_____
_____
_____
_____
_____

MORNING   MOOD: Good-Average-Bad   ENERGY LEVEL: High-Average-Low

REASON _____

Strength	Hope	Spirit	Vision

Awakening	Balance	Energy	Faith	Freedom

AFFIRMATION _____

NIGHT   MOOD: Good-Average-Bad   ENERGY LEVEL: High-Average-Low

REASON _____

Strength	Hope	Spirit	Vision

Awakening	Balance	Energy	Faith	Freedom

DAILY DISCOVERIES _____

_____
_____
_____
_____
_____
_____
_____
_____
_____
_____
_____
_____
_____
_____
_____
_____
_____
_____
_____
_____

HEALTH PATTERNS _____

_____
_____
_____
_____
_____
_____
_____

ACHIEVEMENT _____

ACT OF KINDNESS _____

DIET													
Meat	□	□	□	□	□	□	□	□	□	□	□	□	□
Bread	□	□	□	□	□	□	□	□	□	□	□	□	□
Dairy	□	□	□	□	□	□	□	□	□	□	□	□	□
Vegetables	□	□	□	□	□	□	□	□	□	□	□	□	□
Fruit	□	□	□	□	□	□	□	□	□	□	□	□	□
Water	□	□	□	□	□	□	□	□	□	□	□	□	□
Vitamins	□	□	□	□	□	□	□	□	□	□	□	□	□

PHYSICAL DISCOMFORT

PLAY

Exercise	□	Laugh	□	Read	□
Meditation	□	Dance	□	_____	□
Sex	□	Sing	□	_____	□

CYCLE DAY

_____

DATE_____

Sleep Time ____:____ Wake Time ____:____ Hours of Sleep _____

DREAMS _____
_____
_____
_____
_____
_____
_____
_____

MORNING   MOOD: Good-Average-Bad ENERGY LEVEL: High-Average-Low

REASON _____

Strength   Hope   Spirit   Vision

Awakening Balance   Energy   Faith   Freedom

AFFIRMATION _____

NIGHT   MOOD: Good-Average-Bad   ENERGY LEVEL: High-Average-Low

REASON _____

Strength   Hope   Spirit   Vision

Awakening Balance   Energy   Faith   Freedom

DAILY DISCOVERIES _____

_____
_____
_____
_____
_____
_____
_____
_____
_____
_____
_____
_____
_____
_____
_____
_____
_____
_____
_____

HEALTH PATTERNS _____

_____
_____
_____
_____
_____
_____

ACHIEVEMENT _____
ACT OF KINDNESS _____

DIET

		PHYSICAL DISCOMFORT
Meat	☐☐☐☐☐☐☐☐☐☐☐	
Bread	☐☐☐☐☐☐☐☐☐☐☐	
Dairy	☐☐☐☐☐☐☐☐☐☐	
Vegetables	☐☐☐☐☐☐☐☐☐☐	
Fruit	☐☐☐☐☐☐☐☐☐☐	
Water	☐☐☐☐☐☐☐☐☐☐	
Vitamins	☐☐☐☐☐☐☐☐☐☐	

PLAY

Exercise	☐	Laugh	☐	Read	☐
Meditation	☐	Dance	☐	_____	☐
Sex	☐	Sing	☐	_____	☐

CYCLE DAY

_____

DATE_____

Sleep Time ____:____ Wake Time ____:____ Hours of Sleep _____

DREAMS _____
_____
_____
_____
_____
_____
_____
_____
_____

MORNING   MOOD: Good-Average-Bad   ENERGY LEVEL: High-Average-Low

REASON _____

Strength   Hope   Spirit   Vision

Awakening   Balance   Energy   Faith   Freedom

AFFIRMATION _____

NIGHT   MOOD: Good-Average-Bad   ENERGY LEVEL: High-Average-Low

REASON _____

Strength   Hope   Spirit   Vision

Awakening   Balance   Energy   Faith   Freedom

DAILY DISCOVERIES _____

_____
_____
_____
_____
_____
_____
_____
_____
_____
_____
_____
_____
_____
_____
_____
_____
_____
_____
_____
_____
_____
_____
_____

HEALTH PATTERNS _____

_____
_____
_____
_____
_____
_____
_____

ACHIEVEMENT _____
ACT OF KINDNESS _____

DIET
Meat	☐☐☐☐☐☐☐☐☐☐☐☐☐	**PHYSICAL**
Bread	☐☐☐☐☐☐☐☐☐☐☐☐☐	**DISCOMFORT**
Dairy	☐☐☐☐☐☐☐☐☐☐☐☐☐	
Vegetables	☐☐☐☐☐☐☐☐☐☐☐☐☐	
Fruit	☐☐☐☐☐☐☐☐☐☐☐☐☐	
Water	☐☐☐☐☐☐☐☐☐☐☐☐☐	
Vitamins	☐☐☐☐☐☐☐☐☐☐☐☐☐	

PLAY

Exercise	☐	Laugh	☐	Read	☐
Meditation	☐	Dance	☐	_____	☐
Sex	☐	Sing	☐	_____	☐

CYCLE DAY

_____

DATE_____

Sleep Time _____:_____   Wake Time _____:_____   Hours of Sleep _____

DREAMS _____
_____
_____
_____
_____
_____
_____
_____
_____

MORNING   **MOOD:** Good-Average-Bad   **ENERGY LEVEL:** High-Average-Low

REASON _____

Strength   Hope   Spirit   Vision

Awakening   Balance   Energy   Faith   Freedom

AFFIRMATION _____

NIGHT   **MOOD:** Good-Average-Bad   **ENERGY LEVEL:** High-Average-Low

REASON _____

Strength   Hope   Spirit   Vision

Awakening   Balance   Energy   Faith   Freedom

DAILY DISCOVERIES _____

_____
_____
_____
_____
_____
_____
_____
_____
_____
_____
_____
_____
_____
_____
_____
_____
_____
_____
_____
_____
_____
_____
_____

HEALTH PATTERNS _____

_____
_____
_____
_____
_____
_____
_____

ACHIEVEMENT _____

ACT OF KINDNESS _____

DIET

Meat	☐	☐	☐	☐	☐	☐	☐	☐	☐	☐	☐	☐
Bread	☐	☐	☐	☐	☐	☐	☐	☐	☐	☐	☐	☐
Dairy	☐	☐	☐	☐	☐	☐	☐	☐	☐	☐	☐	☐
Vegetables	☐	☐	☐	☐	☐	☐	☐	☐	☐	☐	☐	☐
Fruit	☐	☐	☐	☐	☐	☐	☐	☐	☐	☐	☐	☐
Water	☐	☐	☐	☐	☐	☐	☐	☐	☐	☐	☐	☐
Vitamins	☐	☐	☐	☐	☐	☐	☐	☐	☐	☐	☐	☐

PHYSICAL DISCOMFORT

PLAY

Exercise ☐   Laugh ☐   Read ☐
Meditation ☐   Dance ☐   _____ ☐
Sex ☐   Sing ☐   _____ ☐

CYCLE DAY
_____

DATE_____

Sleep Time _____:_____   Wake Time _____:_____   Hours of Sleep _____

DREAMS _____
_____
_____
_____
_____
_____
_____
_____
_____

<u>**MORNING**</u>   MOOD: Good-Average-Bad   ENERGY LEVEL: High-Average-Low

REASON _____

Strength	Hope	Spirit	Vision

Awakening	Balance	Energy	Faith	Freedom

AFFIRMATION _____

<u>**NIGHT**</u>   MOOD: Good-Average-Bad   ENERGY LEVEL: High-Average-Low

REASON _____

Strength	Hope	Spirit	Vision

Awakening	Balance	Energy	Faith	Freedom

DAILY DISCOVERIES _____

_____
_____
_____
_____
_____
_____
_____
_____
_____
_____
_____
_____
_____
_____
_____
_____
_____
_____
_____
_____

HEALTH PATTERNS _____

_____
_____
_____
_____
_____
_____
_____

ACHIEVEMENT _____

ACT OF KINDNESS _____

DIET

Meat	☐	☐	☐	☐	☐	☐	☐	☐	☐	☐	☐
Bread	☐	☐	☐	☐	☐	☐	☐	☐	☐	☐	☐
Dairy	☐	☐	☐	☐	☐	☐	☐	☐	☐	☐	☐
Vegetables	☐	☐	☐	☐	☐	☐	☐	☐	☐	☐	☐
Fruit	☐	☐	☐	☐	☐	☐	☐	☐	☐	☐	☐
Water	☐	☐	☐	☐	☐	☐	☐	☐	☐	☐	☐
Vitamins	☐	☐	☐	☐	☐	☐	☐	☐	☐	☐	☐

PHYSICAL DISCOMFORT

PLAY

Exercise	☐	Laugh	☐	Read	☐
Meditation	☐	Dance	☐	_____	☐
Sex	☐	Sing	☐	_____	☐

CYCLE DAY

_____

DATE_____

Sleep Time ____:____ Wake Time ____:____ Hours of Sleep _____

DREAMS _____
_____
_____
_____
_____
_____
_____
_____

MORNING   MOOD: Good-Average-Bad   ENERGY LEVEL: High-Average-Low

REASON _____

Strength   Hope   Spirit   Vision

Awakening   Balance   Energy   Faith   Freedom

AFFIRMATION _____

NIGHT   MOOD: Good-Average-Bad   ENERGY LEVEL: High-Average-Low

REASON _____

Strength   Hope   Spirit   Vision

Awakening   Balance   Energy   Faith   Freedom

DAILY DISCOVERIES _____

_____
_____
_____
_____
_____
_____
_____
_____
_____
_____
_____
_____
_____
_____
_____
_____
_____
_____
_____
_____
_____

HEALTH PATTERNS _____

_____
_____
_____
_____
_____
_____
_____

ACHIEVEMENT _____

ACT OF KINDNESS _____

DIET		**PHYSICAL DISCOMFORT**
Meat	☐☐☐☐☐☐☐☐☐☐☐☐	
Bread	☐☐☐☐☐☐☐☐☐☐☐☐	
Dairy	☐☐☐☐☐☐☐☐☐☐☐☐	
Vegetables	☐☐☐☐☐☐☐☐☐☐☐☐	
Fruit	☐☐☐☐☐☐☐☐☐☐☐☐	
Water	☐☐☐☐☐☐☐☐☐☐☐☐	
Vitamins	☐☐☐☐☐☐☐☐☐☐☐☐	

PLAY

Exercise	☐	Laugh	☐	Read	☐
Meditation	☐	Dance	☐	_____	☐
Sex	☐	Sing	☐	_____	☐

CYCLE DAY

_____

DATE_____

Sleep Time ____:____   Wake Time ____:____   Hours of Sleep _____

DREAMS _____
_____
_____
_____
_____
_____
_____
_____
_____

MORNING   MOOD: Good-Average-Bad   ENERGY LEVEL: High-Average-Low

REASON _____

Strength	Hope	Spirit	Vision

Awakening	Balance	Energy	Faith	Freedom

AFFIRMATION _____

NIGHT   MOOD: Good-Average-Bad   ENERGY LEVEL: High-Average-Low

REASON _____

Strength	Hope	Spirit	Vision

Awakening	Balance	Energy	Faith	Freedom

DAILY DISCOVERIES _____
_____
_____
_____
_____
_____
_____
_____
_____
_____
_____
_____
_____
_____
_____
_____
_____
_____
_____
_____
_____

HEALTH PATTERNS _____
_____
_____
_____
_____
_____
_____

ACHIEVEMENT _____
ACT OF KINDNESS _____

DIET
Meat ☐☐☐☐☐☐☐☐☐☐☐☐   **PHYSICAL**
Bread ☐☐☐☐☐☐☐☐☐☐☐☐   **DISCOMFORT**
Dairy ☐☐☐☐☐☐☐☐☐☐☐☐
Vegetables ☐☐☐☐☐☐☐☐☐☐☐☐
Fruit ☐☐☐☐☐☐☐☐☐☐☐☐
Water ☐☐☐☐☐☐☐☐☐☐☐☐
Vitamins ☐☐☐☐☐☐☐☐☐☐☐☐

PLAY
Exercise ☐   Laugh ☐   Read ☐
Meditation ☐   Dance ☐   _____ ☐   **CYCLE DAY**
Sex ☐   Sing ☐   _____ ☐   _____

DATE_____

Sleep Time ____:____   Wake Time ____:____   Hours of Sleep _____

DREAMS _____
_____
_____
_____
_____
_____
_____
_____
_____

MORNING   MOOD: Good-Average-Bad   ENERGY LEVEL: High-Average-Low

REASON _____

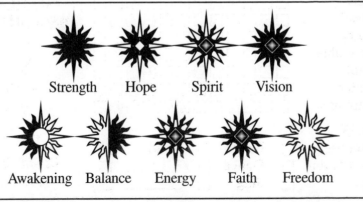

Strength	Hope	Spirit	Vision	
Awakening	Balance	Energy	Faith	Freedom

AFFIRMATION _____

NIGHT   MOOD: Good-Average-Bad   ENERGY LEVEL: High-Average-Low

REASON _____

Strength	Hope	Spirit	Vision	
Awakening	Balance	Energy	Faith	Freedom

DAILY DISCOVERIES _____

_____
_____
_____
_____
_____
_____
_____
_____
_____
_____
_____
_____
_____
_____
_____
_____
_____
_____
_____
_____
_____
_____

HEALTH PATTERNS _____

_____
_____
_____
_____
_____
_____
_____

ACHIEVEMENT _____

ACT OF KINDNESS _____

DIET

		PHYSICAL DISCOMFORT
Meat	☐☐☐☐☐☐☐☐☐☐☐☐	
Bread	☐☐☐☐☐☐☐☐☐☐☐☐	
Dairy	☐☐☐☐☐☐☐☐☐☐☐☐	
Vegetables	☐☐☐☐☐☐☐☐☐☐☐☐	
Fruit	☐☐☐☐☐☐☐☐☐☐☐☐	
Water	☐☐☐☐☐☐☐☐☐☐☐☐	
Vitamins	☐☐☐☐☐☐☐☐☐☐☐☐	

PLAY

Exercise	☐	Laugh	☐	Read	☐
Meditation	☐	Dance	☐	_____	☐
Sex	☐	Sing	☐	_____	☐

CYCLE DAY

_____

DATE_____

Sleep Time ____:____ Wake Time ____:____ Hours of Sleep _____

DREAMS _____
_____
_____
_____
_____
_____
_____

MORNING   MOOD: Good-Average-Bad   ENERGY LEVEL: High-Average-Low

REASON _____

Strength	Hope	Spirit	Vision	
Awakening	Balance	Energy	Faith	Freedom

AFFIRMATION _____

NIGHT   MOOD: Good-Average-Bad   ENERGY LEVEL: High-Average-Low

REASON _____

Strength	Hope	Spirit	Vision	
Awakening	Balance	Energy	Faith	Freedom

DAILY DISCOVERIES _____

_____
_____
_____
_____
_____
_____
_____
_____
_____
_____
_____
_____
_____
_____
_____
_____
_____
_____
_____
_____

HEALTH PATTERNS _____

_____
_____
_____
_____
_____
_____
_____

ACHIEVEMENT _____

ACT OF KINDNESS _____

DIET

Meat	□□□□□□□□□□□□	
Bread	□□□□□□□□□□□□	
Dairy	□□□□□□□□□□□□	
Vegetables	□□□□□□□□□□□□	
Fruit	□□□□□□□□□□□□	
Water	□□□□□□□□□□□□	
Vitamins	□□□□□□□□□□□□	

PHYSICAL DISCOMFORT

PLAY

Exercise	□	Laugh	□	Read	□
Meditation	□	Dance	□	_____	□
Sex	□	Sing	□	_____	□

CYCLE DAY

_____

DATE_____

Sleep Time ____:____ Wake Time ____:____ Hours of Sleep _____

DREAMS _____
_____
_____
_____
_____
_____
_____
_____

MORNING   MOOD: Good-Average-Bad   ENERGY LEVEL: High-Average-Low

REASON _____

Strength   Hope   Spirit   Vision

Awakening   Balance   Energy   Faith   Freedom

AFFIRMATION _____

NIGHT   MOOD: Good-Average-Bad   ENERGY LEVEL: High-Average-Low

REASON _____

Strength   Hope   Spirit   Vision

Awakening   Balance   Energy   Faith   Freedom

DAILY DISCOVERIES _____

_____
_____
_____
_____
_____
_____
_____
_____
_____
_____
_____
_____
_____
_____
_____
_____
_____
_____
_____
_____
_____
_____

HEALTH PATTERNS _____

_____
_____
_____
_____
_____
_____

ACHIEVEMENT _____

ACT OF KINDNESS _____

DIET

Meat	☐☐☐☐☐☐☐☐☐☐☐☐	**PHYSICAL DISCOMFORT**
Bread	☐☐☐☐☐☐☐☐☐☐☐☐	
Dairy	☐☐☐☐☐☐☐☐☐☐☐☐	
Vegetables	☐☐☐☐☐☐☐☐☐☐☐☐	
Fruit	☐☐☐☐☐☐☐☐☐☐☐☐	
Water	☐☐☐☐☐☐☐☐☐☐☐☐	
Vitamins	☐☐☐☐☐☐☐☐☐☐☐☐	

PLAY

Exercise	☐	Laugh	☐	Read	☐
Meditation	☐	Dance	☐	_____	☐
Sex	☐	Sing	☐	_____	☐

CYCLE DAY

_____

DATE_____

Sleep Time ____:____ Wake Time ____:____ Hours of Sleep _____

DREAMS _____

_____

_____

_____

_____

_____

_____

_____

MORNING   MOOD: Good-Average-Bad   ENERGY LEVEL: High-Average-Low

REASON _____

Strength   Hope   Spirit   Vision

Awakening   Balance   Energy   Faith   Freedom

AFFIRMATION _____

NIGHT   MOOD: Good-Average-Bad   ENERGY LEVEL: High-Average-Low

REASON _____

Strength   Hope   Spirit   Vision

Awakening   Balance   Energy   Faith   Freedom

DAILY DISCOVERIES _____

_____
_____
_____
_____
_____
_____
_____
_____
_____
_____
_____
_____
_____
_____
_____
_____
_____
_____
_____

HEALTH PATTERNS _____

_____
_____
_____
_____
_____
_____
_____

ACHIEVEMENT _____

ACT OF KINDNESS _____

DIET												
Meat	☐	☐	☐	☐	☐	☐	☐	☐	☐	☐	☐	☐
Bread	☐	☐	☐	☐	☐	☐	☐	☐	☐	☐	☐	☐
Dairy	☐	☐	☐	☐	☐	☐	☐	☐	☐	☐	☐	☐
Vegetables	☐	☐	☐	☐	☐	☐	☐	☐	☐	☐	☐	☐
Fruit	☐	☐	☐	☐	☐	☐	☐	☐	☐	☐	☐	☐
Water	☐	☐	☐	☐	☐	☐	☐	☐	☐	☐	☐	☐
Vitamins	☐	☐	☐	☐	☐	☐	☐	☐	☐	☐	☐	☐

PHYSICAL DISCOMFORT

PLAY

Exercise	☐	Laugh	☐	Read	☐
Meditation	☐	Dance	☐	_____	☐
Sex	☐	Sing	☐	_____	☐

CYCLE DAY

_____

DATE_____

Sleep Time ____:____ Wake Time ____:____ Hours of Sleep _____

DREAMS _____
_____
_____
_____
_____
_____
_____
_____
_____

MORNING MOOD: Good-Average-Bad ENERGY LEVEL: High-Average-Low

REASON _____

Strength	Hope	Spirit	Vision

Awakening	Balance	Energy	Faith	Freedom

AFFIRMATION _____

NIGHT MOOD: Good-Average-Bad ENERGY LEVEL: High-Average-Low

REASON _____

Strength	Hope	Spirit	Vision

Awakening	Balance	Energy	Faith	Freedom

DAILY DISCOVERIES _____

_____
_____
_____
_____
_____
_____
_____
_____
_____
_____
_____
_____
_____
_____
_____
_____
_____
_____
_____
_____
_____

HEALTH PATTERNS _____

_____
_____
_____
_____
_____
_____

ACHIEVEMENT _____

ACT OF KINDNESS _____

DIET

Meat	☐☐☐☐☐☐☐☐☐☐☐
Bread	☐☐☐☐☐☐☐☐☐☐☐
Dairy	☐☐☐☐☐☐☐☐☐☐☐
Vegetables	☐☐☐☐☐☐☐☐☐☐☐
Fruit	☐☐☐☐☐☐☐☐☐☐☐
Water	☐☐☐☐☐☐☐☐☐☐☐
Vitamins	☐☐☐☐☐☐☐☐☐☐☐

PHYSICAL DISCOMFORT

PLAY

Exercise	☐	Laugh	☐	Read	☐
Meditation	☐	Dance	☐	_____	☐
Sex	☐	Sing	☐	_____	☐

CYCLE DAY

_____

DATE_____

Sleep Time ____:____ Wake Time ____:____ Hours of Sleep _____

DREAMS _____

_____
_____
_____
_____
_____
_____
_____
_____

MORNING   MOOD: Good-Average-Bad   ENERGY LEVEL: High-Average-Low

REASON _____

Strength	Hope	Spirit	Vision

Awakening	Balance	Energy	Faith	Freedom

AFFIRMATION _____

NIGHT   MOOD: Good-Average-Bad   ENERGY LEVEL: High-Average-Low

REASON _____

Strength	Hope	Spirit	Vision

Awakening	Balance	Energy	Faith	Freedom

DAILY DISCOVERIES _____

_____
_____
_____
_____
_____
_____
_____
_____
_____
_____
_____
_____
_____
_____
_____
_____
_____
_____
_____
_____
_____

HEALTH PATTERNS _____

_____
_____
_____
_____
_____
_____
_____

ACHIEVEMENT _____

ACT OF KINDNESS _____

DIET

Meat	☐☐☐☐☐☐☐☐☐☐☐☐☐	
Bread	☐☐☐☐☐☐☐☐☐☐☐☐☐	**PHYSICAL**
Dairy	☐☐☐☐☐☐☐☐☐☐☐☐☐	**DISCOMFORT**
Vegetables	☐☐☐☐☐☐☐☐☐☐☐☐☐	
Fruit	☐☐☐☐☐☐☐☐☐☐☐☐☐	
Water	☐☐☐☐☐☐☐☐☐☐☐☐☐	
Vitamins	☐☐☐☐☐☐☐☐☐☐☐☐☐	

PLAY

Exercise	☐	Laugh	☐	Read	☐
Meditation	☐	Dance	☐	_____	☐
Sex	☐	Sing	☐	_____	☐

CYCLE DAY

_____

DATE_____

Sleep Time ____:____ Wake Time ____:____ Hours of Sleep _____

DREAMS _____
_____
_____
_____
_____
_____
_____
_____
_____

MORNING   MOOD: Good-Average-Bad   ENERGY LEVEL: High-Average-Low

REASON _____

Strength	Hope	Spirit	Vision

Awakening	Balance	Energy	Faith	Freedom

AFFIRMATION _____

NIGHT   MOOD: Good-Average-Bad   ENERGY LEVEL: High-Average-Low

REASON _____

Strength	Hope	Spirit	Vision

Awakening	Balance	Energy	Faith	Freedom

DAILY DISCOVERIES _____

_____
_____
_____
_____
_____
_____
_____
_____
_____
_____
_____
_____
_____
_____
_____
_____
_____
_____
_____

HEALTH PATTERNS _____

_____
_____
_____
_____
_____
_____
_____

ACHIEVEMENT _____
ACT OF KINDNESS _____

DIET

Meat	☐	☐	☐	☐	☐	☐	☐	☐	☐	☐	☐	☐	☐
Bread	☐	☐	☐	☐	☐	☐	☐	☐	☐	☐	☐	☐	☐
Dairy	☐	☐	☐	☐	☐	☐	☐	☐	☐	☐	☐	☐	
Vegetables	☐	☐	☐	☐	☐	☐	☐	☐	☐	☐	☐	☐	
Fruit	☐	☐	☐	☐	☐	☐	☐	☐	☐	☐	☐	☐	☐
Water	☐	☐	☐	☐	☐	☐	☐	☐	☐	☐	☐	☐	
Vitamins	☐	☐	☐	☐	☐	☐	☐	☐	☐	☐	☐	☐	☐

PHYSICAL DISCOMFORT

PLAY

Exercise	☐	Laugh	☐	Read	☐
Meditation	☐	Dance	☐	_____	☐
Sex	☐	Sing	☐	_____	☐

CYCLE DAY

_____

DATE_____

Sleep Time ____:____ Wake Time ____:____ Hours of Sleep _____

DREAMS _____
_____
_____
_____
_____
_____
_____
_____
_____

MORNING   MOOD: Good-Average-Bad   ENERGY LEVEL: High-Average-Low

REASON _____

Strength   Hope   Spirit   Vision

Awakening   Balance   Energy   Faith   Freedom

AFFIRMATION _____

NIGHT   MOOD: Good-Average-Bad   ENERGY LEVEL: High-Average-Low

REASON _____

Strength   Hope   Spirit   Vision

Awakening   Balance   Energy   Faith   Freedom

DAILY DISCOVERIES _____

_____
_____
_____
_____
_____
_____
_____
_____
_____
_____
_____
_____
_____
_____
_____
_____
_____
_____
_____
_____

HEALTH PATTERNS _____

_____
_____
_____
_____
_____
_____

ACHIEVEMENT _____

ACT OF KINDNESS _____

DIET

Meat	☐	☐	☐	☐	☐	☐	☐	☐	☐	☐	☐
Bread	☐	☐	☐	☐	☐	☐	☐	☐	☐	☐	☐
Dairy	☐	☐	☐	☐	☐	☐	☐	☐	☐	☐	☐
Vegetables	☐	☐	☐	☐	☐	☐	☐	☐	☐	☐	☐
Fruit	☐	☐	☐	☐	☐	☐	☐	☐	☐	☐	☐
Water	☐	☐	☐	☐	☐	☐	☐	☐	☐	☐	☐
Vitamins	☐	☐	☐	☐	☐	☐	☐	☐	☐	☐	☐

PHYSICAL DISCOMFORT

PLAY

Exercise ☐ Laugh ☐ Read ☐
Meditation ☐ Dance ☐ _____ ☐
Sex ☐ Sing ☐ _____ ☐

CYCLE DAY _____

DATE_____

Sleep Time ____:____ Wake Time ____:____ Hours of Sleep _____

DREAMS _____
_____
_____
_____
_____
_____
_____
_____
_____

MORNING   MOOD: Good-Average-Bad   ENERGY LEVEL: High-Average-Low

REASON _____

Strength   Hope   Spirit   Vision

Awakening   Balance   Energy   Faith   Freedom

AFFIRMATION _____

NIGHT   MOOD: Good-Average-Bad   ENERGY LEVEL: High-Average-Low

REASON _____

Strength   Hope   Spirit   Vision

Awakening   Balance   Energy   Faith   Freedom

DAILY DISCOVERIES _____

_____
_____
_____
_____
_____
_____
_____
_____
_____
_____
_____
_____
_____
_____
_____
_____
_____
_____
_____
_____

HEALTH PATTERNS _____

_____
_____
_____
_____
_____
_____
_____

ACHIEVEMENT _____
ACT OF KINDNESS _____

DIET

Meat	☐	☐	☐	☐	☐	☐	☐	☐	☐	☐	☐	☐
Bread	☐	☐	☐	☐	☐	☐	☐	☐	☐	☐	☐	☐
Dairy	☐	☐	☐	☐	☐	☐	☐	☐	☐	☐	☐	☐
Vegetables	☐	☐	☐	☐	☐	☐	☐	☐	☐	☐	☐	☐
Fruit	☐	☐	☐	☐	☐	☐	☐	☐	☐	☐	☐	☐
Water	☐	☐	☐	☐	☐	☐	☐	☐	☐	☐	☐	☐
Vitamins	☐	☐	☐	☐	☐	☐	☐	☐	☐	☐	☐	☐

PHYSICAL DISCOMFORT

PLAY

Exercise	☐	Laugh	☐	Read	☐	
Meditation	☐	Dance	☐	_____	☐	
Sex	☐	Sing	☐	_____	☐	

CYCLE DAY

_____

DATE_____

Sleep Time ____:____ Wake Time ____:____ Hours of Sleep _____

DREAMS _____
_____
_____
_____
_____
_____
_____
_____
_____

MORNING   MOOD: Good-Average-Bad   ENERGY LEVEL: High-Average-Low

REASON _____

Strength   Hope   Spirit   Vision

Awakening   Balance   Energy   Faith   Freedom

AFFIRMATION _____

NIGHT   MOOD: Good-Average-Bad   ENERGY LEVEL: High-Average-Low

REASON _____

Strength   Hope   Spirit   Vision

Awakening   Balance   Energy   Faith   Freedom

DAILY DISCOVERIES _____

_____
_____
_____
_____
_____
_____
_____
_____
_____
_____
_____
_____
_____
_____
_____
_____
_____
_____
_____
_____
_____
_____

HEALTH PATTERNS _____

_____
_____
_____
_____
_____
_____

ACHIEVEMENT _____
ACT OF KINDNESS _____

DIET

Meat	☐	☐	☐	☐	☐	☐	☐	☐	☐	☐	☐
Bread	☐	☐	☐	☐	☐	☐	☐	☐	☐	☐	☐
Dairy	☐	☐	☐	☐	☐	☐	☐	☐	☐	☐	☐
Vegetables	☐	☐	☐	☐	☐	☐	☐	☐	☐	☐	☐
Fruit	☐	☐	☐	☐	☐	☐	☐	☐	☐	☐	☐
Water	☐	☐	☐	☐	☐	☐	☐	☐	☐	☐	☐
Vitamins	☐	☐	☐	☐	☐	☐	☐	☐	☐	☐	☐

PHYSICAL DISCOMFORT

PLAY

Exercise	☐	Laugh	☐	Read	☐
Meditation	☐	Dance	☐	_____	☐
Sex	☐	Sing	☐	_____	☐

CYCLE DAY

_____

DATE_____

Sleep Time ____:____ Wake Time ____:____ Hours of Sleep _____

DREAMS _____
_____
_____
_____
_____
_____
_____
_____

MORNING   MOOD: Good-Average-Bad   ENERGY LEVEL: High-Average-Low

REASON _____

Strength	Hope	Spirit	Vision

Awakening	Balance	Energy	Faith	Freedom

AFFIRMATION _____

NIGHT   MOOD: Good-Average-Bad   ENERGY LEVEL: High-Average-Low

REASON _____

Strength	Hope	Spirit	Vision

Awakening	Balance	Energy	Faith	Freedom

DAILY DISCOVERIES _____

_____
_____
_____
_____
_____
_____
_____
_____
_____
_____
_____
_____
_____
_____
_____
_____
_____
_____
_____
_____
_____

HEALTH PATTERNS _____

_____
_____
_____
_____
_____
_____
_____

ACHIEVEMENT _____
ACT OF KINDNESS _____

DIET

Meat	☐	☐	☐	☐	☐	☐	☐	☐	☐	☐	☐
Bread	☐	☐	☐	☐	☐	☐	☐	☐	☐	☐	☐
Dairy	☐	☐	☐	☐	☐	☐	☐	☐	☐	☐	☐
Vegetables	☐	☐	☐	☐	☐	☐	☐	☐	☐	☐	☐
Fruit	☐	☐	☐	☐	☐	☐	☐	☐	☐	☐	☐
Water	☐	☐	☐	☐	☐	☐	☐	☐	☐	☐	☐
Vitamins	☐	☐	☐	☐	☐	☐	☐	☐	☐	☐	☐

PHYSICAL DISCOMFORT

PLAY

Exercise	☐	Laugh	☐	Read	☐
Meditation	☐	Dance	☐	_____	☐
Sex	☐	Sing	☐	_____	☐

CYCLE DAY

_____

DATE_____

Sleep Time _____ : _____   Wake Time _____ : _____   Hours of Sleep _____

DREAMS _____

_____

_____

_____

_____

_____

_____

_____

MORNING   **MOOD:** Good-Average-Bad **ENERGY LEVEL:** High-Average-Low

REASON _____

Strength	Hope	Spirit	Vision

Awakening	Balance	Energy	Faith	Freedom

AFFIRMATION _____

NIGHT   **MOOD:** Good-Average-Bad **ENERGY LEVEL:** High-Average-Low

REASON _____

Strength	Hope	Spirit	Vision

Awakening	Balance	Energy	Faith	Freedom

DAILY DISCOVERIES _____

_____
_____
_____
_____
_____
_____
_____
_____
_____
_____
_____
_____
_____
_____
_____
_____
_____
_____
_____
_____
_____

HEALTH PATTERNS _____

_____
_____
_____
_____
_____
_____
_____

ACHIEVEMENT _____

ACT OF KINDNESS _____

DIET

Meat	☐	☐	☐	☐	☐	☐	☐	☐	☐	☐	☐	☐
Bread	☐	☐	☐	☐	☐	☐	☐	☐	☐	☐	☐	☐
Dairy	☐	☐	☐	☐	☐	☐	☐	☐	☐	☐	☐	☐
Vegetables	☐	☐	☐	☐	☐	☐	☐	☐	☐	☐	☐	☐
Fruit	☐	☐	☐	☐	☐	☐	☐	☐	☐	☐	☐	☐
Water	☐	☐	☐	☐	☐	☐	☐	☐	☐	☐	☐	☐
Vitamins	☐	☐	☐	☐	☐	☐	☐	☐	☐	☐	☐	☐

PHYSICAL DISCOMFORT

PLAY

Exercise	☐	Laugh	☐	Read	☐
Meditation	☐	Dance	☐	_____	☐
Sex	☐	Sing	☐	_____	☐

CYCLE DAY

_____

DATE_____

Sleep Time ____:____ Wake Time ____:____ Hours of Sleep _____

DREAMS _____
_____
_____
_____
_____
_____
_____
_____
_____

MORNING   MOOD: Good-Average-Bad   ENERGY LEVEL: High-Average-Low

REASON _____

Strength   Hope   Spirit   Vision

Awakening Balance   Energy   Faith   Freedom

AFFIRMATION _____

NIGHT   MOOD: Good-Average-Bad   ENERGY LEVEL: High-Average-Low

REASON _____

Strength   Hope   Spirit   Vision

Awakening Balance   Energy   Faith   Freedom

DAILY DISCOVERIES _____

_____
_____
_____
_____
_____
_____
_____
_____
_____
_____
_____
_____
_____
_____
_____
_____
_____
_____
_____
_____
_____
_____

HEALTH PATTERNS _____

_____
_____
_____
_____
_____
_____
_____

ACHIEVEMENT _____
ACT OF KINDNESS _____

DIET

Meat	□	□	□	□	□	□	□	□	□	□
Bread	□	□	□	□	□	□	□	□	□	□
Dairy	□	□	□	□	□	□	□	□	□	□
Vegetables	□	□	□	□	□	□	□	□	□	□
Fruit	□	□	□	□	□	□	□	□	□	□
Water	□	□	□	□	□	□	□	□	□	□
Vitamins	□	□	□	□	□	□	□	□	□	□

PHYSICAL DISCOMFORT

PLAY

Exercise	□	Laugh	□	Read	□
Meditation	□	Dance	□	_____	□
Sex	□	Sing	□	_____	□

CYCLE DAY
_____

DATE_____

Sleep Time ____:____   Wake Time ____:____   Hours of Sleep _____

DREAMS _____
_____
_____
_____
_____
_____
_____
_____
_____

MORNING   MOOD: Good-Average-Bad   ENERGY LEVEL: High-Average-Low

REASON _____

Strength   Hope   Spirit   Vision

Awakening   Balance   Energy   Faith   Freedom

AFFIRMATION _____

NIGHT   MOOD: Good-Average-Bad   ENERGY LEVEL: High-Average-Low

REASON _____

Strength   Hope   Spirit   Vision

Awakening   Balance   Energy   Faith   Freedom

DAILY DISCOVERIES _____

_____
_____
_____
_____
_____
_____
_____
_____
_____
_____
_____
_____
_____
_____
_____
_____
_____
_____
_____
_____

HEALTH PATTERNS _____

_____
_____
_____
_____
_____
_____

ACHIEVEMENT _____
ACT OF KINDNESS _____

DIET

Meat	□□□□□□□□□□□□	
Bread	□□□□□□□□□□□□	**PHYSICAL**
Dairy	□□□□□□□□□□□□	**DISCOMFORT**
Vegetables	□□□□□□□□□□□□	
Fruit	□□□□□□□□□□□□	
Water	□□□□□□□□□□□□	
Vitamins	□□□□□□□□□□□□	

PLAY

Exercise □   Laugh □   Read □

Meditation □   Dance □   _____ □   **CYCLE DAY**

Sex □   Sing □   _____ □   _____

DATE_____

Sleep Time ____:____ Wake Time ____:____ Hours of Sleep _____

DREAMS _____
_____
_____
_____
_____
_____
_____
_____
_____

MORNING   MOOD: Good-Average-Bad   ENERGY LEVEL: High-Average-Low

REASON _____

| Strength | Hope | Spirit | Vision |

| Awakening | Balance | Energy | Faith | Freedom |

AFFIRMATION _____

NIGHT   MOOD: Good-Average-Bad   ENERGY LEVEL: High-Average-Low

REASON _____

| Strength | Hope | Spirit | Vision |

| Awakening | Balance | Energy | Faith | Freedom |

DAILY DISCOVERIES _____

_____
_____
_____
_____
_____
_____
_____
_____
_____
_____
_____
_____
_____
_____
_____
_____
_____
_____
_____
_____
_____
_____
_____

HEALTH PATTERNS _____

_____
_____
_____
_____
_____
_____
_____

ACHIEVEMENT _____

ACT OF KINDNESS _____

DIET
Meat	☐	☐	☐	☐	☐	☐	☐	☐	☐	☐	☐	☐
Bread	☐	☐	☐	☐	☐	☐	☐	☐	☐	☐	☐	☐
Dairy	☐	☐	☐	☐	☐	☐	☐	☐	☐	☐	☐	☐
Vegetables	☐	☐	☐	☐	☐	☐	☐	☐	☐	☐	☐	☐
Fruit	☐	☐	☐	☐	☐	☐	☐	☐	☐	☐	☐	☐
Water	☐	☐	☐	☐	☐	☐	☐	☐	☐	☐	☐	☐
Vitamins	☐	☐	☐	☐	☐	☐	☐	☐	☐	☐	☐	☐

PHYSICAL DISCOMFORT

CYCLE DAY _____

PLAY
Exercise	☐	Laugh	☐	Read	☐
Meditation	☐	Dance	☐	_____	☐
Sex	☐	Sing	☐	_____	☐

DATE_____

Sleep Time ____:____   Wake Time ____:____   Hours of Sleep _____

DREAMS _____

_____

_____

_____

_____

_____

_____

_____

MORNING   MOOD: Good-Average-Bad   ENERGY LEVEL: High-Average-Low

REASON _____

| Strength | Hope | Spirit | Vision |

| Awakening | Balance | Energy | Faith | Freedom |

AFFIRMATION _____

NIGHT   MOOD: Good-Average-Bad   ENERGY LEVEL: High-Average-Low

REASON _____

| Strength | Hope | Spirit | Vision |

| Awakening | Balance | Energy | Faith | Freedom |

DAILY DISCOVERIES _____

_____
_____
_____
_____
_____
_____
_____
_____
_____
_____
_____
_____
_____
_____
_____
_____
_____
_____
_____
_____
_____
_____
_____
_____

HEALTH PATTERNS _____

_____
_____
_____
_____
_____
_____
_____

ACHIEVEMENT _____
ACT OF KINDNESS _____

DIET

Meat	☐	☐	☐	☐	☐	☐	☐	☐	☐	☐	☐
Bread	☐	☐	☐	☐	☐	☐	☐	☐	☐	☐	☐
Dairy	☐	☐	☐	☐	☐	☐	☐	☐	☐	☐	☐
Vegetables	☐	☐	☐	☐	☐	☐	☐	☐	☐	☐	☐
Fruit	☐	☐	☐	☐	☐	☐	☐	☐	☐	☐	☐
Water	☐	☐	☐	☐	☐	☐	☐	☐	☐	☐	☐
Vitamins	☐	☐	☐	☐	☐	☐	☐	☐	☐	☐	☐

PHYSICAL DISCOMFORT

PLAY

Exercise	☐	Laugh	☐	Read	☐
Meditation	☐	Dance	☐	_____	☐
Sex	☐	Sing	☐	_____	☐

CYCLE DAY

_____

DATE_____

Sleep Time ____:____ Wake Time ____:____ Hours of Sleep _____

DREAMS _____

_____

_____

_____

_____

_____

_____

_____

_____

MORNING   MOOD: Good-Average-Bad   **ENERGY LEVEL:** High-Average-Low

REASON _____

Strength   Hope   Spirit   Vision

Awakening   Balance   Energy   Faith   Freedom

AFFIRMATION _____

NIGHT   MOOD: Good-Average-Bad   **ENERGY LEVEL:** High-Average-Low

REASON _____

Strength   Hope   Spirit   Vision

Awakening   Balance   Energy   Faith   Freedom

DAILY DISCOVERIES _____

_____
_____
_____
_____
_____
_____
_____
_____
_____
_____
_____
_____
_____
_____
_____
_____
_____
_____
_____
_____
_____
_____

HEALTH PATTERNS _____

_____
_____
_____
_____
_____
_____
_____

ACHIEVEMENT _____

ACT OF KINDNESS _____

DIET		**PHYSICAL DISCOMFORT**
Meat	☐☐☐☐☐☐☐☐☐☐☐☐	
Bread	☐☐☐☐☐☐☐☐☐☐☐☐	
Dairy	☐☐☐☐☐☐☐☐☐☐☐☐	
Vegetables	☐☐☐☐☐☐☐☐☐☐☐☐	
Fruit	☐☐☐☐☐☐☐☐☐☐☐☐	
Water	☐☐☐☐☐☐☐☐☐☐☐☐	
Vitamins	☐☐☐☐☐☐☐☐☐☐☐☐	

PLAY

Exercise	☐	Laugh	☐	Read	☐
Meditation	☐	Dance	☐	_____	☐
Sex	☐	Sing	☐	_____	☐

CYCLE DAY

_____